Spatialising Politics

Spatialising Politics

Culture and Geography in Postcolonial Sri Lanka

Edited by

Cathrine Brun
Tariq Jazeel

First published in 2009 by

SAGE Publications India Pvt Ltd
B1/I-1 Mohan Cooperative Industrial Area
Mathura Road, New Delhi 110 044, India
www.sagepub.in

SAGE Publications Inc
2455 Teller Road
Thousand Oaks, California 91320, USA

SAGE Publications Ltd
1 Oliver's Yard, 55 City Road
London EC1Y 1SP, United Kingdom

SAGE Publications Asia-Pacific Pte Ltd
33 Pekin Street
#02-01 Far East Square
Singapore 048763

Published by Vivek Mehra for SAGE Publications India Pvt Ltd, typeset in 10/12 pt Times New Roman by Star Compugraphics Private Limited, Delhi and printed at Chaman Enterprises, New Delhi.

Library of Congress Cataloging-in-Publication Data

Spatialising politics: culture and geography in postcolonial Sri Lanka/edited by Cathrine Brun and Tariq Jazeel.

p. cm.

Includes bibliographical references and index.

1. Sri Lanka—Ethnic relations—History. 2. Ethnic conflict—Sri Lanka—History. 3. Sri Lanka—Politics and government. I. Brun, Cathrine. II. Jazeel, Tariq.

DS489.2.S625 954.9303—dc22 2009 2008055255

ISBN: 978-81-7829-929-7 (HB)

The SAGE Team: Elina Majumdar, Gargi Bhattacharya, Amrita Saha and Trinankur Banerjee

Contents

List of Figures

List of Abbreviations

ADB	Asian Development Bank
ARIA	Antagonism through Resonance, Intervention and Action
BCE	Before Common Era
CECB	Sri Lanka's Central Engineering Consultancy Board
CPA	Centre for Performing Arts
EU	European Union
FP	Federal Party
GA	Government Agent
ICES	International Centre for Ethnic Studies
IDPs	Internally Displaced Persons
IEG	Institute of Economic Growth
IMF	International Monetary Fund
INGO	International Non-Governmental Organisation
IPKF	Indian Peace Keeping Forces
JHU	Jathika Hela Urumaya (National Heritage Party)
JVP	Janatha Vimukthi Peramuna (People's Liberation Front)
LTTE	Liberation Tigers of Tamil Eelam
MP	Member of Parliament
NGO	Non-Governmental Organisation
PPF	People's Peace Front
PULSE	Peradeniya University Lecture Series
SLMC	Sri Lankan Muslim Congress
TECH	The Economic Consultancy House
TULF	Tamil United Liberation Front
UK	United Kingdom
UN	United Nations
UNESCO	United Nations Educational, Scientific and Cultural Organization

UNF	United National Front
UNP	United National Party
US	United States
UTHR	University Teachers for Human Rights

Acknowledgements

The cover image for this volume is an untitled piece by the Toronto-based Sri Lankan artist Geevan, a.k.a. Nanda Kandasamy. The image depicts a figure whose gaze faces *not quite* upwards, downwards, towards us, or away from us. Not only is her gaze difficult to read, but the forms inside her head seem to reference shapes within shapes—spaces intersecting one another—and a dense complex of lines and textures. The composition of the image—its framing of a figure with immaculate poise and balance—give the lie to legibility, but the rich layerings of form, orientation, and trajectory in and around her head seem to us to indicate the contradictions and complexities of spaces imagined. The painting indicates the complexities of the many spatial forms, orientations, trajectories, and histories of contested nationalisms in contemporary Sri Lanka that are lived, experienced, imagined on the ground, by people. The cover image offers the perfectly troubling visual introduction to this book on spatial politics in the Sri Lankan context. To Geevan, thank you for allowing us to use this image here.

This collection of essays grew out of a series of off-stage conversations amongst friends and colleagues at the Annual Sri Lankan Studies Conference some years ago in Matara. We are extremely grateful to Kanchana Ruwanpura, Sharon Bell, Camilla Orjuela, Isak Svensson, and Benedikt Korf for conversations both sane and inspiring. For us, as editors, these conversations provided the basis for continued forms of creative collaboration, experience, and dialogue that have ultimately led to this collection.

Along the way, many people have offered us sound advice and critical commentary at different stages. Many thanks to Maite Conde, Steve Pile, Jenny Robinson, John Allen, Denis Cosgrove, Jennifer Hyndman, Satish Kumar, Nira Wickramasinghe, and Nick Van Hear. At SAGE, we would like to thank four individuals who have nurtured this project, Tejeshwar Singh, Ashok R. Chandran, Gargi Bhattacharya, and especially Elina Majumdar, whose enthusiasm has been infectious. We also thank the anonymous reviewers for comments along the way that have sharpened the collection. Finally, we want to express our thanks to all the contributors to this collection. Without their hard work and patience this book would not have come together.

Cathrine Brun
Tariq Jazeel

1

Introduction: Spatial Politics and Postcolonial Sri Lanka

Tariq Jazeel and Cathrine Brun

This book brings together a collection of essays that take as their theme the spatial politics of Sri Lanka. Most observers will be aware of the importance of space in the ongoing ethnic conflict that has fuelled civil war in the country. Claims and contestations over the integrity of island space, the legitimacy of the spatiality of the nation-state, and of 'homeland' and territory are at the centre of a dense cluster of disputes that swirl around the referent 'Sri Lanka'. The waves of war from 1983 up to the present, and the resulting unacceptable loss of life, have been fundamentally about the control of the northern and eastern territories of the island, and federalism and devolution have been at the heart of the faltering peace talks that started in 2002. Clearly, geography matters in this contested context.

Importantly, however, space and spatiality also matter in a number of ways that are less frequently evoked in the political science and anthropological literatures that engage with politics and ethnicity in this particular South Asian context. The production of ethnic enmity, and the deeply entrenched, embodied senses of self, other, 'race', class, and sex, are not just produced in a de-materialised haze of abstract and contested political imagination. Encounters on the ground, in and through the spaces of everyday life, also play their role in the production of social relations. The complexities and rhetoric of the political realm and of 'history', permeate the everyday in Sri Lanka; these forces give form to the everyday, moulding and shaping the contours and topologies of dynamic spaces that continually (re)produce subjectivities through social encounter. It is to these often occluded spatial formations of everyday encounter, the spaces through which everyday life in Sri Lanka is negotiated, and the spaces that are (re)produced through those negotiations and encounters, that this volume pays particular attention.

At the heart of the argument that this book develops is the contention that to think through cultural politics is to think spatially. The production of racialised modes of identity, difference, and violence is not an organic phenomenon that occurs in otherwise empty and passive, container-like space. Rather, this volume explores the ways that (essentialised) difference is produced *through* meaningful space; space that acts, and therefore, must be imbued with some kind of agency in Sri Lanka's contested politics of ethnicity. But meaningful space is itself produced, and politically we believe that because of its agency, the contingent histories of space must be unravelled. Each chapter variously teases out the social implications of working Sri Lanka's cultural politics through spatial registers—as *spatial politics*. Each chapter evokes the spatial forms and fantasies through which a culture makes its presence (see Carter 1987).

Spatialising politics is intensely material. It involves teasing out the relationships between spatialities, subjects, and institutions in a highly differentiated and varied geography that does not focus solely on territory, but rather regards territory as merely one amongst many spatialities through which the nation-state is instantiated and contested. The book explores the relationship between the spatial politics and lived experiences through which difference has been, and continues to be, produced across a range of scales both coarser and finer than the colonial/nation-state itself. Together, contributors to this volume explore the taken-for-granted spaces and spatialities that are often so familiar to us as citizens, refugees, researchers, men, women, children, disinterested observers, and foreigners, that we rarely stop to think about how they impinge(d) upon us and our forbears, how they (re)produce us and our otherness as we move through, negotiate, and dynamically reproduce them ourselves: architecture and cities, landscapes, diasporas, knowledge spaces, spaces of peace work and (post-)imperial spatialities, to name a few that are explored in the chapters that follow.

Ultimately, this book evokes a politics of identity and power that is articulated through space and is fundamentally about space. Bringing into focus these geographical incarnations of power is a step towards a more holistic understanding of the production of difference, and its often violent manifestation; a step that acknowledges space as far more than a contested stage, or a container, that is so easily carved into territories or compartments, and instead, as the very fabric through which nationhood, identity, and violence are produced.

Locating Postcolonial Sri Lanka: Postcolonial Geography and Identity

In this context, the effort to engage the complexities of the striated world through which identity and difference are produced necessitates a critical and conceptual engagement with histories of colonisation in South Asia, and specifically the ideological and material legacies of Ceylon's colonial encounter. To signify this engagement, we have quite purposely employed the problematic term 'postcolonial Sri Lanka', which warrants some explanation. We are wary of the premature celebration implied by the temporalities that inhere in the very term 'postcolonial' (Nash 2002: 220). In Sri Lanka, the postcolonial must be made to mean much more than after-the-colonial, for it also urges a critical disposition to engage, think, and live the nation-state in ways that remain attuned to the historicity of its many different stories-so-far. Postcolonial Sri Lanka, therefore, does not refer to a space–time or object as such; it is not post-independence Ceylon. For us, it is a term whose very uneasiness holds in productive tension the ways that the nation-state cannot, must not, be thought or mobilised without the types of historical sensitivity that refuse to stop troubling away at exactly how the multiplicities of the present condition have been produced. It is, in this sense, a methodological approach rather than an essential place—one that takes seriously and understands the challenge of what Gayatri Spivak (1996) has referred to as the impossibility of breaking free from—of saying no to—the ground beneath our feet. The time-lag, the dwelling of the colonial in the present, renders this no impossible; yet we argue, it is through a lens that recognises the ground beneath our feet as historical, not essential, that we hope to locate 'postcolonial Sri Lanka', to bring its various and contested dimensions into focus.

It is the spatial engagements of this problematic that concern the contributors to this volume. Although, famously, it was Edward Said (1978) who first alerted us to the potent geographical imaginations that inhered in the colonial project, recent postcolonial geographical scholarship has drawn attention to the myriad different ways that colonialism, postcolonialism, and geography are intimately linked (Blunt and McEwan 2002; Sidaway 2000; Yeoh 2001). Spatial engagements of postcolonial theory and scholarship have revealed not just the many social and spatial structures, patterns, flows, and contiguous power imbalances that bear testimony to colonialism's afterlife, but also the political potential of critically engaging these structures. For many postcolonial geographers, it is the very awkwardness of the 'post' in postcolonialism that has necessitated a continued political and intellectual engagement with the spatialities and spatial fixities signified by colonialism (see Gregory 2004, for example). The 'post' remains a useful irritant that inhibits a comfortable move beyond the colonial, a reminder of its very persistence and the need for an ongoing political and spatial engagement with its results (Nash 2002: 221).

But one of the critiques most often levelled at postcolonialism is of the levels of abstraction at which its critical interventions are made. The disjuncture between an approach whose theoretical and empirical lineage emerges from discourse analyses undertaken in the comfortable (often Western) academic spaces of literary and textual studies, and the conditions and materialities of the visceral, often sanguinary, tensions swirling around lived experiences of identity, citizenship, exclusion, and otherness in postcolonies such as Sri Lanka, are a problematic that, some argue, renders postcolonial theory difficult to connect to the specific concrete and local conditions of everyday life in this 'real' world (Jacobs 1996: 158). Political execution, mob violence and rioting, arson, and suicide bombing are, of course, neither imaginative nor textual. Neither should the visceralities and trauma of conflict be trivialised by clever conceptual manoeuvres and abstractions. However, by simultaneously historicising space and subjectivity, and by exploring the spatial production of identity, postcolonial geography is positioned to re-materialise postcolonialism, to critically explore the lived experiences of postcoloniality (McEwan 2003: 3), to be able to explore how, as Achille Mbembe (2001: 5) asserts, colonial discourses and representations are imbued with materiality, and how they connect irreducibly to practice.

Vikki Bell suggests the purchase of this type of approach in the analyses of fascistic, racist, sexist, and homophobic terrains, by arguing how such a perspective, '"instead of attempting to determine what we should do on the basis of what we essentially are, attempts, by analysing what we have been constituted to be, to ask what we might become." This is precisely not to understand one's identity as a given, an a priori, in short an *essence*' (1999: 123, emphasis original). In this configuration, different modes of identity, including contested modes of 'Sri Lankan-ness', are best regarded as engagements and negotiations with the complexities of living the position of a partially objectified subject. Importantly, these objectifications are lived in and through the striated spaces of everyday life, whose roots this volume traces and variously weaves through Ceylon's colonial encounter and post-independence trajectories; space becomes part of an ever-shifting social geometry of power and signification in which the material and ideological are co-constitutive (Jacobs 1996: 5). In her feminist reflections on the embodiment of identity, Vikki Bell draws heavily on the postcolonial, psychoanalytic writings of Franz Fanon, particularly his existential negotiations of the blackness imposed on his own body by the objectifying, racialising gaze of the colonising regime. In his much cited essay 'The Fact of Blackness', Fanon (1982), she notes, realises the futility of his struggle to reject the thematisation of his body in order that he might just be 'a man among men' in a world of imperial and colonial space where his body is already mapped and objectified. These are themes the psychiatrist Fanon (1965) also takes up in his notes on mental disorders amongst Algerians during the colonial war of independence with France. Crucially, in all this Fanon recognises that embodiment moves, is produced, through a value-laden world (Bell 1999: 128)—an insight that evokes considerable potential for us in tracing and undoing some of the value-laden Sri Lankan geographies through which different Sri Lankan bodies move. Sri Lankan identities emerge as: 'a structuring of the self, a formation, *within the world* that is about the sense of becoming familiar with the co-ordinates of one's own living body *within space*' (ibid.: emphasis added).

It is this within-the-worldness to which our postcolonial geography attends, because the proliferation, and sometimes violent manifestation, of difference in modern Sri Lanka, is shaped in space, and given form through the colonial encounter and the unfolding projects of state and nationhood. Just as Fanon, through his career, maintained a sense of commitment to Algeria through his critical engagements with French colonialism, and its affects on Algerian society and psyche, we also hope that the chapters that follow raise questions over the political instantiation and effect of postcolonial Sri Lanka. We hope the volume 'speaks to' Sri Lanka. In order to do so there is a need to critically sketch a formal history of the uncompromising and essential spaces that constitute Sri Lanka's territorially contested formal present.

A Social History of Uncompromising Spaces *in* Sri Lanka

The formation of a centralised Sri Lankan nation-state derived from a classical pattern, from the existence of pre-colonial, relatively autonomous spatio-political units married through colonialism to form, first, a territorial colonial island-state, and then an independent nation-state, both of whose geopolitical and ideological roots can be traced through 17th-century

Westphalian templates of clearly defined, centrally controlled, independent social and political entities, and the development of 19th-century romantic nationalisms. Prior to the European colonisation of the island's spaces, for more than three centuries, it consisted of kingdoms, the most important of which were Kotte, Kandy, and Jaffna. One interpretation of the island's pre-colonial history claims that the kingdoms were organised on very different principles from those which underlie the modern nation-state, where they were loosely structured, self-sufficient, and self-contained entities (Nissan and Stirrat 1990). Political power and territorial boundaries in the kingdoms were not fixed, but diffused and marked by zones of intermittent influence. It was the power of each kingdom's centre that determined their reach and their territories (Perera 1999; Tambiah 1986). According to Nissan and Stirrat (1990), ethnic and linguistic differences between 'culture language areas' were not used as the bases for inclusion or exclusion; at various times groups would speak alternative languages, practice alternative religions, and claim alternative identities. So, notwithstanding the fact that relatively little is known about pre-colonial 'Ceylonese' space, it seems that neither territory nor territorialised 'ethnic' identities then were the spatial registers through which antagonistic notions of difference were produced and lived.

The Jaffna kingdom was the first to fall to the Portuguese colonial powers who ruled part of the island from 1505 to 1683, when the Dutch came and expanded their control to cover the entire coastline. Both the Portuguese and Dutch nations were mercantile powers, their imperialist interests focused primarily on dominating the coastal areas in order to extract revenues from international trade. In addition to the mercantile activities, one central impact of Portuguese colonialism was the introduction of Catholicism (Fuglerud 1999). When the British arrived in 1796, they initially established a colonial administration only over the island's peripheral kingdoms. Europeans, however, had been 'mapping' a unified island spatiality here since Ptolemy's *Geography*. Thus, the 'island-colony' existed in the British imperial imagination long before it was actually realised as a material space. In 1815, the British eventually conquered the Kandyan kingdom, at last bringing the whole island under a single colonial administration. Sri Lanka, or Ceylon, as it was then, became a single 'unified' political territory, which the British promptly divided into administrative provinces and districts, all subject to a single, English-speaking administration based in Colombo. Each district was headed by British officers. This system effectively subordinated the 'indigenous' political power and cultural identities that formerly emerged through the kingdoms, and the new socio-political, organisational, and administrative unit was designed to suit the economic and imaginative needs of the colonial regime (Perera 1999; Pfaffenberger 1994; Phadnis 1989). Political centralisation was facilitated by the construction of a centripetal transport system, roads and railways that all led to Colombo, and were designed to facilitate the extraction of raw materials from the island-colony's peripheries for export to Britain (Pfaffenberger 1994). This administrative and infrastructural system remains roughly the same today, and the colonial administrative boundaries of north, north-east, and north-west are still the cartographic boundaries through which militant Tamil nationalism, and its armed struggle for the homeland, Eelam, are articulated even today; one such spatiality through which the colonial remains dangerously present.

In building an administrative system, the colonial authorities, faced with having to rule a large 'native' population, integrated elite members of the local groups into their political and economic systems from the mid-19th century onward. According to Shastri (1997), leading members of the Sinhalese community were given positions and titles in the colonial system of government and village administration. Key members among the Ceylonese Tamil sought jobs in the civil service in Colombo. Other Ceylonese Tamils, along with members of the Muslim community, went into trade and finance. In rural parts of the country, leading members of each group (excluding upcountry Indian Tamils—indentured plantation labourers) continued to exercise influence as landowners, while the large majority in each community lived as peasants. The social cleavages were dominated by class and caste, not ethnicity (Singer 1964; also see Jayawardene 2000).

Many aspects of society changed during the British colonial period. Together with the unified centralised state, and the commercial and social transformations of society, these changes included the institutionalisation of ethnic differences and a new system of political representation. The institutionalisation of ethnic differences emerged principally in relation to the British colonial administration's need to deal with very different groups of people. British policy was highly influenced by the racial theories of the time that pervaded an empire of science, and within Ceylon social heterogeneity was dealt with by attempts to categorise people in biological terms, by racialising society (Nissan and Stirrat 1990). In the mid-19th century there were significant developments in Ceylonese racial theory amongst colonial scientists—differences that were aired in the *Journal of the Royal Asiatic Society of Ceylon* (Angell 1998; Guneratne 2002).

Not only were Tamils, Sinhalese, and Muslims (with subgroups) categorised as different races, the Sinhalese Aryans were beginning to be hierarchically positioned over Tamil Dravidians (Angell 1998). These categorisations laid the foundation for an institutionalisation of group politics; they were the 'bound serialities' of colonial governmentality that provided the templates for ethnicised communitarianism, which as Partha Chatterjee (2004: 22) argues, is precisely what relentlessly drives the pervasive politics of ethnicity. The colonial government recognised variations in certain contexts, and allowed differences of practice to continue. For example, the areas with predominantly Sinhala speakers were administered in Sinhala, while the areas with a predominance of Tamil speakers were administered in Tamil (Nissan and Stirrat 1990), thus consolidating and territorialising ethnic difference where there was already established coexistence.

Towards independence in 1948, the spread of franchise and the discussion over political representation also increased tensions between these nascent racialised communities. The core of the tensions was the discussion over whether the basis of political representation should follow communalist representation or territorial representation. Tamil parties advocated fifty-fifty representation, meaning that one half of the seats in the parliament should go to Sinhalese members, who represented about three-quarters of the population, and the other half to representatives of the various minority communities, constituting about one-quarter of the island's population. However, this proposal was rejected, and instead a Westminster-type cabinet system was introduced based on territorial representation and a one-man, one-vote system. It was a system of political representation that favoured the densely populated areas of the south, now increasingly territorialised *as* Sinhalese, and it was a system that did not give adequate constitutional protection to minorities (Phadnis 1989; Stokke 1998).

Unlike in British India, Ceylon's passage toward independence was peaceful, characterised by a relatively smooth transition to independent statehood. Britain and Ceylon's late colonial relationship was characterised by a 'trustee' philosophy that implied 'Britain was in Africa and Asia for the Africans' and Asians' good: that her aim was to develop them to a stage where they could fend for themselves' (Porter 1984: 313). However, despite the political ease with which Ceylon won independence (for more, see Madden and Darwin 1994), the independent nation-state's first constitution lacked a bill of rights affording effective formal protection for minorities. As a consequence, one of the first actions of the new government was to disenfranchise the Indian Tamils who had been brought by the British colonial management and construction companies from South India to work on the coffee—and later tea—estates in the hill country. While at this time the Tamil politicians did not try to prevent the disenfranchisement because politics was concentrated along a left–right axis rather than around ethnic questions, during the 1950s, a much more polarised ethnic political environment developed. S.W.R.D. Bandaranaike was elected Prime Minister in 1956 and came to power on a programme of populist Sinhalese nationalism that promoted an ethnicity based on language and religion, and soon after Sinhala was promoted to the status of the official language of the country, prompting the first of a series of ethnic riots. This marked the beginning of the inability of the nation-state to represent and include different groups.

From independence up until the 1950s, the Sri Lankan economy had grown rapidly, but from 1956 onward, it steadily deteriorated, leading to increased social unrest (Stirrat 1988). Population growth, together with an economy that failed to create enough employment, affected the younger generation in particular. Reforms to the economy, welfare measures, and reforms in the education system all contributed to increased frustration among the youth in the south and north of the island. In the south, Sinhalese ultra left-wing movements induced violent riots led by the Janatha Vimukthi Peramuna (JVP, meaning People's Liberation Front), a group dominated by educated rural unemployed or underemployed youth. The unrest and violence that followed took hold in different ways in the north and south. During the 1970s, there was increased insecurity for Tamils all over the country, leading many Tamils to move northwards. At the same time, the north was becoming more militarised, and tensions increased between the Sri Lankan security forces and a number of Tamil militant organisations (of which the Liberation Tigers of Tamil Eelam [LTTE] established in 1974 later became the strongest [see Fuglerud, this volume]). Increased tension and militarism culminated in July 1983 with the worst pogrom against Tamils in Sri Lanka's history. What has since been termed 'black July' marked the beginning of the first phase of the prolonged war.

Today, 'history' is an integrated part of everyday Sri Lankan life that bears responsibility for producing essentialist claims about the past (Spencer 1990). Popular understandings of Sri Lankan history have produced specific essentialised spaces of difference, fear, and mistrust, resulting in particular and territorialised, ethnically exclusive imaginations that proclaim primordial and immutable difference in terms of ethnicity between Muslims, Tamils and Sinhalese.[1] However, these understandings, interpretations, and spacings of history cannot, we contend, be mobilised without acknowledging the colonial processes of history-writing (Gunawardana 1995), Orientalist philological translation and archaeological restoration (Jazeel, this volume, Jeganathan 1995), and colonial racial science (Angell 1998) that have effectively narrativised Sri Lanka's now institutionalised foundational fictions.

In no small way egged on by these colonial encounters and their legacies in the post-independence era, ethnic identities fuelled by potent and uncompromising historical and territorial imaginations have become the central issue driving a conflict between competing, antagonistic, and incompatible Tamil and Sinhalese nationalisms. The assertion of one is widely perceived to be a denial of the other (Rotberg 1999; Tiruchelvam 2000b). Although Sinhalese and Tamil nationalists oppose one another politically, like most nationalisms and counter-nationalisms, they have very much in common because of the theoretical and ideological frameworks they use (Bastian 1996). Regarding national and cultural-historical origins, both ideologies make explicit references to 'the past' in order to explain and justify current nationalist sentiments and practices. Advocates of both nationalisms portray their own nation as a primordial unit revolving around fixed essences of language, religion, ethnic origin, and territory (Stokke 1998). Arguments about seniority, antecedence, and therefore, legitimacy, are especially strong: those who came to an area first, irrespective of who have settled there later, believe themselves to have natural rights to the territory (Hellmann-Rajanayagam 1990).

For the Sinhalese, the ancient Buddhist chronicles of the *Mahavamsa* and *Culavamsa* are used to demonstrate the virtues and rewards of a particular political relationship between Buddhism and the pre-colonial polity, though again we must be at pains to assert that these chronicles were only translated from Pali and Sanskrit in the 19th century by European Orientalist scholars. The attendant riders around the problematics of the translation of meaning and the narrativisation of the past therefore apply. In general, Sinhalese nationalists claim that even if they were not the first inhabitants of the island—a status they allow for the aboriginal Veddhas—they were at least the first 'civilised' settlers of Sri Lanka (Nissan and Stirrat 1990). Through the poetic interpretation of colonial translations of ancient chronicles and inscriptions, the Sinhalese gradually became known as an ancient race, descendants of Indo–Aryan settlers from north India, and as such different in blood, origin, and kind from their Tamil neighbours.

The Sinhalese nationalists view Sri Lanka as a sacred island where Buddhists have a responsibility to preserve Buddhism and associated concepts of race, territory, and nation—an idea known as *Dhamma Deepa*, the land in which Theravada Buddhism had been preserved in its untouched purity (Tiruchelvam 2000a).

The parallel processes of nationalism and the making of Tamil identity lack a single clear historical source equivalent to the Buddhist chronicles. The search for the traditional homeland has come to dominate relatively recent writings on the Tamil past. Hellmann-Rajanayagam (1990) traces the concept of the 'Tamil homeland' back to the 1930s when it was often coupled with the notion of the traditional: traditional homelands of the Tamils being regions where Tamil-speaking people have traditionally lived. The traditional homelands of the Tamils in the north and east are today the territories cognate with the Tamil separatist case, of which the main advocate and force has become the insurgent group, the LTTE. Demands for a separate homeland for the Tamils in the north and east clearly opposes Sinhalese nationalism; if the island was separated, it would be regarded as a violation of the Sinhala-Buddhist *Dhamma Deepa*. Additionally, Sinhalese nationalists have been able to rely on what Tiruchelvam (2000a: 199) termed 'the dominant colonial constitutional discourse' that conceptualises the modern democratic nation-state as one based on the singularity and centralisation of political and administrative space.

The Sri Lankan conflict is commonly explained as a bipartite one between the majority Sinhalese and the minority Tamils. However, this view must be refined; and although the origins of the conflict may to a large extent involve mostly Tamils and the Sinhalese, the conflict has spread beyond the Sinhalese–Tamil ethnic boundary to involve the Muslim population, also affecting the consolidation of Muslims as an ethnic category. The emergence of a Muslim ethnic identity has resulted today in a very tense relationship between Muslims and Tamils in the east and the north of the island. Many Muslims are worried about whether their rights will be secured within this framework, and some Muslim politicians are instead advocating the needs of Muslims as a separate ethnic group. One proposal has been to recover from the 1980s the promotion of a separate Provincial Council or administrative unit for Muslims in the north and the east. It seems that today all groups are looking for solutions based on ethnicised forms of segregation, and a pervasive majority/minority thinking, none of which offers up possibilities for the resolution of conflict on the basis of political pluralism (Uyangoda 2003).

Uncompromising Spaces, Material Outcomes

For people on the ground, forced and voluntary movement, as well as conventional warfare and killings, suicide attacks, the destruction of economic targets, and political violence have been fairly common experiences that have resulted from Sri Lanka's particular social and spatial history. The profound and rapid rupture and social change of people's lives throughout the island is not uncommon. Displacement of people and loss of livelihoods represent the major social, economic, and human costs of the war. By the end of 2000, between 750,000 and 800,000 were living as internally displaced persons in Sri Lanka, while the same number of people were living as refugees and asylum seekers abroad. It is estimated that up to 1.7 million people have been displaced one or more times since 1983 (Danish Refugee Council 2000). While many internally displaced people returned to their homes during the fragile ceasefire of 2002, more than 200,000 were forced to be on the move again during the first six months after hostilities resumed in the first months of 2006. The displaced people's camp has become a common experience for many people during the war.

Moreover, the 2004 Indian Ocean tsunami that hit the coasts of the country left 31,000 people dead; 6,300 are still missing according to the Asian Development Bank (ADB 2005), and 443,000 people were displaced in Sri Lanka alone. The material losses after war, the ongoing violence, and the tsunami are immense. International assistance in the first six months after the three waves hit the coasts of the island (also termed the fourth wave) was massive, and not only were the divisions, tensions, and cleavages between communities revealed and reified in the aftermath of the tsunami, these divisions—between the north and south, between LTTE-controlled areas and government-controlled ones, and between ethnic groups—have created particular material outcomes for people on the ground. An attempt to set up a common mechanism for the LTTE- and government-controlled areas to coordinate assistance after the Indian Ocean tsunami, with headquarters established in Kilinochchi , the capital of the LTTE-controlled areas, failed after the Supreme Court ruled the mechanisms unacceptable as 'ordinary citizens would not have access to the region' (Relief Web 2005).

Since the tsunami, a disproportionate share of assistance has been directed towards the Sinhalese-dominated south. Over 2,000 more houses than were needed were reportedly built in Hambantota (current President

Mahinda Rajapakse's district), whilst the island-wide process of recovery has been hampered by lack of funds, materials, workers, and a very slow government process to allocate land in the north and east. Due to a pending war, the situation of inequality in everything from education and housing to material wealth will increase between discrete nations within the island boundary. Yet in the international arena, which accounts for Sri Lanka's rates of post-tsunami recovery at the scale of the nation-state, the island looks statistically to be doing well in the wake of the disaster. Postcolonial sensitivities to the enduring colonial spatialities of the nation-state are the sorts of analytical perspective that can usefully reveal the spatial inequalities and spatial divisions of aid and assistance that pervade the contemporary nation-state.

Although the north and east are commonly considered the war zones in Sri Lanka, there are no limits to the spaces through which the war has been fought. People living in the south have also lived with the war and destructive violence, albeit in very different ways to people in the north and east. In the cities, particularly in Colombo, control and surveillance of bodies—particularly Tamil bodies—at checkpoints by the government forces (see Hyndman and de Alwis 2004), coupled with the omnipresent threat of the LTTE's suicide bombers, have been constant reminders of a conflict and of a tense relationship with an 'other' group. In the rural areas of the south, the war economy has also had particular outcomes. The 30,000-strong army in 1986 had increased to nearly 129,000 by 1996, and to 143,000 by 1999 (Kelegama 1999; Rotberg 1999). An increasing number of Sinhalese rural poor from the south of the country have been depending on war income sent through remittances from household members fighting as soldiers in the north and east (Dunham and Jayasuriya 1998).

Connections between youth militancy in the north and south of the country point to other aspects of the relational spaces of war and violence. While Gunaratna (1998) claims that the Tamil militant groups were inspired by the JVP in the early 1970s, Uyangoda (1999) claims that the JVP insurgency from 1987 to 1989 was inspired by the 1983 riots and violence in the north. In Uyangoda's view, violence seems to not only have bred further violence, it has also reinforced the belief, equally held by both the Sinhalese government and the LTTE, that a decisive outcome on the battlefield might have a direct bearing on a future political settlement.

Ethnic imaginations revolving around contemporary Sri Lanka proliferate on a range of geographical scales, and not just those subsumed within the current juridical boundaries of the nation-state that we have been mobilising so far. Intense and diffuse transnational connections are continually shaping and challenging the postcolonial nation-state. Indeed, our own very engagements in this volume represent just one dimension of the complex intertwining of 'national' and 'outer-national' spatialities that continually (re)produce the island itself. In terms of the global Sri Lankan diaspora, Tamils[2] who left Ceylon to work and study during the colonial period, those who decided to stay abroad when conditions and life chances proved increasingly limited for Tamils during the period between 1950s and 1970s, and those who left Sri Lanka amidst increasing violence from the 1970s onward, have together shaped a Tamil diaspora that stretches across numerous countries all over the world. Venugopal (2003) estimates that in 2001 the Tamil diaspora numbered between 600,000 and 800,000. Having family members in exile in Canada, the UK, Switzerland, Norway, and India while the family is living as internally displaced in Sri Lanka is not unusual for today's transnational Sri Lankan Tamil. Individual and social remittances from the diaspora to the north and east regularly sustain family members, local communities, and the LTTE; therefore, the political economy of postcolonial Sri Lanka and its contested spatialities must be thought transnationally.

The LTTE has been a strong force in the diaspora, and much of their military and political strength has been sustained by economic support within the diaspora. The diasporic activities of fundraising, cultural and religious practices have also been instrumental in maintaining the geographical imagination of the Tamil Eelam; a Tamil nation whose spatiality fractures that very taken-for-granted island-ness inherited from colonial encounter by evoking the ethnic, cultural, historical, and even geological links between the north and east of Sri Lanka and the south of India. However, global geopolitical changes and a militant and global, neo-liberal commitment to declaring a 'war on terror' in the wake of 9/11 has resulted in the listing of the LTTE as a terrorist organisation and the consequent banning of members of LTTE visiting the EU in 2005. At the same time there is an incipient space for critical discourse around the LTTE in the diaspora, which has possibly affected the strength of the LTTE abroad and the diaspora support for the LTTE's activities in Sri Lanka. Whilst currently the banning of the LTTE in other countries seems to have had a negative impact on the initiatives to make peace, the diasporic spaces—and the spaces stretching outside Sri Lanka's territory—may enable contestation of the uncompromising spaces created by war.

Spatialising Sri Lankan Politics

We suspect the nation

(Jeganathan and Ismail 1995: 2)

Interrogating the instantiation of the postcolonial Sri Lankan nation-state requires suspicion towards the claims and consequences of the very project of nationhood. Sri Lanka is politically homogenising, constraining, oppressive, and eviscerating. Uncompromising. Violence inheres in its ongoing (re)production because of the fundamental attributes on which it has been built: fixed sovereignty and territorial borders, as well as fixed demands of political loyalty and obligation from its citizenry (Uyangoda 1998), all of which were forged in the crucible of colonial encounter. And these fundamental attributes have produced particular and popular understandings of the geographies of Sri Lanka. The perception is that the nation is as an autonomous island-state, comprised largely of contested and ethnicised territories. But the authors in this volume believe that politics has many different spatial incarnations. So, rather than taking this uncompromising version of the spatiality of the nation-state for granted, this volume sets out to disrupt those popular spatial stories. The chapters that follow all variously engage spaces and spatialities both coarser and finer than simply the contested territories that comprise the nation-state. Collectively they explore the kaleidoscope of spatial politics through which the nation has been actively, relationally, and fluidly built, lived, (re)produced, and contested. The utility then, of a postcolonial lens to frame this project, stems from a concern to get to grips with the ongoing political effects of the spatial forms and transmutations of colonialism in the present.

Nira Wickramasinghe's chapter on material culture and the imagined spaces of Empire provides a way into thinking about how fluid, non-territorial understandings of space and spatiality matter in the politico-cultural constitution of the postcolonial nation-state. Her careful historical analysis of consumption in late 19th- and early 20th-century Ceylon shows how the colonial state was performed and conjured into existence through the use of newly available consumer goods in a domestic market shaped by colonialism. But geographically, her chapter also does much more. It shows how such negotiations of new consumer goods and the liveliness of the goods themselves helped to lock Ceylonese people into an imagined and fluid 'space of empire', a spatiality that one cannot ignore when mobilising or locating postcolonial Sri Lanka. Sri Lanka's uncompromising territorial spatialities must be set against this historical context. It was, Wickramasinghe suggests, through everyday and mundane practices, like the use of imported Singer sewing machines, the drinking of tea and the application of European cosmetics, that the colonial island-state was not just borne, but spatially and imaginatively orientated within routes that connected it to the imperial metropolis.

This type of careful and contextual historical and geographical analysis reminds us that the very formation of the modern nation-state cannot be comprehended through narratives of organic, seed-like growth, and gestation from within, like those geographical imaginations employed so often by Sinhala nationalist movements. And this is precisely the point James Duncan teases out with the 'simultaneous stories-so-far' that he tells of Ceylon's 19th-century highland coffee plantations. If the histories of the coffee plantations are a history of Ceylonese or Sri Lankan modernity, the modernity that effectively built the colonial and the nation-state's successful plantation economy, then Duncan's chapter stresses the importance of geographically situating these stories within the transnational cultural, economic, and scientific eddies that umbilically connected Ceylon with Britain. The development of a highland plantation economy in Ceylon could only emerge because of, amongst a complex of other things, an emergent taste for this hot, bitter, black drink in bourgeois British metropolitan society. So, just as Duncan reminds us that European modernity must be seen as one of many coeval, intersecting trajectories, Ceylonese and Sri Lankan economic modernity was, and is, coeval with what happens on the island's constitutive outsides. What happens here cannot be disassociated from what happens there; modernity works differentially across transnational spatial registers, and, importantly, it has spatially differential effects.

But to talk of the nation's 'constitutive outsides' presupposes a certain ease with which one can be either in or out of the postcolonial nation-state, either be or not be Sri Lankan, belong or not belong. Diaspora and transnational studies have taught us that such distinctions are problematic indeed. Sharon Bell's auto-ethnographical reflections on her own connections, disconnections, and proximities through Sri Lanka's turbulent post-independence history and through her own career as a 'foreign' researcher within Sri Lankan studies remind us of the problems of drawing these lines of distinction. As researchers within the broad field of Sri Lankan studies, we all move through an array of knowledge spaces, and we all struggle to find a voice with which to intervene in debates over the politics of ethnicity or nationhood, to 'abide by' or 'speak to' Sri Lanka without neo-colonially 'speaking for' and anthropologising it as merely an object or case study (Ismail 2005). Bell's chapter reminds us that no matter where we are geographically positioned as researchers, we are all at various points in our own careers both inside and outside. What inscribes itself on us is our commitment as researchers to continue to generate the conversations we feel there is a need for, however awkward this may be at times.

To try and define who gets to speak is to revert to the dangerous prioritisation of an 'authentic Sri Lankan' voice, which so often implies a singular, hegemonic spatial present. This we reject. Similarly, it is those authoritative, exclusive, and organicist articulations of 'Sri Lankan space' that Benedikt Korf rejects in his lucid critical engagement with the contemporary geographical research by the Sri Lanka-based scholars G.H. Pieris and Madduma Bandara. Both of these respected scholars of Geography have recently mobilised the authorial effects of the discipline's 'scientific' discourse—discourses that are, of course, freely available to all of us who are lucky enough to work in a discipline that straddles the social and physical sciences—to first dispute claims for a Tamil homeland, and second assert claims for an island-wide Sinhala nationhood. Korf's aim is to highlight the ways that Peiris and Bandara's geographical scholarship operates *as* a discourse that has political effect. His careful and important intervention in a particular scholarly, geographical debate shows us how politics is always already spatialised, how space is always already political. But, like Bell, Korf is mindful of the tightrope that any 'foreign' researcher is made to walk when one engages (especially critically) such Sri Lankan scholarship: we must balance carefully lest our engagements be construed as 'foreign intervention' of the 'meddling' variety. Here then, at stake is not just Sri Lankan geographical scholarship itself, but the knowledge spaces that comprise that scholarship. As Bell suggests, a commitment to the necessity, substance, and quality of the debates and interventions themselves must take precedence over exclusivist decisions made by self-elected gatekeepers on who gets to speak. This is essential if we are to sustain productive dialogues within a broad field of Sri Lankan studies that is both provincial and credible.

In postcolonial Sri Lanka, then, the question of who gets to speak of or for the nation-state is political itself. Not just in scholarly research, but also in a field of literary and cultural production so heavily marked by diasporic movement. Authors like Michael Ondaatje have been much criticised in the domestic press over charges of exoticism or 'inauthenticity', but as Tariq Jazeel argues in his reading of Ondaatje's *Anil's Ghost*, if we accept that the historical and ongoing constitution of postcolonial Sri Lanka cannot easily be disassociated from its constitutive outsides (as the first four chapters argue so strongly in different ways), and further that the very role of the writer of fiction is to probe, interrogate, ask questions, then we can entertain the possibility that *Anil's Ghost* opens new angles through which to explore Sri Lanka's spatial politics. In particular, Jazeel's reading suggests that the novel sheds light on how a particular form of everyday Sri Lankan space—that is, meaningful Sri Lankan landscape authored as Sinhala, as Buddhist—actually shapes a politics of identity and plays an important role in the instantiation of the postcolonial (Sinhala) nation. But, importantly, his reading also suggests that the inscription of these landscape histories lies squarely within colonial histories of land management and archaeological survey. The very fabric of space itself has been authored, which urges us to question the very form of the nation-state, its naturalisations, and taken-for-granted topographies.

There are, of course, many more ways through which space has been shaped by colonial encounter across the island-state, and Camilla Orjuela's chapter draws attention to another lasting spatial presence of colonialism that often goes unrecognised in the burgeoning industry of peace-work that inflects contemporary Sri Lankan society. She focuses on the over-determining presence of Colombo-based institutions, NGOs and peace strategies, and the ways that this centre/periphery geography of peace work exercises unequal power relations in attempts to build civil society. What is at stake here are the polarisations of ethnicity and class that map onto this colonial centre/periphery binary that dwells so strongly in the present. If Colombo remains the seat of governance, and the business of government remains so heavily classed and constitutionally ethnicised, then—Orjuela argues—one must question the centrifugal peace-work emanating from this hub. How can peace-work *work* if it replicates the geographical polarisation of Sinhala and Tamil ethnicities? But if much is known about the unequal power relations exercised by the very structure and omnipresence of Colombo in Sri Lankan society and in the Sri Lankan psyche, then relatively little has been written on everyday life in, and the urban geographies of, the Jaffna peninsula. This is where Nihal Perera offers a series of illuminating reflections on the performance and habitation of urban space in and around the peninsula. His chapter provides a much-needed corrective to accounts and descriptions of Sri Lankan urban structures that allow Colombo (or Kandy) to somehow stand for the nation-state (in scholarly research as much as in glossy, 'Barefoot', coffee-table books). Jaffna's unique urban structures and architectures come into representation through Perera's writing. But more than this, if Orjuela argued that the polarisation of ethnicity is sustained at least in part *by* geography, then Perera's accounts of the hybrid spaces that have emerged through practice (spaces characterised now not by ethnic polarisation but by ethnic ambivalence) offer a glimmer of hope that the performance of space can also drive change. His chapter suggests the myriad ways that spatial practices inscribe themselves within the binary geographical imaginations that pervade Sri Lankan society, offering the potential to shatter the very binaries themselves.

Through all this we wish to emphasise again our commitment to what we call 'lively and heterogeneous spatialities', our commitment to rebuking a single spatial present. Which brings us to Eelam. Locating postcolonial Sri Lanka is not to negate the existence of Eelam. Rather, our aim is to open up and interrogate the spatialities that have instantiated the nation-state, to intersect its trajectories with alternative spatial imaginations, like, for example, Eelam. To argue for the multiplicity of space and spatial imaginations is to vehemently resist being forced to choose *between* Sri Lanka and Eelam, and this is the underlying subtext to Øivind Fuglerud's exploration of the orientations, operationalisation, and performance of the LTTE's state-to-come. As he argues, despite the LTTE's sophisticated modes of civil and urban governance (playing also at Western understandings of peace building, and universal rights to self-determination), they have failed to build a broad-based and inclusive concept of the Tamil nation. In fact, the conflict and the fight for a Tamil Eelam has moved from a bipolar ethnic imagination to a complex relationship between groups on the island; relationships between Tamils and Muslims, between Tamils in the north and Tamils in the east, between the Tamils still located on the island and the Sri Lankan Tamils abroad. These are just some examples that destabilise the understanding of the singularity of Eelam's—or indeed Sri Lanka's—spatial present.

To have to choose, then, is to be coerced into picking between competing singular spatial presents: 'Sri Lanka or Eelam?', the politicians ask. And this is the point: space offers us so much more. So part of the purpose of bringing these chapters together is to debunk the notion that we need to choose a singular spatial present. We hope the chapters generate questions around the spatialities through which Sri Lanka's cultural politics operate, and we hope that in doing so they suggest the political possibilities of more lively heterogeneous, less static spatial imaginations. We hope they allow us to hold in productive tension the multiplicity of (spatial) narratives, orientations, and imaginations that comprise this postcolonial Sri Lanka. This will be a small step towards unpicking the present 'national' and rebuilding it in more spatially inclusive ways. Our postcolonial geographies are hopeful.

Notes

1. Of Sri Lanka's approximately 19.5 million citizens, about 5 per cent are Indian Tamils, 8 per cent are Muslims, 4.5 per cent are Sri Lankan Tamils and 82 per cent are Sinhalese, in addition to a small number of other groups (Peace in Sri Lanka 2006). There has been no census since 1981 in the north and east of the country, so the numbers are only estimates by the government. Despite the fact that the war is not immediately about ethnic differences, it is often presented as an ethnic conflict fought between the predominantly Sinhalese Sri Lankan armed forces (government forces) and the LTTE.
2. Tamil and Sinhalese migration abroad followed similar patterns during colonial and early post-independence times, but with increasing experience by Tamils of discriminatory politics and war, they soon outnumbered the Sinhalese in leaving the country.

References

Angell, M. (1998). 'Understanding the Aryan theory', in M. Tiruchelvam and C.S. Datthathreya (eds), *Culture and Politics of Identity in Sri Lanka*, pp. 41–72. Colombo: International Centre for Ethnic Studies.

Asian Development Bank (ADB). (2005). *From Disaster to Reconstruction: A Report on ADB's Response to the Asian Tsunami*, Available online at http://www.adb.org/Documents/Reports/ADB-Tsunami/default.asp, accessed 3 October 2008.

Bastian, S. (1996). 'Control of State Land: The Devolution Debate', in ICES, *Sri Lanka: The Devolution Debate*, pp. 61–86. Colombo: International Centre for Ethnic Studies.

Bell, V. (1999). *Feminist Imagination*. London: Sage Publications.

Blunt, A. and C. McEwan (eds). (2002). *Postcolonial Geographies*. New York and London: Continuum.

Carter, P. (1987). *The Road to Botany Bay: An Essay in Spatial History*. London and Boston: Faber and Faber.

Chatterjee, P. (2004). *The Politics of the Governed: Reflections on Popular Politics in Most of the World*. Columbia University Press: New York.

Danish Refugee Council (2000). *Program Document: DRC Sri Lanka 2000–2003*. Anuradhapura: Danish Refugee Council.

Dunham, D. and S. Jayasuriya (1998). 'Is All So Well with the Economy and with the Rural Poor?' *Pravada*, 5(10/11): 22–27.

Fanon, F. (1965 [1961]). *The Wretched of the Earth* (trans. Constance Farrington). London: Macgibbon and Kee.

———. (1982 [1967]). 'The Fact of Blackness', in *Black Skin, White Masks* (translated by C. L. Markham), pp. 109–40. New York: Grove Press, Inc.

Fuglerud, Ø. (1999). *Life on the Outside: The Tamil Diaspora and Long Distance Nationalism*. London: Pluto Press.

Gregory, D. (2004). *The Colonial Present*. Oxford: Blackwells.

Gunaratna, R. (1998). *Sri Lanka's Ethnic Crisis & National Security*. Colombo: South Asian Network on conflict Research.

Guneratne, A. (2002). 'What's in a Name? Aryans and Dravidians in the Making of Sri Lankan Identities', in N. Silva (ed.), *The Hybrid Island: Culture Crossings and the Invention of Identity in Sri Lanka*, pp. 20–40. London, New York and Sri Lanka: Zed Books and The Social Scientists' Association.

Gunawardana, R.A.L.H. (1995). *Historiography in a Time of Ethnic Conflict: Construction of the Past in Contemporary Sri Lanka*. Colombo Social Scientist's Association.

Hellmann-Rajanayagam, D. (1990). 'The Concept of a "Tamil Homeland" in Sri Lanka: Its Meaning and Development', *South Asia*, 13(2): 79–110.

Hyndman, J. and M. de Alwis (2004). 'Bodies, Shrines and Roads: Violence, (Im)mobility and Displacement in Sri Lanka', *Gender, Place and Culture*, 11(4): 535–57.

Ismail, Q. (2005). *Abiding by Sri Lanka: On Peace, Place and Postcoloniality*. Minneapolis: University of Minnesota Press.

Jacobs, J. (1996). *Edge of Empire: Postcolonialism and the Future*. London and New York: Routledge.

Jayawardene, K. (2000). *Nobodies to Somebodies: The Rise of the Colonial Bourgeoisie in Sri Lanka*. Colombo: Social Scientist's Association and Sanjiva Books.

Jeganathan, P. (1995). 'Authorizing History, Ordering Land: The Conquest of Anuradhapura', in P. Jeganathan and Q. Ismail (eds), *Unmaking the Nation: The Politics of Identity and History in Modern Sri Lanka*, pp. 106–36. Colombo: Social Scientists' Association.

Jeganathan, P. and Q. Ismail (1995). 'Introduction: Unmaking the Nation', in P. Jeganathan and Q. Ismail (eds), *Unmaking the Nation: The Politics of Identity and History in Modern Sri Lanka*, pp. 2–9. Colombo: Social Scientists' Association.

Kelegama, S. (1999). 'Economic Costs of Conflict in Sri Lanka', in Robert I. Rotberg (ed.), *Creating Peace in Sri Lanka: Civil War and Reconciliation*, pp. 71–88. Washington, DC: Brookings Institution Press.

Madden, F. and J. Darwin (eds). (1994). *The Dependent Empire 1900–1948: Colonies, Protectorates and Mandates—Select Documents on the Constitutional History of the British Empire and Commonwealth*, Vol. VII. Connecticut and London: Greenwood Press.

Mbembe, A. (2001). *On the Postcolony*. Berkeley, Los Angeles and London: University of California Press.

McEwan, C. (2003). 'Material Geographies and Postcolonialism', *Singapore Journal of Tropical Geography*, 24(3): 340–55.

Nash, C. (2002). 'Cultural Geography: Postcolonial Cultural Geographies', *Progress in Human Geography*, 26(2): 219–30.

Nissan, E. and R.L. Stirrat (1990). 'The Generation of Communal Identities', in J. Spencer (ed.), *Sri Lanka: History and the Roots of Conflict*, pp. 19–44. London: Routledge.

Peace in Sri Lanka (2006). 'Facts and Figures'. Available online at http://www.peaceinsrilanka.org/peace2005/Insidepage/FactsandFigures/FactsandFigures.aspm, accessed 22 February 2007.

Perera, N. (1999). 'Colonialism and National Space: Representations of Sri Lanka', in S. Gamage and I.B. Watson (eds), *Conflict and Community in Contemporary Sri Lanka: 'Pearl of the East' or the 'Island of Tears'?* pp. 23–48. New Delhi: Sage Publications.

Pfaffenberger, B. (1994). 'Introduction: The Sri Lankan Tamils', in C. Manogaran and B. Pfaffenberger (eds), *The Sri Lankan Tamils: Ethnicity and Identity*, pp. 1–27. Boulder, CO: Westview Press.

Phadnis, U. (1989). 'Sri Lanka: Crises of Legitimacy and Integration', in L. Diamond, J.J. Linz and S.M. Lipset (eds), *Asia: Democracy in Developing Countries*, Volume 3, pp. 143–86. Boulder, CO: Lynne Rienner Publishers.

Porter, B. (1984). *The Lion's Share: A Short History of British Imperialism 1850–1983*. London and New York: Longman.

Relief Web (2005). 'Sri Lanka's Top Court Blocks Sections of Tsunami Aid Deal between Government, Rebels', Available online at http://www.reliefweb.int/rw/rwb.nsf/db900SID/EVIU-6EBCUJ?OpenDocument, 15 July, 3 October 2008.

Rotberg, R.I. (1999). 'Sri Lanka's Civil War: From Mayhem toward Diplomatic Resolution', in R.I. Rotberg (ed.), *Creating Peace in Sri Lanka. Civil War and Reconciliation*, pp. 1–16. Washington, DC: Brookings Institution Press.

Said, E. (1978). *Orientalism*. London: Penguin.

Shastri, A. (1997). 'Government Policy and the Ethnic Crisis in Sri Lanka', in M.E. Brown and S. Ganguly (eds), *Government Policies and Ethnic Relations in Asia and the Pacific*, pp. 129–63. Cambridge, MA: Centre for Science and International Affairs.

Sidaway, J. (2000). 'Postcolonial Geographies: An Exploratory Essay', *Progress in Human Geography*, 24(4): 591–612.

Singer, M.R. (1964). *The Emerging Elite: A Study of Political Leadership in Ceylon*. Cambridge, MA: MIT Press.

Spencer, J. (1990). 'Introduction: The Power of the Past', in J. Spencer (ed.), *Sri Lanka: History and the Roots of Conflict*, pp. 1–18. London: Routledge.

Spivak, G.C. (1996 [1990]). 'Poststructuralism, Marginality, Postcoloniality and Value', in P. Mongia (ed.), *Contemporary Postcolonial Theory: A Reader*. pp. 198–222, New York, London: Arnold Press.

Stirrat, R.L. (1988). *On the Beach: Fishermen, Fishwives and Fishtraders in Post-colonial Lanka*. Delhi: Hindustan Publishing.

Stokke, K. (1998). 'Sinhalese and Tamil Nationalism as Post-colonial Political Projects from "Above", 1948–1983', *Political Geography*, 17(1): 83–113.

Tambiah, S. (1986). *Sri Lanka: Ethnic Fratricide and the Dismantling of Democracy*. Chicago: Chicago University Press.

Tiruchelvam, N. (2000a). 'The Politics of Federalism and Diversity in Sri Lanka', in Yash Ghai (ed.), *Autonomy and Ethnicity: Negotiation Competing Claims in Multi-ethnic States*, pp. 197–218. Cambridge: Cambridge University Press.

———. (2000b). 'Devolution and the Elusive Quest for Peace in Sri Lanka', in K.M. de Silva and G.H. Peiris (eds), *Pursuit of Peace in Sri Lanka: Past Failures and Future Prospects*, pp. 183–202. Kandy: International Centre for Ethnic Studies.

Uyangoda, J. (1998). 'Biographies of a decaying nation-state', in M. Tiruchelvam, and C.S. Dattathreya (eds), *Culture and Politics of Identity in Sri Lanka*, pp. 168–86. Colombo: International Centre for Ethnic Studies.

———. (1999). 'A Political Culture of Conflict', in R.I. Rotberg (ed.), *Creating Peace in Sri Lanka: Civil War & Reconciliation*, pp. 156–68. Washington, DC: Brookings Institution Press.

———. (2003). 'Pluralism, Democracy and Ethnic Conflict Resolution: Trajectories in Sri Lanka'. Paper presented at 'Democratizing and Developing Post-conflict Sri Lanka' Conference, Oslo, 6 May.

Venugopal, R. (2003). 'The Global Dimension of Conflict in Sri Lanka'. QEH Working Papers 99, Queen Elizabeth House, University of Oxford.

Yeoh, B.S.A. (2001). 'Postcolonial Cities', *Progress in Human Geography*, 25(3): 456–68.

2

The Imagined Spaces of Empire

Nira Wickramasinghe

The united luxuries of Europe and Asia are displayed in superfluous abundance. (Cordiner 1807: 111)

Introduction

When Ceylon became part of the British Empire, its material cultures underwent a drastic but selective transformation. New products that entered the market, were immediately consumed or took root in the living spaces of some sections of the Ceylonese population. These new objects and artefacts surrounded them, and possibly redefined their dream world, transformed their bodies, and reshaped their lives and those of their descendants. Since they were purchased and used, we can assume that some of these objects—although they were not fabricated in Ceylon—reflect (directly or indirectly) their beliefs, or at least a shift in their beliefs in time. Indeed, objects consumed became part of a culture in the making where they played an important part in mediating social and spatial relationships. Consumption generated an active mode of relations, not only with other goods, but also with the domestic collectivity, and Empire to which that domestic collectively notionally 'belonged' (Baudrillard 1968).

When these objects entered the homes of the people of Ceylon/ Sri Lanka the Empire was already present as a tangible reality as is evident from British civil servant John Ferguson's fascinating account of Queen Victoria's 1883 Jubilee celebrations in Ceylon on the Galle Face Green Esplanade. On that day, services in four languages—English, Sinhalese, Tamil, and Portuguese—were held in all places of worship. The Queen's letter requesting that prayer and thanksgiving be offered was sent to all pastors demonstrating the Empire's willingness to personalise its rule. A large number of the poor in towns and villages were fed, each getting a measure of rice and five cents (one penny), or a piece of calico. This act of charity was followed by great celebrations at the Galle Face Esplanade where 15 to 20 *pandal*s (large decorative structures that describe the life of the Buddha and his teachings) were erected. They were decorated with loops of plantain and coconut leaf, green moss and fern, and yellow *olas (*palm leaves). Approximately 25,000 people were present to hear the governor read the record of the chief events of the 50 years. The Royal Standard was hoisted and a salute of 50 guns was heard. The royal anthem was sung. A procession of 2,000 people followed, including 27 Buddhist monks and Arabi Pasha—who had led a revolt against the British in Egypt and would remain in Ceylon as an exile for 19 years—and three fellow exiles (Ferguson 1887: 176). When school children sang 'God save the Queen', a young monk chanted a number of Pali stanzas composed by the learned Sumangala in honour of the monarch, the high priest of Adam's peak and the president of Widyoda College.

The Empire was clearly a performative act: it was saluted and sung by all its subjects in an atmosphere suited to its majesty. But it was also made of a series of prosaic acts—in 1905 if a Ceylonese subject posted a letter to any part of the British Empire (except the Commonwealth of Australia) s/he would pay 6 cents for the stamp, while to all other foreign countries the cost was 15 cents, nearly three times higher. It was also through such everyday acts and practices that the Empire was made real for its subjects, rich, poor, colonised and colonisers (*Ferguson's Ceylon Directory* 1905: 249).

In its heyday, the British Empire governed roughly a quarter of the world's population, covered the same proportion of the earth's land surface, and dominated nearly all its oceans. By the time of the British conquest of Ceylon that followed the Portuguese in the 16th century and the Dutch in the mid-18th century, there were in the western and south-western regions of the island signs announcing the burgeoning of modernity: the growth of towns, a moving labour force, the spread of the use of money, the rise in production and the expansion of long-distance trade had broken the isolation and insularity of many people. More than any other Empire in history, the British Empire promoted the free movement of goods, capital, and labour. Its growth was powered by commerce and consumerism.

Life moved at a slower pace for rural folk than for city dwellers. But if the large majority lived their lives in the village or district of birth, some moved and wandered away following the economic booms of the period: plumbago, graphite mining, and coconut. A few adventurous men and women even boarded ships that took them to Malaysia or Australia. Natives too were moving. In the 1901 census, for the first time, information concerning the place of birth of the inhabitants of the island appeared. People were still very sedentary since 90 per cent lived in the district of their birth: 'The Ceylonese are not naturally of a roving disposition and they seldom leave their homes if without so doing they can procure a moderate subsistence' (*Census of Ceylon 1901* 1902: 118).

The port of Galle in south Ceylon was an important port of call for schooners and steamships until the later part of the 19th century when with Ceylon's expanding tea industry Colombo took precedence as a port. Foreign contact with sailors and captains probably provided information about the bountiful lands on these trade routes. These contacts would have encouraged young people to leave. A few did leave for other lands. Most 19th century Sinhalese migrants to Malaya and as far afield as Tanganyika, Uganda, Kenya, Siam, Shanghai, Hong Kong, Australia, and Thursday Island were from Galle and Matara, and their hinterlands in the southern coast of Ceylon: 'The emigration of young men to the Straits, Burma and other places in search of employment continues to be on the increase' (ibid.).

They were part of the Empire, subjects of the largest system of domination in the world. Even those who did not leave knew something of this world through the foreign news despatches in the fledgling Sinhala press, sporadic contacts with British government agents, or through rumours that started in the workplace or in the teashops and spread at the speed of a bullock cart. The vagaries of a war in the Cape or in Europe, or news of violence perpetrated on Muslims in the Orient reached them, but did not perturb them. For those working in the new export industries, changes in the world economy were, however, clearly felt. World War I, for instance, affected the growth of the coconut industry. The island was, in that sense, closely connected to the rest of the world through ties of domination and economic exchange.

This chapter explores the connections between modernity, material culture, and Ceylon's emergent imperial geographies through a foray into new consumption patterns in Ceylon/Sri Lanka in the early 20th century. It will explore the entry and circulation of some new objects produced in the British Empire as part of the transformation of the material culture in late colonial Ceylonese society. If objects define nature and ourselves, if they change the world, create it anew, and if we constantly rediscover and redefine the world through objects, as Hannah Arendt suggests in the *Human Condition* (Lubar and Kingery 1993: 197), one can suppose that objects of Empire opened up the horizons of the common person. Thus, transformations in material culture signalled a transformation of the native body, and his/her relation to the time and space of both community and Empire, a transformation that was largely incomplete but significant enough to be mentioned in the colonial texts.

The consumption of goods and objects cannot, however, be looked at in isolation, a tendency quite common among students of material culture. The facility with which these new objects were accepted in the homes of the people must be linked to a variety of enabling circumstances. Among these the rituals and practices through which the colonial state created a sense of allegiance to the idea of Empire and eventually a new cognitive space are crucial. The creation of a cognitive space of Empire through news items in the press and advertisements would have facilitated the entry of new objects from familiar places into the homes of the literate middle classes. But the worldview of the non-literate classes is more difficult to fathom. We shall never know with certainty what their dreams were made of or what emotions they harboured, but the study of the objects they bought and consumed give us a few clues on their inner life.

Another factor that would have helped the adoption of foreign goods by the people of Ceylon was the human traces of Empire in the small crown colony that was Ceylon. Indeed, men and women from different countries—all subjects of the Empire—lived, worked, and were exiled on the island. Lives had become interconnected across territories, seas, and oceans. The exile of prisoners and rebels to other British colonies was a common practice in the Empire. Arabi Pasha and some of his followers were sent to Ceylon after he fomented an anti-colonial revolt in Egypt, while the Kandyan chief Ehelepola was sent to serve his term of exile in Mauritius after the Kandyan revolt against British rule was put down in 1818. Other troublemakers were sent to India and kept under house arrest. Ceylon was itself home to prisoners of war who were sent to serve their term in penitentiaries far away from their homelands. The largest contingent of foreigners in the early 20th century came to Ceylon in the wake of the Boer War. The first batch of South African prisoners of war arrived in August 1900 and others followed up to June 1900. Altogether, 4,914 prisoners were interned in Ceylon chiefly at camps in Diyatalawa, Ragama, and Mount Lavinia. Some were kept on board the hospital ship *Atlantian* in Colombo harbour, and some were on parole in the rest of the island.[1]

Import of Goods from Britain and the Rest of the Empire

From the 16th century onwards British expansion proceeded steadily, and the Empire was the product of the new world systems built in the aftermath of the 'discoveries'—world systems that were rooted in colonial growth. The expansion of the British Empire, from that time onward, was interrupted by the War of American Independence and a significant loss of territory and influence, with a consequent diminution of enthusiasm on the part of the British for colonial adventures. By the time of the Napoleonic Wars, however, Britain was recovering such interest, and by the 1820s, having made considerable territorial gains, ruled 26 per cent of the world's total population. Between 1840 and 1860 the value of Britain's trade with the world had tripled. British manufacturers exported their goods to the rest of the world on British ships and railways, backed by British insurance and banking services. They depended on the 'rest of the world' to supply raw materials and foodstuff. The economic dependence was mutual, but the power relation unequal (Hall 2000: 7). In this Empire, Partha Chatterjee (1994) has argued, the variety of forms of rule was underpinned by a logic that he calls 'the rule of colonial difference'. This was the rule that distinguished the colonisers from the colonised, that was predicated on the power of the metropole over its subject people (Hall 2000: 6–7). When it comes to consumption patterns, however, the rule of difference was shaded with ironic tints. The coloniser and colonised would buy the same jam for the same cost, but consume it in either similar or different ways, either with butter and toast in one instance, or with *pol roti* in another.

From within the Empire and outside the privileged trade partners differed in time and according to the products, as in the case of imported clothes. In the early 20th century goods were imported from a variety of different countries. Half of the products still came from the United Kingdom and one-third from British colonies. But Japan and Germany sent a considerable proportion of the cheaper qualities of cotton clothes such as *banian*s, shirts, and undergarments. In bleached and printed piece goods England had a practical monopoly, but Japanese imports of printed goods were on the rise. England and Holland supplied large quantities of sarongs, probably produced in Indonesia. In grey piece goods England supplied three-fourths of the quantity and the USA, British India, and Japan the remainder. Handkerchiefs, scarves, and shawls came from the United Kingdom and Japan. Japan sent three-fifths of the total amount of silk and satin after British India. Even a few woollen goods were imported: blankets from British India, cloth items and flannel from the United Kingdom, and scarves and shawls from Japan (Turner 1922: 43). From the writings of the early 20th century, the trade figures point to an influx of foreign goods. It was quite clear that Ceylon was now part of the world system, and that the decline of its own already weak textile industry was irreversible.

New Consumption Patterns

The capital city too was changing and growing into a more metropolitan space. The expansion of Colombo harbour and the building of a breakwater that was completed in 1884 confirmed Colombo as the major business centre of the island. A massive demographic change followed. People migrated from the countryside to the city looking for employment and greater economic opportunities, and in so doing were confronted with new, worldly 'cultural' offerings that they were unused to in the isolation of the village. From 1901 to 1911 the rate of population increase in Colombo was more than double that of the islands as a whole (Panditharatne 1964: 206). In 1921, while the total population was 4,505,000, there were 33 principal towns, out of which 11 had a population more than 10,000 and 15,000 villages. With urbanisation modernity found a privileged terrain.

Turner (1922: 4) has described the changes that took place in the cities quite predictably in the language of progress and development:

> Of the towns of Ceylon, the most important and progressive is the capital Colombo. It is the main business centre of the island, the seat of the government and its principal officials and the headquarters of the chief mercantile firms. It is consequently the most westernised of all the towns and possesses most of the refinements of modern civilisation, up to date hotels, electric lights, fans and ramways an excellent water supply, an up to date system of water borne drainage, an extensive emporia of goods of all kinds.

Although in 1911 the urban–rural divide was still pronounced, with the large majority of the population living in rural areas, town life was no longer unknown to villagers. For example, wealthy villagers sent their children to school in the nearest large town, and in 1912, E.B. Denham (1912: 158) commented, 'The wants of a town have been created amongst the rural population.' The isolation of the village had been breached with the new Colombo–Galle road and the coastal railway. But the rates of the railway in the late 19th century were such that older modes of transport survived. In 1895 carters were competing successfully over short distances with the southern railway in Galle. In the Western Province the bulk of Kalutara traffic to Colombo went by other means than railway even by 1898. Most of the arrack and furniture produced in Kalutara and Moratuwa were transported in boats to Colombo (*Ceylon Administrative Report* 1895; *Ceylon Observer*, 4 December 1897; Public Record Office 1888).

Rituals of Empire: Changing the Internal Space

Ceylon (as it was then called) became a Crown colony in 1802 after being ruled for a few years from Madras. Although we can only regretfully surmise what people of the time thought of the idea of Empire in the century and a half that followed, we can clearly identify the different ways in which the idea modified the everyday life of people of the island. For one, the space in which they dwelt and functioned was a constant reminder that they were part of an Empire that spread across the seas. But mostly there were rituals that were enacted to celebrate the Empire and its rulers at regular points in time. One such ritual of belonging was the 1885 Jubilee of Queen Victoria's coronation as Empress of India. This foundational moment was preceded and prepared as it were by less important events such as the royal visits of the Duke of Edinburgh in 1870, of the Prince of Wales in 1875, and the young Princes Albert and George of Wales in 1881. According to Ferguson (1887: 170), 'on each occasion the loyalty and devotion of the people to the British crown and their warm personal interest in the happiness and welfare of their sovereign were very conspicuous.' This connection was intimately soldered through the redrawing of the calendar where government holidays were either Christian religious feasts or commemorative events related to the British royal family, for example, 24 May: Queen's birthday; 28 June: Queen's coronation day; 26 August: Prince Albert's birthday; 9 November: Prince of Wales's birthday (*Ceylon Almanach and Annual Register* 1861:10).

Empire as Spatial Identity: Names, Things, Places

The city became a site for the celebration of Empire and for the performance of rituals of belonging. It is in cities that the new objects of consumption first found a welcoming terrain. The people of Colombo and other cities in the island gradually found that the space in which they lived was acquiring a new identity. Roads, buildings, and provinces were renamed, the imprint left by the Portuguese and Dutch erased forever. Nihal Perera (1999) has analysed these transformations of space and the way in which British rule consolidated its control over the land of conquest through semantic appropriation. Building on his comments, we can try to find out if the idea of Empire, of a space that spread beyond the boundaries of the island, entered the process of renaming. A number of streets of the Fort of Colombo were renamed during the years of British rule so as to evoke the connection with the metropolis, the most conspicuous being Queen Street, Prince Street, Chatham Street, and York Street (ibid.: 49). In Kandy, a driveway was constructed around the lake and named after the Empress Victoria, as was the esplanade in front of the temple (ibid.: 56). Most significant was Victoria Park, the sumptuous green space in the middle of the capital city where British residents could take an evening stroll.

When addressing the issue of how names are read and perceived by passers-by, Michel de Certeau (de Certeau 1988: 104) perceptively writes that the words that hierarchise and semantically order the surface of a city 'slowly lose, like worn coins, the value engraved on them, but their ability to signify outlives its first definition'. What he means is that words become 'liberated spaces that can be occupied' that articulate 'a poetic geography on top of the geography of the literal, forbidden or permitted meaning' (ibid.: 105). So although the spaces of the city were 'imperialised', they were lived and perceived by the residents as a personal and totally ineffable experience. More importantly, these spaces had by the early 20th century shed their cultural anchorages and entered the floating realm of modernity, a realm in which the machine punctuated these symbolic, imagined geographies.

The Machine

The rural areas resolutely laid claim to modernity with the conquest of the sewing machine and the gramophone. While the gramophone that had become visible in the colony through advertisement and showrooms became a significant organising principle of a modern British colonial and Ceylonese upper-class private home in urban areas, the sewing machine could be found in the most remote rural areas of the island. It epitomised the intoxication of modernity and its transitory character: it was easy to work, noisy, faster than humankind, and an instrument of standardisation. It could create replicable serials at a much greater speed than a person.

In this sense, it was as much part of the driving power of modernity as photography or print, whose commodified production in books, novels, and especially newspapers, Benedict Anderson (1991) argues, made possible the dissemination of a national consciousness, by organising distant and proximate events according to a calendrical simultaneity—of 'empty, homogeneous time' that enabled their readers to coordinate social time and space, and thus to conceive of relations to others across countries and continents (Wilson 2000: 159–60). It is in this context that material cultures underwent significant changes.

With the sewing machine, the human touch was subordinated to the machine's will, the particular was replaced by a reproducible model (Anderson 1991: 182–83). Sari blouses, for instance, could be made in vast quantities as each person had a block pattern to which the tailor referred. The sewing machine contributed to the *coup de grâce* of traditional weaving by its art of replicating rather than creating unique products.

In the late 19th century a number of companies were vying for the market. Among them was Wrenn Bennet and Company, which advertised 'the ideal sewing machine selling by thousands in England' (*Ceylon Examiner*, 23 March 1896). The referent was Britain, the mother country of the imperial Raj. Of the trading companies, however, Singer, of American origin, was by far the most successful. Interestingly, the American identity of Singer was never highlighted by its proponents or users, and gradually seems to have been subsumed in a wider 'modern Western imperial' identity. While 'for those living outside the United States, owning American products was a sign of Western modernity', international advertisements for Singer products suggested that less civilised people could become more civilised and more modern, more developed with the use of American products (Domosh 2004: 457). The first shop and office of the Singer Sewing Machine Company was established in Colombo in 1877 at No. 27 Main Street Pettah. In 1851 Singer introduced the first practical sewing machine with two roller feeds. Subsequently, it developed domestic straight stitch hand-operated models. The machines were marketed through Singer-owned retail outlets. After the first shop in Pettah branches were opened in Kandy, Galle, and Hatton. Thereafter, the Singer Sewing Machine Company was established and branches were opened in many towns throughout the island. People accepted the machines with open arms because Singer offered it on easy payments from the inception.

Advertisements in the fledgling press were avidly consumed, just as much as the news accounts relating to countries where the products originated from. Approximately 40 per cent of males and 10 per cent of females enumerated in the Census of 1911 were able to read and write. Many people who could not read were read to at the workplace or after the workday was over. These people too would have been touched by the new ideas contained in the press of the time. New objects such as the gramophone and the sewing machine imaginatively and physically entered the homes of the people of Ceylon as their worldviews were shaped by the press of the day. The terrain for the acceptance of the foreign object in their home was prepared by the Ceylonese public's gradual awareness of the rest of the world and its understanding as being part of the Empire. Literacy was an important factor that facilitated changes in worldviews.

The world was there in the newspapers and the books that were read in English and in translation. Thanks to the new telegraphic lines, the reader was now in touch with the news from all parts of the world and the Western products advertised in the printed news. The *Ceylon Observer* contained the latest telegraphic news by the Indo–European line, Singapore and Australian lines, as well as from India. It was the first 'Indian journal on Reuter's list' and had correspondents in different parts of the world ('Catalogue of Newspapers, Periodicals, Books, Maps', compiled by *Ferguson's Directory* 1985).

Newspaper items literally and figuratively mapped imperial aspirations. They also organised time and space in ways that welded the national and imperial interest, while effacing the crueller aspects of Empire, colonialism and trade. In the past, as today, the reader is obviously not passive. Every reading modifies its object:

> He invents in texts something different from what they intended. He detaches them from their (lost or accessory) origin. He combines their fragments and creates something un-known in the space organized by their capacity for allowing an indefinite plurality of meanings. (de Certeau 1988: 169)

If one accepts with de Certeau that the reader is a poacher, one can think, for instance, that for some readers foreign news might have led to the production of a mercantilist worldview in which trade and the accumulation of wealth appeared as the highest national good; for others it might have led to a sense of belonging and loyalty to the Empire; for still others it might have made manifest the sombre realities of great power politics. Indeed, since the idea of a community formed in a homogeneous time is a utopia that scholars such as Partha Chatterjee have spelt out, the cognitive space of Empire can only be characterised by heterogeneity.

It is in this context that the consumer of newspaper advertisements and buyer of sewing machines must be understood.

An advertisement in the Sinhala paper *Lakmina* for Singer warned against imitations and expounded the after-purchase servicing as well as the easy payment scheme (*Lakmina Pahana,* 4 January 1895). Its first users were housewives and tailors. The first clothes sewn were jackets, shirts, and sarongs. A typical Singer advertisement went as follows:

> If you wish to reduce your tailoring expenses
> If you wish to save your time
> If you wish to see your family neatly dressed
> If you wish to see your ladies engaged in useful and intelligent work at home (*Ceylon Independent*, 6 February 1904)

The appeal was clearly to the housewife as consumer, and displayed a conventional perception of what a useful occupation was for the womenfolk of the country. As Domosh (2004: 458) has shown in her work on five American companies, gender ideology was crucial to the configuration of culturally acceptable forms of mass consumption. The native stockist and buyer were, however, positioned as male, as the term 'your ladies' indicates. Indeed, at that time urban upper middle-class women were getting involved in Victorian leisure activities, such as piano playing, which were not considered useful by many nationalist critiques. The sewing machine reinscribed colonial Victorian templates of female respectability—such as confinement to the home, caring and looking after one's husband and children, and reproductive labour in the private sphere of the lower middle classes. Interestingly, the sewing machine that embodied the Victorian values of work and thrift—unlike the piano, a frivolous machine—soon shed its foreign image and became part of the transformed material culture of the common people. The singular fact that Singer was an American company did not appear in the advertisements, whose creators clearly understood the immersion of the future buyers in a Victorian/imperial culture of work and values.

Some tailoring establishments, such as Whiteaway Laidlaw and Company, and Drapers and Outfitters advertised themselves as users of sewing machines—an added proof of quality tailoring in 1918. With the conquest of the sewing machine, the tailor too became modernised. Hannalis, the caste of Sinhalese tailors, had never been numerous, since they worked mainly in the court of the kings. In the early 19th century they were described by Davy as being 'very few' in number. A century later tailoring had mainly become the preserve of Tamils and Burghers as the newspaper advertisements indicate (Ryan 1993: 113–14).

Competing with Singer were other brands such as National and Pfaff, the former having regularly advertised its product in the Sinhala papers:

> New National sewing machine
> No home is complete without this machine.

The machine was sold less as a useful item and more as a status symbol (*Lakmini Pahana,* 19 January 1918). In that sense it contributed to consolidating more recent social hierarchies that were no longer based on class or name. The sewing machine was consumed as a sign either that consolidated one's belonging to the group or brought distinction from erstwhile groups and reference to a higher social group (Baudrillard 1968: 79). Pfaff sold its product as an ideal Christmas or wedding present (*Ceylon Independent*, 6 February 1903: 7). The sewing machine would gradually become a central part of the dowry of a middle-class woman in Ceylon.

The appeal of the sewing machine also came from its unassuming size. Unlike other machines of the modern age such as trains or cars, the sewing machine was human in its size and appearance. It was small, convenient, and mobile enough for the home, to be placed and used inside the colonialised and feminised spaces of domestic and reproductive labour.

Food

In 1894, an account of the Ceylon customs describes the various types of foodstuff imported to Sri Lanka from other countries belonging to the Empire: butter, cheese, ham and bacon, beef, salted pork, biscuits, and bread from Australia; curry stuffs, *ghee*, onions, and potatoes from India; sago from the Straits; fruits unpreserved from the UK, Austria, Arabia, India, and Australia; salt from the UK, India, and the Maldives; and soap from India, the UK, and Germany (*Ferguson's Directory* 1895: 607–08). New consumables of international origins, from the Empire as well as other countries, were now available for people to buy and for others to desire.

Food habits among the wealthier classes changed with the import of foreign products. The middle classes drank imported gin, brandy, and whisky and, as one would expect, they led the lifestyle of English gentlemen and women, or what they thought was their lifestyle. Aerated waters were consumed commonly and manufacturers had sprung up in the island to meet the demand. Cream soda was among the most popular of drinks. *Ferguson's Directory* (1903: 326) provides a list of manufacturers for

1903. Particularly interesting is the extent of the spread of soda water and ice manufactures throughout the island: there were 15 ice and soda water mills in the Western Province, one soda mill manufacturer in the Central Province (Ampititiya) and Matale, and three soda water manufacturers each in the Eastern Province and Uva.

The consumption of meat increased considerably as the rise in the number of butchers and in the number of cattle thefts prove. At weddings of wealthy villagers meat was now being served. Through the sharing of food at festivals a new basis for the social was being created. It was, however, in predominantly Christian communities that meat was regularly eaten. Changes were taking place in the people's daily diet too: tea, coffee, and milk were gradually replacing rice *conjee,* cold rice water, and buttermilk. Tea stalls were springing up everywhere, especially near the railways. The 100 per cent increase in the amount of condensed milk imported between 1901 and 1911 reflected the change in consumption habits. The tea-drinking world was expanding: in 18th century America, the central item in a rapidly changing society was tea as it replaced stronger drinks such as the popular rum punch. While by the end of the 19th century tea, a product grown thousands of miles away on plantations in the hill country of Ceylon or India, had become, as Stuart Hall (1991: 39) relates, the symbol of English identity, the act of drinking tea in Ceylon or in other colonies was a kind of inverse performance of belonging to the Empire through the consumption of the sign of Englishness in the territories from which the raw materials for the 'cup of tea' came.

> Taking tea became a recognized ritual requiring the correct cups and saucers, sugar bowls and a collection of pots.... For all these Americans, drinking tea required cups that could hold extremely hot liquids and that in turn forced them to import the technically advanced ceramics that originated in Staffordshire. (Breen 1986: 488)

A decision to buy tea led to other purchases: for example, an imported pewter or silver bowl. This trend was discernible in Ceylon in middle-class households; the poorer classes would have used whatever utensils they had, adapting them to new modes of consumption.

In the same way, people of means were buying prepared foods for children such as malted milk, and Mellin's and Allebury's foods in an effort to emulate the eating habits of the British. The popularity of tinned soups, meats, and sardines was such that every bazaar was stocked with these products. In the city, Cargills and Company, established in 1844 as general importers and warehouse, was the largest department store, and was known to have a particularly well-stocked wine and spirit department.

> As regards the food supply, every care is taken that the beef and mutton supplied are imported. Australian frozen mutton is issued to prisoners of war and troops alike once a week, instead of beef. (*Census of Ceylon 1901* 1902: 165)

But most food habits remained the same in a country of rice eaters, or were more forcefully intruded upon by foods from the subcontinent: *appa* and *indi-appa* came to Sri Lanka with Malayalee workers and became part of the national cuisine more so than any food from the West. In that sense, the Empire had less influence on the fabric of everyday life than say, for instance, the Portuguese colonisers who left in Sri Lanka the chilli, the foundation of the national food regime.

Hygiene and Home

The body was a key site of the colonial encounter, as recent works in the field of colonial studies have suggested. Policies on the body in the Javanese colonial situation have been shown to have spawned 'a set of behaviours, a template for living, a care of the self, an ideal of domesticity' (Stoler 2002: 1). But in many of these studies the focus is the colonial encounter and genealogies of the intimate in the domestic space of the coloniser rather than of the colonised. Although this signals a paradigm shift in colonial studies, there is still a need to narrate the transformation in the worldviews, habits, and material cultures of the colonised, and describe as what James Duncan (2002: 317–36) calls their 'embodied practices' through a reading of the margins of colonial documents. We know, for instance, that before the advent of 'colonial soap', people in Sri Lanka, a land generally endowed with natural lakes, rivers, waterfalls, and hydraulic tanks, used to wash their bodies and clothes frequently with natural products such as sandalwood. 'No soap is used for washing clothes, dipping garments in water and striking them against a flat stone' was the most common method as described in 1807 by Reverend James Cordiner (1807: 118). Colonial documents are silent on the reactions of the native Ceylonese to the new products and the types of concerns that were voiced, although the native body was an imagined space that generated pervasive concern in official, settler, missionary, and planter's discourse and practices epitomised in the British civil servant E.B. Denham's (1912: 170) detailed account of the material culture of the natives in 1911.

In the colonial state, the colonised body was transformed gently, as well as coerced and disciplined into becoming a docile body. Just as in South-East Asia where the body of the native was described as different—Ann Stoler (2002: 6) describes how Javanese nursemaids were instructed to hold their charges away from their bodies so that the infants would not 'smell of their sweat'—in Ceylon native bodies were considered lacking in hygiene and discipline. The plantations workers resisted attempts to transform them into abstract, docile bodies by rejecting the highly routinised plantation regime through the few weapons of the weak—desertion, thefts, minimising work—they had at their disposal. But in a situation of unequal power relations they had to comply overtly (Duncan 2002).

Through the contact with cosmetics, the body of the native man and woman became both a desiring body and a healthier body more adapted to labour. This feature was important since the goals of the colonisers were essentially economically motivated. In the villages and cities, hygiene was sold as a consumer product, while in the plantations, a combination of Western hygiene and control transformed the Tamil labourer from a 'weak, stupid, ill-fed, badly clad person' through being 'well housed, well cared for, well fed, and employed at regular and sufficient work' into 'a strong, intelligent, lusty labourer' (ibid.: 326). Highly perfumed soap was in great demand in the first decade of the 20th century. Even in the interior villages Cherry Blossom and Famra soap and powder were available in small shops and sold widely. Soap was sold at 35 cents a cake and talcum powder at 40 cents a tin. Among the popular perfumed powder was the one called White Rose (Denham 1912: 170), a name that married in one image the white colonial master and the rose, evoking the gentleness of his civilisation.

A letter to the editor of the *Sinhala Jatiya* castigated this new trend in women, which was 'to waste money unnecessarily to beautify themselves, following the latest fashions and using strange things like perfume' (*Sinhala Jatiya*, 1 February 1923). Society's equilibrium that was between the *dharmista* and un-*dharmista* was clearly acquiring the traits of a consumption society where the equilibrium was between consumption and its denunciation (Baudrillard 1968: 79). This critique of wastage made a value judgement based on the distinction between necessities and luxuries. What was feared, indeed, was the gradual imposition of a consumer culture as had happened in Europe. Modern consumption would produce a passive, subordinated population, which would no longer be able to realise its 'real needs'. The consumer was now presented with a choice of soaps, each adapted for a particular situation. An advertisement of the Chiswick Soap Company mentions a variety of soaps, including imperial and red poppy, odourless soft soaps, snowflake potash soap, saddle soap, saddle paste, and Chiswisk compound (*Ferguson's Directory* 1895: 870b). Later in the 20th century in Africa institutional forms of communication more advanced than those in Sri Lanka in the early years of the century were used to spread the gospel of cleanliness and other colonial forms of propaganda—demonstration and cinema vans, radio, African newspapers, women's clubs, health lectures, mission schools, beauty contests, and fashion shows (Burke 1996: 189–212). The spread of soaps and powders in rural Sri Lanka as well as more direct 'lessons of hygiene' in Africa were part of the general attempt to promote 'civilised' manners and discipline in the comportment of the self and the practice of everyday life in different colonial situations. Thus, with the acquisition of new hygienic habits and the entry of new products into the homes of the natives throughout the Empire, a process of homogenisation was taking place.

The homes of the rich and the poor had undergone many transformations under Portuguese and Dutch rule. One of the few detailed accounts of the furniture in an 'ordinary villager's house' is given in Denham's report of 1912. With the sense of detail of an apothecary, he described the furniture in the house of a villager in the Colombo *mudaliyar*'s division.[2] The furniture was mainly functional but of good quality, for instance, a satinwood almairah and jakwood bed was mentioned. The wall had a few Buddhist pictures and the only concessions to frivolity were the mirrors, wineglasses, and a clock. In Kalutara a villager's house contained pictures of the Buddha published and sent out by the Mellin's Food Company as an advertisement of their foods, together with a portrait of the late John Kotalawela. Religious memorabilia reproduced *en masse* was fast becoming for commercial companies a useful means of promoting their goods for mass consumption. The pictures on the walls in other simple households were also generally of a religious nature: saints or the Virgin and Child or birth and renunciation of Prince Siddhartha. Pictures of kings and queens of Europe too were popular and available even in shops in interior villages.

These images linked colonised subjects across the subcontinent in an imagined community of servants of the Raj. In the house of a *vidana arachchi* (village level head officer), Japanese pictures hung on the walls. Western-style hygiene was also entering the home with dressing tables in bedrooms, combs, and hairpowder boxes. The custom had been to have the toilet and bathroom separated from the rest of the house. The entry of these new objects into the life of the people of Ceylon was both guided by individual choice, as well as forced upon by market trends. The consumption of foreign textiles was the best example of the latter. The impact of these objects in their materiality and presence in the homes of people is difficult to fathom. There seemed to have been a fashion for foreign goods. G. A. Marinitish and Company based in Queen Street, Colombo, advertised goods in a manner that stressed a foreign origin: Austrian pine flooring and ceiling boards, Austrian pine tea-chests, French Portland cement, Italian ornamental flooring tiles, Austrian iron safes. The impact of these foreign goods, it has been suggested, went beyond simple changes in the layout of homes. In 18th-century America 'consumer goods became topics of conversation, the source of a new vocabulary, the spark of a new kind of social discourse' (Breen 1986: 496). This might have been the case, but their impact in colonial Ceylon must not be overemphasised. Indeed, the changes these objects brought must be weighted against all that did not change in the material culture of the people: in the home, people still slept on mats, ate on the ground with their fingers, slept in sarongs, oiled their hair, and drank the local brew rather than gin and tonic.

Conclusion

For Walter Benjamin, urban objects—relics of the 19th century, like dream images—were hieroglyphic clues to a forgotten past (Buck-Morss 1991: 39). Objects consumed by the Ceylonese under late colonialism tell us of a growing bourgeois consciousness typified by commodity fetishism. But unlike in the metropolis, modernity in the colony came with a sense of outwardness rather than inwardness. This perception of the 'outside' world was not limited to reaching out to the Empire at large, but infused older currents with new energies. In the late 19th century, the awareness among Buddhists of a worldwide community of their co-religionists was sparked by the movement spearheaded by a lay preacher called Anagarika Dharmapala, to protect and restore Buddha Gaya, the holiest Buddhist shrine. In 1891, during his pilgrimage to Buddha Gaya, he began correspondence with Buddhists of Ceylon, Burma, Siam, Japan, China, Arakan, and Chittagong. The Maha Bodhi Society established in that same year had a clear pan-Buddhist approach. Dharmapala travelled the world to mobilise public opinion against the destruction of the holy site, and even raised money from Buddhists of Ceylon and Burma to purchase the Maha Bodhi village at Buddha Gaya (Dharmapala 1965: 615–26). Newspapers made frequent allusions to other Buddhist countries, especially Siam, even in non-religious issues as, for instance, in July 1900 in the news item relating how the king of Siam was trying to do away with the slave trade (*Lakmini Pahana,* 21 July 1900).

People's consciousness of being Buddhist in a modern world was shaped by the outwardness of it new bourgeois propagators, such as Anagarika Dharmapala, who travelled the country in an automobile to convey the message of Buddhism for the new age. In contrast, the Empire in Ceylon was imagined as an Empire of objects and goods, of tea, jam, and Bovril, an Empire founded on needs rather than one made of men and women who settled on the island—which explains perhaps both the facility with which it was dismantled—and the resilience of ties between the former colonial power and former colonies to this day. Political ties changed, but material cultures remained deeply embedded. The little farmers of Chesapeake County declared their independence from consumer goods just as the working people of Boston did when they dumped the tea into the harbour, and the Sinhalese nationalists did when they called on their compatriots to refrain from wearing the clothes of white men and adopt the *Arya* dress instead. Once that symbolic link between England and America, and later Sri Lanka, had been severed, once common men and women asserted their control over the process of acculturation, the political ties of Empire quickly unravelled (Breen 1986: 499). But the Empire remained as a representation, and as a space identified by different names; as the Commonwealth, English-speaking, 'civilised' world, it lingers on.

Notes

1. Among the prisoners were representatives of 24 different races, 31 countries, and 152 occupations. Some of the nationalities of the prisoners of war were: Free Staters (3,209), Transvaal Burghers (782), Boers (594), Dutch (107), Frenchmen (23), and Americans (18) (*Census of Ceylon 1901* 1902: 165).
2. The *mudaliyar* was the chief headman and the administrator of a *korale* (a unit of administration consisting of the part of a district) in British times.

References

Anderson, B. (1991). *Imagined Communities: Reflections on the Origin and the Spread of Nationalism*. London and New York: Verso.

Baudrillard, J. (1968). *La Société de Consommation*. Paris: Gallimard.

Breen, T.H. (1986). 'An Empire of Goods: The Anglicization of Colonial America, 1690–1776', *Journal of British Studies*, (25)4: 467–99.

Buck-Morss, S. (1991). *The Dialectics of Seeing: Walter Benjamin and the Arcades Project*. Harvard, MA: MIT Press.

Burke, T. (1996). 'Sunlight Soap Has Changed My Life: Hygiene, Commodification, and the Body in Colonial Zimbabwe', in H. Hendrickson (ed.), *Clothing and Difference: Embodied Identities in Colonial and Post-Colonial Africa*, pp. 189–212. Durham, NC, and London: Duke University Press.

Census of Ceylon 1901 (1902). Vol. I, Containing the Review of Census Operations and the Results of the Census of Ceylon 1901. Colombo: H.C. Cottle, Acting Government Printer.

Ceylon Administrative Report (1895). Colombo: Ceylon Government Printer.

Ceylon Almanach and Annual Register (1861). Colombo: William Skeen, Government Printer.

Chatterjee, P. (1994). *The Nation and Its Fragments. Colonial and Postcolonial Histories*. Princeton: Princeton Unversity Press.

Cordiner, J. (1807). *A Description of Ceylon*. London: Longman, Hurst, Rees and orme, Paternoster Row and A. Brown, Aberdeen.

de Certeau, M. (1988). *The Practice of Everyday Life*. Berkeley: University of California Press.

Dharmapala, A. (1965). 'Buddha-gaya: The Holiest Buddhist Shrine', in Ananda Guruge (ed.), *Return to Righteousness: A Collection of Speeches, Essays and Letters of the Anagarika Dharmapala*, pp. 615–26. Colombo: Ministry of Educational Cultural Affairs.

Denham, E.B. (1912). *Ceylon at the Census of 1911*. Colombo: H.C. Cottle, Government Printer.

Domosh, Mona (2004). 'Selling Civilization: Toward a Cultural Analysis of America's Economic Empire in the Late Nineteenth and Early Twentieth Centuries', *Transactions Institute of British Geographers*, 29(4): 453–67.

Duncan, James (2002). 'Embodying colonialism? Domination and Resistance in Nineteenth Century Ceylonese Coffee Plantations', *Journal of Historical Geography*, 28(3): 317–36.

Ferguson, John (1887). *Ceylon in the Jubilee Year*. London: John Haddon, and Colombo: A.M. and J. Ferguson.

———. *Ferguson's Directory* (1895). Colombo: A.M. and J. Ferguson (1903). Colombo: Ceylon Observer Press.

———. *Ferguson's Ceylon Directory* (1905). Colombo: Ceylon Observer Press.

Hall, C. (ed.). (2000). *Cultures of Empire: A Reader—Colonizers in Britain and the Empire in the Nineteenth and Twentieth Centuries*. New York: Routledge.

Hall, S. (1991). 'Old and New Identities, Old and New Ethnicities', in Anthony D. King (ed.), *Culture, Globalization and the World-system: Contemporary Conditions for the Representation of Identity*, pp. 41–68. Binghamton, NY: State University of New York.

Lubar, S. and D.W. Kingery (eds). (1993). *History from Things: Essays on Material Culture*. Washington and London: Smithsonian Institution Press.

Panditharatne, B.L. (1964). 'Trends of Urbanization in Ceylon 1901–1953', *Ceylon Journal of Historical and Social Studies*, 7(2): 203–17.

Perera, N. (1999). *Decolonising Ceylon: Colonialism, Nationalism and the Politics of Space in Sri Lanka*. New Delhi: Oxford University Press.

Public Record Office (1888). CO 54/580, Under-Secretary of State, 10 July.

Ryan, B. (1993). *Caste in Ceylon*. New Delhi: Navrang Publishers.

Stoler, A.L. (2002). *Carnal Knowledge and Imperial Power: Bourgeois Civilities and the Cultivation of Racial Categories in Colonial Southeast Asia*. Berkeley, University of California Press.

Turner, L.J.B. (1922). *Handbook of Commercial and General Information for Ceylon*. Colombo: H. Ross Cottle, Government Printer.

Wilson, K. (2000). 'Citizenship, Empire, and Modernity in the English Provinces, c. 1720–90', in C. Hall (ed.), *Cultures of Empire: A Reader—Colonizers in Britain and the Empire in the Nineteenth and Twentieth Centuries*, pp. 157–86. New York: Routledge.

Other Periodicals

Ceylon Examiner, 23 March 1896.

Ceylon Independent, 6 February 1903.

Ceylon Independent, 6 February 1904.

Ceylon Observer, 4 December 1897.

Lakmina Pahana, 4 January 1895.

Lakmini Pahana, 21 July 1900.

Lakmini Pahana, 19 January 1918.

Sinhala Jatiya, 1 February 1923.

3

Coffee, Disease, and the 'Simultaneity of Stories-So-Far' in the Highlands of 19th-century Ceylon

James Duncan

Introduction

My concern in this chapter is to briefly develop a case study within the broad topic of the spatialisation of the history of modernity in relation to British colonialism.[1] Doreen Massey (2005: 63) calls for a rethinking and reworking of modernity 'away from being the unfolding, internal story of Europe alone'. She sees European modernity as one of many coeval, intersecting trajectories, 'the simultaneity of stories-so-far' as she calls them. By opening out the history of modernity spatially and repositioning it within intersecting Asian, European, and North and Central American trajectories, one can add complexity and differentiation, and reveal multiple dimensions to the story of modern liberal governmentality that a focus on Europe alone can obscure, and this as Massey (ibid.) says, 'undermines the very story [Europe] tells about itself'.

I look at coffee as one of the most important world commodities, a product that gathered around itself a vast assemblage of sites, routes, ecologies, technologies, and human and non-human agents (Duncan 2007). Coffee plantations in the Ceylonese highlands were particularly interesting sites of experiments in modern bio-political practices of power during the 19th century. The plantation can be seen as a laboratory for developing modern technologies of the bureaucratic administration of a colonial population where 'race' was seen as a critical marker by which subjects of rule were understood. Plantations were sites where new methods were sought to manage, discipline, and regulate populations of migrant labourers by guiding and encouraging modern and efficient modes of conduct, and by applying scientific methods of delivering health and welfare. One could even argue that the regulation and improvement of the estates and the lives of migrant labourers became a principal *raison d'être* of the colonial state, albeit one that was often contested by those with economic interests in merely exploiting the labour of the Indian migrants.

First, I give a brief sketch of the rise and fall of coffee production from the 1830s to the 1880s in terms of the meeting up of histories through interpenetrating networks of nature/science/governmentality/culture. In doing so, I hope to show through the story of coffee that there are many different types of coexisting agents, material preconditions, and spatialities that must be considered in order to undermine the story of capitalist modernity as centred in Europe. I will then outline a number of interrelated issues: the role of coffee as an important element in the forging of the intersecting trajectories of Britain, Ceylon, and South India; the role of capitalist coffee production in the radical transformation of the ecology and disease environments of the highland interior of Ceylon; the destabilisation of subsistence farming in this highland region; the aggressive re-territorialisation of populations from India to Ceylon; and the perceived need for the public management of their lives and deaths by British planters and colonial administrators. In order to do this, I outline global networks of coffee production and consumption, the fatal networks of plant and human disease transmission, and intersecting knowledge flows concerning the containment of these diseases. I briefly map these extra-insular spatialities and far-reaching networks by tracing the human and non-human agency—not only of the British state and other colonial institutions that sought authority, but the relational formations of European and South Asian societies, including the various populations in Ceylon, the climate, disease, science and technology, and the spatially extensive and historically deep-rooted political economies that animated these networks, as they worked to radically reassemble and transform them.

London and Highland Ceylon: The Coffee Connections

Coffee had been used medicinally in Arabia since the 10th century, but it did not become a popular drink in the Islamic world until the 15th century. By the mid-17th century increasing world trade had cultivated a taste among the bourgeoisie in Europe for Orientalia, and exotic luxuries such as coffee, tea, chocolate, and tobacco. Coffee became popular in Europe in part because contaminated drinking water limited people to fermented beverages and those made with boiled water, such as tea or coffee. By the mid-17th century in many circles, coffee was favoured over beer as it had acquired a reputation as the 'great soberer', an anti-erotic medication and stimulant of the intellect. This led to the development of a gendered geography of coffee houses as sites of enlightened public discourse reserved predominantly for men. Coffee houses in Europe were important as new public spaces where men could gather to discuss scientific and political ideas and conduct business.

The first coffee house in England opened in 1650, while the most famous was established by Edward Lloyd in 1688 as a meeting place for men in the maritime trades who came there to hear trade news and buy insurance. By the early years of the 18th century coffee houses in London outnumbered taverns, overshadowing them in importance as places of public intercourse and important sites of knowledge transfer and decision making. During the 18th century, insurance brokers rented booths in Lloyd's to transact business, and by the end of the century it became known as Lloyd's of London, the insurance brokerage firm. The London Stock Exchange similarly emerged from Jonathan's Coffeehouse where a list of stock and commodity prices was posted, and organised trading in marketable securities began. Similarly, the East India Company based itself in Jerusalem Coffeehouse, also in London, and the Royal Society, the most influential scientific institution, was founded in a coffee house in Oxford. Thus, on a variety of levels coffee houses were important nodes in Britain's global commercial network.

In Britain towards the end of the 18th century, coffee houses began to be eclipsed by men's clubs as social spaces in which to transact business. However, by this time, coffee had become a domestic drink for men and also for women who established ladies' coffee circles as a kind of anti-coffee house (Schivelbusch 1993: 69). This greatly increased its consumer base. Although outstripped by tea, the consumption of coffee rose dramatically throughout the 19th century, sustaining the coffee networks that entwined the fate of planters, subsistence farmers, migrant labourers, merchants, and colonial administrators throughout Britain's tropical empire. However, non-human agents such as disease also circulated within these networks, threatening their continuing stability and viability. Establishing rational control over highland ecologies and populations, as we shall see, remained an ongoing unfinished struggle.

The Plantation Economy

Until the late 17th century, Europeans had purchased coffee from Arabia. But as the demand for coffee increased, the French, the Dutch, and the British sought to produce coffee in their own colonies. This move was fuelled by mercantilist fears of an outflow of capital and desire to increase state control over plantation production. The French planted coffee in the Antilles. The Dutch successfully planted it in Java, and attempted to grow it in Ceylon, though with little success as they failed to negotiate control over the cool mountainous interior of the island. The British had established plantations in the West Indies based upon slave labour; however, these had become fundamentally disabled by the abolition of slavery in 1834. By the end of that decade, British coffee production had declined substantially; in Jamaica alone 465 coffee plantations totalling more than 188,000 acres were abandoned. The British government responded by passing legislation favourable to coffee production in other British possessions. British planters moved production to these other regions where the climate, terrain, and the costs of production were thought to allow greater profitability. Ceylon was to become such a location due in large part to its good climate and mountainous terrain. (Coffee trees, which need cool, humid climates without frost are limited to tropical highlands.) Furthermore, its proximity to India facilitated the seasonal (and thus cheaper) use of labour (Kurian 1989: 13).

Lowland coastal Ceylon had for many centuries served as an important node in a trading network, dominated first by Muslims, and after the 16th century by Europeans (the Portuguese, Dutch, and British East India Company), linking East Asia and Europe. In 1802 it became a British crown colony. However, the highland coffee-growing region (which consisted of small holdings of peasant cash crop cultivation that included coffee as an important export crop) continued to remain under the control of the Kandyan king who successfully resisted European attempts to annex his lands until the British deposed him in 1815. This highland kingdom had long been in contact with the wider capitalist world. Although ethnically fairly homogeneous, it had experienced other cultural influences from India and lowland Ceylon as Indian princes had at times occupied the throne, and lowlanders and Muslim traders had moved in to escape European rule. In resistance to these outside interventions, the kingdom had set itself up as a zone of protection for Ceylon's ancient Buddhist civilisation (Bandarage 1983: 18). It managed to retain control over its own economy during the period that the Portuguese-controlled lowland

Ceylon. The region supplied food to the lowlands and two-thirds of exports from the island were from the Kandyan hills (Bandarage 1983: 44). The Kandyan kings controlled some seaports during that time. However, the kingdom's economy fared less well during the time the Dutch occupied the coastal lowlands. The Kandyans struggled to retain control over their own external trade at first, but were subsequently forced to trade only through the Dutch at prices well below market value. Bandarage (ibid.: 45) states:

> It is clear that the effect of Dutch mercantilism on the Kandyan economy was forced isolation and involution, rather than economic expansion. This meant that with the decline of commerce, the money supply of the state, which had not been great to begin with, was further reduced. It meant also that the state had to pay its officials increasingly with land grants in lieu of money [even though]… land was the basis of political authority in Kandyan society.

Under British control the Kandyan region was further exposed to distant events as it became restructured into a vast colonial network that it was forced to join as an expanded export-oriented region. By the 1830s a plantation economy was established and became the primary *raison d'être* of Ceylon as a British colony. Early British mercantilist policies, which concentrated on trade monopolies and tax revenue rather than production, had discouraged large-scale European or native capital investments outside of Colombo. By the 1830s, however, such mercantilist policies were increasingly challenged by competing theories of free enterprise, and, consequently, the political rationality of British colonialism began to change.

Ceylon became increasingly looked upon as a permanent base for plantation production. The colonial administration of plantations, and the pastoral care of the bodies and souls of plantation labour became a central focus of a new governmental rationality, or governmentality as Foucault (2000) termed it.[2] As one author puts it:

> Within the short space of a few years coffee had made itself responsible for almost a third of the government's income. The stake was large enough to render it the State's most favored child. In the years that followed the planters' problems came to be regarded as synonymous with those of the country. (Van den Driesen, quoted in Snodgrass 1966: 17)

This change of focus on the part of the British in Ceylon is described by David Scott (2005: 29), who writes:

> With the formation of the political rationality of the modern colonial state, not only the rules of the political game but the political game itself changed—not only did the relation of forces between colonizer and colonized change, but so did *the terrain* of political struggle itself. (emphasis added)

Here Scott refers to the beginnings of modern colonial governmentality and its displacement of older mercantilist forms of political rationality (David Scott 2005: 37). While modern governmentality adopted as its general focus the everyday working and moral lives of the colonised populations, especially plantation workers, the rationality of power, or what Foucault has called the micro-practices of power, in fact had to be worked out differently in each institutional domain. Prakash (2000: 190) has introduced the question of whether colonialism was the tropicalisation of modernity. It is clear that the British who ruled Ceylon took the idea of tropicality and tropical difference very seriously (Driver and Yeoh 2000). The question of what race is, and what difference it makes to 'natural rights', was not seen in the 19th century as simply a question of biology alone; nor was it primarily about culture in the sense of customs and mores. Rather, it was seen as fundamentally about environment—and in the case of Ceylon, the tropical environment. During this period 'natural rights' were also seen to be severely challenged by many of the British and—indeed—some of the natives in authority because the hegemony of the British was insecure, modern European visions of civil society had not been established, and cultural and racial differences were thought to be significant to the practical working out of such ideals.

Although plantation agriculture required much more capital investment than transit trade, it was believed that by controlling plantation agriculture the British could gain more control over the volume of that trade. Plantations were now expected to produce a net profit for the government. The governors, therefore, encouraged the establishment of export agriculture. An early governor, Sir Edward Barnes (1824–31), who wished to encourage the British to develop permanent economic interests in the island, established his own model plantation, abolished export duties on coffee, and built a network of roads, bridges, canals, and a postal service connecting the highlands to the coast (Bandarage 1983). In 1841, the Ceylon Bank was opened to finance the expanding coffee plantation enterprise. One contemporary observer even referred to the government as an 'appendage of the estates [plantations]'.

Although the first European commercial plantations in the highlands were created in the 1820s, the British colonial officials who set these up generally lacked experience and eventually suffered many failures and loss, often to other more experienced British planters.[3] In the meantime, however, they had used their official positions to set up an infrastructure favourable to the establishment of large-scale coffee planting. The removal of export duties on coffee and taxes on coffee lands (that lasted for 12 years), and the building of transportation networks during the rule of Governor Barnes were examples of state intervention on behalf of the plantation economy. Also significant was the relocation of the government botanical research station from the capital in Colombo to Peradenya near the plantations where scientific research on the growing of coffee plants and their diseases was carried out.

It is not surprising that for such a large-scale transformation to be accomplished in the highlands, related events of great moment would have happened elsewhere. The first was the abolition of slavery in the West Indies in 1833, which severely disrupted the supply of West Indian coffee to Europe. The second was the passage of two key pieces of legislation. One was the equalisation of duty on West Indian and Ceylonese coffee in 1835 (before which time coffee from South Asia had been charged a 50 per cent higher tariff), and the other was the Crown Lands Encroachment Ordinance of 1840, which seized for the British Crown all land that had not been continuously under cultivation and for which no deed or tax receipt could be shown. Together, these comprised the key events in the creation of a boom in the highland plantations attracting farmers from Britain and planters from other British colonies.

The Crown Lands Encroachment Ordinance was disastrous for the Kandyan peasantry in certain areas where few had satisfactory documentation (Van Den Driesen 1957b: 40). It meant that they lost much of the land they had used for shifting cultivation (*chena*), a vital supplement to their rice lands. In one day alone in 1840, 13,275 acres of land were transferred to British officials at a meagre five shillings an acre. Although a sizeable percentage of coffee lands were in the hands of native farmers, much of this was in smallholdings. There were only a few (Meyer 1992: 207) Sinhalese and Tamil plantation owners in these early years. Their numbers were limited in part by British-owned banks and agency houses that either refused to loan them sufficient funds[4] or charged them higher rates than were charged to British entrepreneurs.

Production skyrocketed during the early 1840s and then crashed in 1847 when a general depression in Europe from 1847 to 1849 coincided with the removal of the preferential duty on coffee. The price for coffee plummeted from 130 shillings per hundred weight in 1840 to 43 shillings in 1847. Consequently, 90 per cent of investors from the 1830s and 1840s were bankrupted. Between 1850 and 1870 coffee production again prospered. Banderage (1983: 77) states that by 1,857 new technologies allowed an acre of forest land to be brought under cultivation for one-tenth of its cost in 1844. The price of coffee climbed to 55 shillings per hundred weight, a return that allowed only a very modest profit, but as we will see, by 1870 Ceylon coffee planting was subjected to a devastating conjuncture of events: the Great Depression in England from 1879 to 1884, strong competition from Brazilian coffee, and, most notably, the spread of the coffee fungus disease.

Perhaps most important to the introduction of plantation enterprise in Ceylon were the Colebrooke–Cameron Reforms. Banderage (ibid.: 59) states:

> It was the Colebrooke–Cameron Reforms of 1833 that provided the politico-juridical framework for the 'modernization', specifically capitalist development of Ceylon, and provided a definite watershed in the history of the island.

He also argues that it was Bentham's liberal brand of utilitarianism that emphasised the necessity to achieve cultural hegemony, and the role of the state as a guardian of a population rather than John Stuart Mill's more authoritarian version that was most influential in the setting up of a political rationality for Ceylon through these reforms. The main thrust of the reforms was to ensure the transition of the British administration of the island from direct engagement in the economy to becoming a facilitator of the large-scale capitalist enterprise there. David Scott (2005) argues that, with the Colebrooke–Cameron Reforms, the British adopted a new strategy of government oriented towards 'improving the conditions of social life including moral conduct', replacing an older mercantile orientation towards territorial expansion, and the extraction of revenue and forced labour in the form of *rajakaryia*. Scott (ibid.: 44) states:

> What was at stake in the governmental redefinition and re-ordering of the colonial world was to paraphrase Jeremy Bentham once more, to design institutions such that, following only their own self-interest, natives would do what they ought.

Although in theory the new role of the state was to provide a conducive environment for the development of capitalism, including, importantly, the reproduction of the population of migrant labourers, in actuality, as we will see, it took quite an interventionist role whenever such enterprise appeared to be threatened (Banderage 1983: 63). These Colebrooke–Cameron Reforms put in place a system of government agents and a legislative council (filled initially by British planters and later included Westernised native elite) whose authority took precedence over the native administrative structure. As Banderage (ibid.: 61) points out, this further diminished the power of the Kandyan headmen and village councils by deepening the connections between the Kandyan region and the wider world.

The British strategy for governing the various populations in Ceylon was two-fold. First, they allowed the pre-colonial feudal hierarchy to remain and to keep many of its political functions. They found these feudal lords extremely useful in mediating between themselves and the Kandyan peasantry (ibid.: 157). Nevertheless, they collaborated with them in ways that ultimately destabilised the feudal land system itself. For example, the chiefs found that it was advantageous to them to participate in the commercial land market. They sold off their lands to outside interests without respect for the users' rights. The new landlords often claimed rights to the services of tenant cultivators, creating great hardship (ibid.). Second, British settlers and administrators were encouraged to gradually introduce British laws, institutions, manners, religion, and morals. Education in English language and culture was established in order to create a class of Westernised elite, and to spread Christianity and European civilisation among the native populations. This was accomplished to a certain extent; a Western-educated Sinhalese elite did find it to their advantage to act as agents of European theories of modernisation, often espousing the same doubts as to the health, hygiene, and discipline of their fellow Sinhalese and the Indian migrants as did the British (Prakash 2000: 205). They constituted what has been called 'political society' by Partha Chatterjee (2000: 42–43)—a mediating space between the people and the state. They took up the task of attempting to bridge the seemingly unbridgeable gap between the colonial administrators and the Indian masses who were looked upon as a population[5] of racialised bodies to be studied and controlled more than as a civil society in the classic normative European sense of the term.

Nevertheless, there arose vociferous debates among political thinkers and politicians about the extent to which a programme of cultural imperialism could and should be accomplished. Among the British and native elite there were many different opinions on what the role of state medicine or public health in producing healthy and productive colonial subjects should be, and about the range of possibilities given the racial and cultural differences between South Asian populations and Europeans. Many retained a view more akin to James and John Stuart Mill than Bentham, believing that colonial rule must be despotic and paternal rather than democratic, that the perceived frailties of the South Asian body and character justified authoritarian colonial power over the masses. The South Indian masses had to be governed by a different set of rules until they were able to properly understand European norms and values. Theories of racial and environmental difference impacted on liberal and utilitarian philosophies of colonial government, allowing despotism to be justified as long as the end was the improvement of a population, and also, as Mill (1962: 73) puts it, if the means were justified by 'actually effecting that end'. These evolving political rationalities became the basis for colonial governmentality in Ceylon during these years.

The result of these ideological struggles concerning the purpose, possibilities, and limitations of tropical peoples and environments meant that modernity in Britain's colonies would be discontinuous from that in Europe. In fact, Prakash (2000) goes so far as to argue that it became structurally impossible for there to be an uncolonised domain of self-constitution, because it was believed that centralised decision-making and bureaucracy was necessary to carry out the sanitary and other reforms necessary to keep the populations of places like Ceylon safe from disease and their own unsanitary habits. He (ibid.: 192) states:

> Fundamentally irreconcilable with the development of a civil society, the colonial state was structurally denied the opportunity to mobilize the capillary forms of power. Thus, colonial governmentality developed in violation of the liberal conception that the government was part of a complex domain of dense, opaque, and autonomous interests that it only harmonized and secured with law and liberty.

The development of plantation production in Asia was intimately connected to industrialisation in Europe. Not only were plantations sources of cheap raw materials, they were also sites of the adaptation and development of industrial methods and other Western technologies of rationalisation, calculation, and discipline (Courtenay 1980; Kurian 1989). It has often been claimed that in the mid- to late-19th century, Europe's tropical colonies were laboratories of modern governmentality, and within these colonies the 'industrial plantations were especially important experimental sites (Gregor 1965). Such modern plantations were established nearly simultaneously in British South Asia, the Dutch East Indies, French Indochina, and the Philippines, and as Kurian (1989: 10) points out, there was an intense international competition among industrial plantations, with each having its own somewhat different trajectory. Consequently, producers had little control over market prices, which were established in Western Europe. Thus, places like Ceylon were not simply self-contained, self-sufficient nodes in a global network, they were both active and reactive as participants in various coeval, but entangled projects of modern capitalism.

The Kandyan highland plantations were sites for the testing of new ideas of governmentality; for new technologies for reconfiguring and rationalising space; for the forcible bringing together of culturally heterogeneous populations in order to attempt to strip them of their former social attachments and reconstitute them as self-disciplined 'modern' workers. Scott (1999: 26) speaks of this governmentality as an emergent form of power that was:

> ...*not merely coincident with colonialism*—which was concerned above all with disabling old forms of life by systematically breaking down their conditions, and with constructing in their place new conditions so as to enable—indeed, so as to *oblige*—new forms of life to come into being. (Emphasis original)

It was also a place where modern bio-political ideas of tropical disease management and public medicine were tried out.[6] These aims were accomplished through the use of newly developed space–time strategies of monitoring and control of workers. Scientific explanations and theories of administration were shaped in large part by ongoing debates about race, morality, and public responsibility for health and welfare. The spatially extensive methods of labour recruitment, the liminal legal status of migrant labourers, and the uncertainties over the difference that race makes to specific capabilities and vulnerabilities, as well as the general lack of knowledge on the part of the British about tropical environments, led to many unintended and unexpected difficulties and failures of government. Important among the challenges facing planters and colonial administrators was the circulation of fatal human and plant diseases, especially cholera and the coffee leaf rust fungus *Hemileia vastarix*. In 1870, Ceylon was exporting 100 million pounds (45 million kg) of coffee a year. By 1889, production was down to 5 million pounds (2.3 million kg). In less than 20 years, many coffee plantations were destroyed, and production had essentially ceased principally due to this devastating disease of the coffee leaf.

Networks of Labour

British planters had hoped to employ Kandyan villagers to work on the plantations, but found few who would accept the low wages they offered.[7] There were various reasons why this was so. The Sinhalese population had declined during the British invasion of the Kandyan kingdom and again during the suppression of a rebellion in 1818–19. The native population was further weakened by hunger and the disruption of water supplies, which caused a severe outbreak of dysentery. Furthermore, continuing high death rates in the second quarter of 19th century due to various diseases greatly reduced the available labour pool. Peasant agriculture was generally sufficient for Sinhalese needs. Working for the British was seen as an unattractive option because the rates of pay were very low and the working conditions known to be poor. Residence on the plantation was normally required, wages were retained, and planters' and overseers' treatment of workers was notorious.

The systematic recruitment of Tamil labourers from south India began in 1839, coinciding with the beginning of the boom in coffee production. The average number of annual arrivals for 1839–42 was 5,300. This rose to 115,416 between 1873 and 1879, and then dropped to 46,152 between 1880 and 1886 when coffee was in its final decline. A complex circulatory network was established by planters and *kanganie*s, middlemen who recruited migrants and largely controlled the network, which connected villages in Madras to the plantations in the Kandyan highlands.

The socio-economic conditions in southern India, particularly in rural villages, were very poor, especially in years of famine. The *kanganie*s were able to exploit this situation by developing a relatively unregulated system of debt bondage (Kurian 1989: 93). The plantation owners in Ceylon placed orders with *kanganie*s for labourers. The *kanganie*s or their assistants used their caste and kin group networks to gain the confidence of villagers. They lent the labourers money for their travel expenses, and negotiated wages and terms once they arrived at the plantations. Although this was not officially an indenture system, all Tamil labourers arrived in Ceylon in debt to the *kanganie*s and were not allowed to leave the estate until their *tundu* (note) of indebtedness was cleared. Guards were responsible for keeping them on the estate. Government police were also recruited to help with the problem of runaways.

There were various reasons for the Tamils' willingness to migrate. Some were related to the British control over Madras, some to relations with the local south Indian elite, and others related to the weather. First, the local population grew as the result of a British-imposed peace in the area, producing an increase in the number of landless labourers. Second, poverty in the region was exacerbated by the decline of village weaving, as Indian cloth manufacture could not compete with the British cotton that had flooded the market. Third, as demonstrated in Gough's (1981) study of Thanjuvur, an area of seasonal migration to the coffee plantations, the freeing of slaves in the 1830s created a poor low-caste group in search of employment. This coincided with the interests of local Indian landlords who wished to retain only a certain percentage of the labour force in debt bondage. Kurian (1989: 58), following Gough, writes:

> When they were needed for cultivation in their villages, the landlords operated their authority of debt bondage to retain them in India. When they were not necessary for that purpose, it was also in the interests of landlords to allow them to work on the plantations in Ceylon. The workers caught between the dictates of plantation capitalism and debt bondage had little choice of place of work or seasonality of employment.

Finally, the seasonality of cropping and yearly variable weather patterns in both India and Ceylon affected migration flows. The labourers were pulled and pushed along networks joining India and Ceylon by fluctuating demand for rice in India and coffee in Ceylon. These forces were largely beyond their control. The harvesting of rice in South India took place in January and March. Labour was most needed on coffee plantations between August and November, with the greatest demands during the harvesting of the crop in November. In theory, labourers could participate in the coffee harvest in November and return to India for the rice harvest in January. But when the rains were delayed, problems of timing would arise. Also, when the rice harvests were good in India, workers felt less compelled to come to work in Ceylon and planters suffered shortages of labour. Conversely, in a year when the monsoons were insufficient or failed to arrive, labourers flocked to the plantations in Ceylon. The viability of coffee plantations in Ceylon not only depended on local factors, but also on the monsoons and their impact on South Indian agriculture. The entanglement of the two economies was especially obvious when the south of India suffered famine. There were seven famines in the Madras Presidency during the 19th century, two of which, (during 1850s and the 1870s) occurred during the plantation coffee period in Ceylon. While the principal cause of the famines was either a lack or an overabundance of rain, other contributing factors were the collapse of local industry due to competition with factories in Britain, changes of land tenure, and a failure of local wages to keep pace with price increases, again due to the influence of distant events. As a consequence of the social-environmental conditions in Madras, there was a fairly persistent wage differential between Madras and Ceylon throughout the coffee-growing period.

The plantations were constructed as sites of what Henri Lefebvre (1991) has termed abstract space: the commodification and bureaucratisation of everyday life.[8] As an ideal, abstract space requires the construction of 'abstract bodies' to conform to it.[9] Abstract bodies are bodies that are made docile, useful, disciplined, rationalised and normalised, and controlled sexually (Foucault 1979). Such bodies are seen as economic resources to be protected and utilised to capacity. The successful production of abstract bodies in a place like Ceylon would have required the creation of a re-cultured worker.[10] The poor Tamil villagers displaced from southern India were at least partially torn from their traditional social networks: their social, judicial, religious, and medical support systems. However, the attempt to produce rationalised bodies for plantation space was undermined because elements of the workers' networks and ways of life remained intact and served as important bases for resistance.[11] The only partially rent Tamil networks were able to lend support to the workers' resistance to attempts to re-acculturate them. Stoler (1986: 124) argues that plantations rarely transformed peasants into full-fledged proletarians.[12] Rather, the plantation system allowed—and even encouraged—some elements of peasant life, such as the cultivation of private garden plots. As such, the modern plantation can be understood as a site of heterogeneous networks, radically reconstituted into a new socio-material configuration, with some degree of economic stability and success achieved at a very high social cost, borne principally by the Tamil workers, but also by the planters themselves.

The European planters adopted certain strategies and technologies in an attempt to produce and regulate abstract space and bodies on coffee plantations. However, they never fully achieved the condition of disciplinarity as internalised control that is necessary for the production of docile bodies.[13] In part this was because plantation owners and managers saw workers as short-term, expendable, racialised, commodities that were still so thoroughly embodied by their raw 'animal' nature and lack of exposure to European civilising forces that self-discipline was barely possible.[14] Hence, rather than educating workers through formal English schooling, the most that they hoped for was an appreciation of 'the dignity of labour'. Most worker discipline was imposed through direct surveillance by Europeans and their supervisors through the threat of physical force, based on the current environmental determinist view of race, which assumed that coercion was required to ensure that tropical races worked efficiently (Arnold 1996: 160). The refusal of workers to discipline themselves was not, however, a passive refusal. Rather, they actively engaged in what Scott (1985) has termed 'the weapons of the weak'—a set of tactics of resistance to the demands placed upon them within the experimental space of the plantation.[15] Unable to consistently instil discipline through anything other than constant surveillance and punishment, the planters continually sought more effective ways of producing workers. This was achieved in part by involving the colonial state in the disciplining process. Not only were the planters brought into conflict with the workers and the *kangany* networks of power and authority, but also with other bureaucratic forces such as British government agencies and humanitarian groups who campaigned against the planters' cruel use of force. Adas (1986) argues that non-confrontational resistance on plantations can be divided into what he terms everyday resistance, exit strategies such as desertion, and retribution such as damaging crops and equipments. He claims that everyday resistance is simultaneously the most common form and the most difficult to study, in part because it involves individual rather than collective action, and in part because it entails 'calculated errors' and incompetence rather than sustained protest.

Networks of Disease

The British thought of the forested highlands as centres of disease. They blamed high rates of mortality from diseases like malaria, smallpox, and beriberi on the nature of the forested environment, especially in the early years of settlement. They were unfamiliar with many of the fauna and flora in the highlands and found these threatening. They believed that diseases and fevers were a product of miasmas—poisonous vapours given off by damp, rotting tropical vegetation (Johnson and Martin 1846: 88). Since the 1830s, the British sanitarian movement had favoured an environmental notion of disease, and supported the idea of medical topographies involving the mapping of unhealthy places and the systematic collection of statistics that were experimented with in Ceylon at the time. In fact, sanitary reform could, in the words of Prakash (2000: 196), be considered 'a new order of knowledge and power'. He says that unlike climate and other uncontrollable environmental factors, sanitation was seen as potentially controllable.

The jungles were in reality dangerous in various ways to human health, and the British programme of clearing for plantations did lead to a decrease in some diseases, such as malaria. However, as we will see, there were some ecologically disastrous effects of cutting down the rainforest that modern British scientific knowledge was unable to predict. As it happened, the miasmatic theory of disease also dovetailed conveniently with utilitarian beliefs that such deadly wastelands and jungles should be transformed by modern European practices and technologies to make them economically productive (Webb 2002). Samuel Baker, a pioneer who opened up the high mountains around Nuwara Eliya for British settlement, posited a connection between European capitalism and the eradication of disease, which, even if wrong in the exact attribution of causes, correctly predicted the correlation:

> The felling and clearing of jungle, which cultivation would render necessary, would tend in great measure to dispel fevers and malaria always produced by a want of free circulation of air. In a jungle covered country like Ceylon, diseases of the most malignant character are harboured in those dense and undisturbed tracts, which year after year reap a pestilential harvest from the thinly scattered population. Cholera, dysentery, fever, and smallpox all appear in their turn, and annually sweep whole villages away. (Baker, quoted in Webb 2002: 52)

Without the knowledge of bacteria or the role of vectors such as mosquitoes or lice, the focus of medical concern was on the environment. Air was seen as a fundamental medium of fevers, hence meteorology was of great interest to physicians. The British sought 'salubrity'. Ventilation took on an almost mythical status, hence the emphasis on clearing forests. Although the British may have removed some of the conditions conducive to malaria, they opened the highlands to other diseases. For example, they reintroduced smallpox to the highlands in 1819 after a two-decade absence from the area (ibid.: 29). More deadly still, the labour demands of the plantation economy resulted in the introduction of cholera from India through the recruitment of Tamil labourers.

The Portuguese and the Dutch had generally had great respect for Sinhalese medicine, and although the Sinhalese in turn valued European drugs,[16] the exchange of knowledge flowed largely from the Sinhalese to the Europeans. One Dutch governor argued that the pharmacopoeia of Ceylon was so complete that there was no need to send any medicine from Holland (Uragoda 1987: 68). European hospitals in Ceylon at that time were largely run by the military for the military and other Europeans. They generally felt little responsibility for the health of the native population. However, 19th century proved to be one of some very widespread and dangerous epidemics, and this began to impress upon the British that the states of health of the various populations, including themselves, were interlinked. This would over time lead them from state medicine[17] to a much broader conception of public health.

In the early years of British rule, hospitals were run by the military. However with new 19th century views of pastoral governmentality and growing pressure from the plantations, which, as indicated eariler, the British saw as the principal *raison d'être* of the colony, the health of the native population and migrant workers eventually became an important humanitarian and economic concern. At first the British saw native medical practitioners as knowledgeable because they understood the local conditions of disease and as the British theories of disease at that time were still strongly environmental, they felt they had much to learn from the locals (Arnold 1996).

By mid-century, however, the British began to place more emphasis on contagion and developing multi-factoral models of disease. Increasingly they believed that native medicine was irrational and dangerous. This view was but one instance of a more general critique of folk knowledge in Europe and elsewhere that was current at that time (Arnold 1993: 51). The irony of this European arrogance was that Europeans still did not understand the causes of major killer diseases of the tropics such as cholera, dysentery, smallpox, and malaria, and they realised this.

In the early years, missionaries and individual doctors undertook to provide British medicine to the least fortunate sectors of society—the lepers, the mentally ill, and the prisoners (Uragoda 1987: 88). In 1858 the government set up a Civil Medical Department, which was independent of the military. Historian of medicine in Ceylon, C.G. Uragoda (ibid.: 93) states that this separation was a landmark in the development of public health: 'It heralded a spate of activities by which medical facilities were extended within a short time to a large sector of the population, both urban and rural, through a network of hospitals and dispensaries.'

David Arnold (1993: 292–93) makes the point that Western medicine was more than simply a tool of empire; European doctors working in South Asia found it to be an excellent laboratory for the study of variation in disease as medicine increasingly began to operate through racialised categories. He (ibid.: 8) has argued that, 'Colonial rule built up an enormous battery of texts and discursive practices that concerned themselves with the physical being of the colonised.' While such a concern was based in liberal and humanitarian ideas of governmentality, it can also be understood in terms of the more immediate economic and enculturating goals of the colonisers. Hygiene and medical theories were specifically tailored to theories of racial difference and tropical environments. Tamil plantation workers were thought to be sickly by nature and consequently short-lived. They were also seen to mature quickly, as one planter put it, 'In the East…a youth of nine or ten is mentally as precocious as our boys at double that age' (A Planter 1886: 12). Thus, it was thought that their labour should best be utilised efficiently before they sickened and died. Given the short-term requirements of labour on the plantations, this was not seen as a serious problem. Such beliefs also naturalised the use of child labour and relatively high death rates. However, there were debates about what exactly the death rate among the labourers was and about what rate could be considered morally acceptable. Planters were sensitive to charges of causing high death rates among Tamils because there were powerful factions both in Britain and India who took a great interest in the welfare of Indian migrant labourers. The *Ceylon Observer* (1849) estimated that between 1841 and 1848, 70,000 workers—or 25 per cent of those who came to the island—died.

Southern India was seen as a reservoir of epidemic diseases such as cholera whereas Ceylon being an island, had been relatively free of the disease until the arrival of annual migrations of workers from south India. Arnold (1993: 159) describes cholera as a 'highly political disease' in that it was seen as alien, and the failure of the British to bring it under control threatened their control. Between 1842 and 1878, 72,999 people died of the disease in Ceylon (*Administration Reports*, *Ceylon* 1878). W.R. Kynsey, Principal Civil Medical Officer and Inspector General of Hospitals, posed what was widely seen as the great dilemma of plantation coffee production when he wrote in 1876:

> Intimately connected as the subject of the immigration of coolies is with the great coffee industry and the material progress of the Colony, it is equally connected with, and I am sorry to state answerable for, the introduction and dissemination of no small amount of such infectious diseases as cholera and smallpox throughout the island. (*Administration Reports* 1876)

He went on to point out that cholera was only found in districts visited by coolies. The problem for the government was how best to exclude those who were visibly ill, insulate the native population from the immigrants, and treat those coolies who fell ill while on the island. However, programmes for minimising the spread of cholera to the island's population such as quarantine and devising routes through sparsely populated areas operated only with consideration for the plantations' demand for ready labour. Commissions were appointed to study new potential immigrant routes scientifically planned to effectively use the empty space strategy and to protect the health of the coolies on their journey (*Papers Laid Before the Legislative Council of Ceylon* 1878: 9). The former was, of course, a prime consideration to stop the spread of disease and to quieten the opposition among residents to the coolie presence.

There were debates among planters, doctors, and government administrators over how much medicine workers should be given. It was assumed that they did not need the same level of care as Europeans, but exactly how much was appropriate was considered to be both scientifically unestablished and morally debatable. Should European medicines be forced on those who refused them? There was a constant battle with the local government administrators and Parliament in Westminster over these issues and who was to blame for the unusually high death rate. The planters tended to place the blame on unsanitary habits, refusal of Western medicine, and exploitation by the Indian hiring agents during the long trips from India to the plantations. Government officials persistently challenged the planters' assumptions about what constituted adequate health care. Nevertheless, planters made economic calculations concerning the value of labour and how much was economically rational to spend on keeping workers alive. These costs were weighed against those of locating new labourers and receiving bad press in Britain.

As there was nearly always a ready supply of labour available, it was thought unnecessary to spend very much on medicine. Similar calculations were made regarding food; there was a fine balance to be achieved between the cost of food and the productivity of labour. Planters debated among themselves the question of how much food a worker needed, and how much and how often they should consume hot food. Theories concerning these bio-political issues circulated among members of planters' associations in Ceylon and elsewhere in colonial plantation economic regions.

Disease and Coffee Plants

Until 1815, the Kandyan kingdom had been protected from the invasion of armies by a massive rainforest belt. It was a policy to keep the forest impenetrable for defence purposes. The high cost of porterage kept Kandy relatively peripheral to major Asian networks of trade and to the spread of disease (Webb 2002: 19). The 19th century saw the transformation of much of this rainforest into agriculture. In response to the demands of a greatly enlarged export economy, Kandyan peasants burned even more forest than British planters as they sought to extend their *chena*, or shifting cultivation plots, for coffee production and to claim tenure. By the end of the 19th century, the barrier forest had disappeared.

As plantations spread and coffee was planted in previously uncultivated or mixed-use peasant-owned land, coffee plants became ecologically vulnerable. Mono-cultivation promoted outbreaks of diseases and allowed them to spread. Pests and diseases greatly increased when the same fields were repeatedly used for the same crop. In 1843, coffee bugs of a variety of species began to spread, but were often halted by forest breaks between plantations as a certain amount of forest still existed at that time. In 1869, the orange coffee leaf rust fungus *H. vastarix* was first noted. The origin was unknown; it may have been endemic in wild coffee plants and spread in the late 1860s to cultivated coffee. By then most of shatterbelts were gone (ibid.: 2002). Fungal pathogens dispersed by monsoon winds found ideal conditions due to mono-cultivation and the vastly increased intensity and duration of sunlight due to deforestation made the leaves much more susceptible. The disappearance of the shatterbelts caused further problems, for as coffee plants became weakened by disease, high winds could more easily strip them of their leaves (ibid.: 115). Coffee yields declined until they became negligible, and plantations failed. These abandoned estates then became transmission centres from which the disease could spread even more freely. It also spread to south India through networks of coolies, on their clothing, and eventually on to South Africa, East Africa, Java, Fiji, and Queensland, Australia (ibid.: 116).

The Royal Botanic Garden at Peradeniya, which was used for research on diseases and their prevention, in its turn added to the ecological disaster. Its researchers, who were in close contact with other imperial botanic gardens, including Kew Gardens in London, decided to import some Liberian coffee to see if it might prove disease resistant. The devastating outcome of this experiment was a scale bug, *Lecanium viride*, which spread widely from this sample to Ceylonese coffee, and after 1885 became the final ecological blow to the industry.

Depression

In the 1880s, as disease ravaged production in the highlands, depression struck world economies and was especially hard on colonial export economies. Demand dropped greatly at a time when planters were struggling with reduced yields. Compounding the problems of disease and decreased demand was a surge in production of Brazilian coffee after 1879, which had the effect of decreasing world prices. As it became clear that sources of coffee in British colonies were disappearing, the British government once again removed preferential duties on colonial coffee. This was the final straw in the series of ecological and economic blows to Ceylon coffee, knocking it out of the international network of coffee producers.

By the mid-1880s, with production nearly wiped out by the various coffee plant diseases, another round of bankruptcies occurred, and the only plantations that survived were those that switched to cinchona or tea. The average area planted to coffee dropped from a high of 125,000 ha between 1875 and 1879 to 45,000 ha by 1886. By the late 1880s an old coffee hand had this to say as he saw the industry collapse around him:

> Many of the plantations were deserted, the capitalists took fright, and superintendents were thrown out of employment and set off to other countries. There was a regular migration to Northern Australia, Fiji, Borneo, the Straits, California, Florida, Burma and elsewhere. I should say that out of 1700 planters we lost at least 400 this way. (Ferguson 1887)

As plantations began to fail, wages were not paid. While non-payment had been a perennial problem, it was made worse by the coffee disease and the changing fortunes of the planters. And so labourers deserted. The planters persuaded the government to punish desertion with a term of up to three months of hard labour. So prevalent was desertion, and so effective was the state in recapturing the deserters, that in the words of the Queen's advocate, 'The jails are crammed with scores and hundreds of men, women, and children arrested on warrants of desertion' (Digby 1879).

Because of the taxation system, peasants had been able to avoid some land taxes by farming *chena* lands as opposed to wet rice. The British government had encouraged peasants to grow coffee. Peasant production doubled between 1820 and 1824; it doubled again between 1826 and 1833. In 1829, the government released coffee producers from annual labour service, but by mid-1830, the government began to become concerned about peasants cutting forest land and competing with planter interests. In fact, the peasants produced the bulk of the coffee grown in Ceylon well into the late 1840s. The government decided to tax peasants on their land at a rate that could only be paid readily if the rice harvest was very good or if coffee was grown as an important supplementary cash crop. With the failure of coffee, peasants were often unable to pay their taxes and after several years of non-payment, the government confiscated their lands in lieu of payment. This in turn led in some instances of widespread hunger and the issue of the 'Ceylon starvation question' was raised in Parliament. A taxation policy had been created around a set of environmental expectations that were then radically changed by disease.

There has been a tendency in the literature on the coffee industry in 19th century Ceylon to assume a dualistic economy in which the plantations represented an enclave economy that was so separate from the peasant economy that it had little impact on it (Snodgrass 1966: 56). Meyer (1992: 204) argues to the contrary that:

> The village–estate continuum was in many cases significant enough to 'blur the border' between the two sectors, that in a micro-perspective, intersectoral flows played a decisive role in the socio-economic life of most villages in the plantations areas, and that economic depressions in the world market resulted in a dramatic deterioration in the so-called 'peasant sector'.

There were in fact significant interactions between the village and plantation economies, which as mentioned earlier, included commercial transactions between these two sectors and the employment of peasants (albeit a small percentage in comparison to imported labour). As I have also indicated, there had been commercial agriculture supported by the kings of Kandy before the British period and the peasant sector of coffee production, both gardens and small-scale plantations, accounted for the majority of exports even after the arrival of British management and capital until the 1840s. However, the British plantations began to overtake the peasant economy as the state supported the British entrepreneurs far more than the locals in terms of land, legislation, finance, infrastructure, labour control, and taxation (ibid.: 202). This left the locals much more vulnerable to downturns in the market, especially the depression during the 1880s. Thus, as Bandarage (1983: 325) and Meyer (1992: 202) say, the plantation system grew at the expense of the peasant sector.

Conclusion

I have traced such networks and imbrications as associated with the rise and fall of the coffee economy in Ceylon during the 19th century. I have looked at Ceylon and the British coffee plantations there as experiments in governmentality. Highland Ceylon was one place where the bio-political responsibilities of colonial rule were first realised in all their varied implications of looking after the lives of the populations and the ecologies on which their economies depended. It was a place where it became painfully obvious that these populations and ecologies were highly interconnected in ways that their scientific knowledge could not have predicted, and that these were causally entangled with many other places in the world as well. As Foucault (2000: 208–9) states:

> What government has to do with is not territory but, rather, a sort of complex composed of men and things. The things, in this sense, with which government is to be concerned are in fact men, but men in their relations, their links, their imbrication with those things that are wealth, resources, means of subsistence, the territory with its specific qualities, climate, irrigation, fertility, and so on.

Those British and native colonial administrators, the doctors, the planters, and the scientists who tried their experiments in governmentality in 19th century Ceylon discovered that the complex imbrications of people and nature, and the extensive spatial links that Foucault speaks of were beyond their ability to successfully predict and control. Coffee collapsed primarily due to the untreatable fungus *H. vastarix*. The fungus pathogen had long existed in Ceylon, but it did not have devastating effects until the coffee region approached a condition of near mono-cultivation. Then it was able to spread rapidly as plant density is a major factor in dissemination. It is clear that the full impact of a local agency was actualised by non-local agents and distant events. As the local agent of disease became entangled in new networks of demand and supply, it united the highlands of Ceylon with markets in Europe and with other coffee-producing places. It was these networks that produced the mono-cultivation that made the disease spread. Hence, the despair of bankrupt planters, and the grinding poverty of Tamil workers and Sinhalese peasants was caused by a particular conjunction of nature/culture: by a fungus of the coffee plant that long existed on the island, but which spread uncontrollably due to decisions made both locally and in faraway places. It was caused by earlier shifts in local tax policy that operated on unsubstantiated environmental expectations regarding peasant and colonialist coffee production. It was caused by the unforeseen effects of mono-cultivation and the inadvertent introduction of a new pest while seeking a cure for the fungus. It was caused by shifting financial conditions in Europe and by conditions of production in other nodes of the network such as Brazil. There can be no easy distinction between nature and culture, or the local and the global in these long networks of causation. Rather, the question becomes one of exploring how nature/culture interpenetrate, and how various actors and localities become vulnerable and also complicitous in a network in ways that are so complex that they escaped governmental or scientific management at the time. Such complexity is even difficult for us to evaluate and fully disentangle with the benefit of hindsight and subsequent advances in science.

This short case study of the spatiality of modernity attempts to describe the deep entanglement of Ceylon with Britain and its empire. I have argued that due to the importance of coffee as a commodity, the remaking of space in highland Ceylon had far-reaching causes and consequences within the 19th century world economy. Ceylon proved to be a particularly interesting site of experiment in modern bio-political practices and governmentality in a tropical environment. It was equally a site of experiments in non-state governmentality, as the planting community was able to usurp a good deal of power from the state because coffee production was seen as a primary *raison d'être* of the colony. Here we witness the tensions between the sovereignty of the state and the quasi-sovereignty of the plantations in the working out of state and private economic interests, the management of the health of the immigrant labouring population of Ceylon's plantations, and decisions concerning the moral acceptability of high death rates. The coffee plantations served as laboratories for the bureaucratic management of a racialised labouring population, which was the subject of highly contested theories of race, environment, health, and welfare. The plantations were also sites of largely unsuccessful experiments in the rationalisation of agricultural practices, and the management of plant and human diseases. I have attempted to trace extra-insular spatialities and networks of human and non-human agency, including British state and non-governmental institutions, migrant and native populations of Ceylon, the climate, disease, science, technology, and the spatially extensive and historically deep political economies that enlivened and transformed these networks.

Notes

1. This chapter is based on a larger research project on coffee plantations in 19th-century Ceylon (see Duncan 2007).
2. Governmentality is a modern form of decentred power that includes both self-control and pastoral control of populations with the aim of improving welfare and the conduct of everyday life. This distinctively modern and expanded view of instructing, managing, disciplining, and regulating the self and others under one's control assumed that such aims could be accomplished through the displacement of traditional practices and unscientific beliefs

by modern rationality and improved 'habits of mind'. This form of power depended on the use of census and surveys, and various other bureaucratic technologies for monitoring a population. Although the bureaucratic control over the health and welfare of populations was based on genuine humanitarian concerns, it was also seen as an economic necessity, and it is not surprising that different interests within the colonial world did not always agree on the exact calculations of the costs and benefits of such pastoral concern. On governmentality, see Foucault (2000).

3. After the 1850s the colonial government embarked on a systematic effort to recruit new planters with previous experience in managing farms or plantations (Forrest 1969).
4. It costs a minimum of £3,000 to establish the typical estate in Ceylon during the 1840s (Snodgrass 1966).
5. Chatterjee (2000: 43) says of Foucault that he 'has been more perceptive than other social philosophers of recent times in noticing the crucial importance of the concept of population for the emergence of modern governmental technologies'. For Foucault's definition of population, see Foucault (1979: 216–17), Chatterjee (2000), Legg (2005), and Prakash (2000: 204).
6. Also see Prakash (2000: 191) and Arnold (1993: 9) on India as a site of biopolitical experimentation.
7. Meyer (1992: 207) argues that the role of Sinhalese labour has often been underestimated. He says that in fact some level of employment of Sinhalese peasants 'was important to the economic processes of both the villages and the estates, at least during certain periods and in certain areas'. Nevertheless, even Meyer himself does not deny that only a relatively small percentage of plantation labourers were Sinhalese, especially after the initial clearing work was completed.
8. Lefebvre (1991) applies the notion of abstract space to capitalism in Europe, I would argue that it was equally a goal in industrial plantations in tropical colonies. There, however, it was cross-cut by race and south Indian social relations.
9. Michael Landzelius, personal communication. See also Poovey (1995) and Duncan (2002).
10. Planters viewed the 'native' as a product of a degrading climate and moral condition, who, it was believed, European capitalism could transform. For a discussion of the discourse of the degraded 'native', see Arnold (1993, 1996), Livingstone (1991) and Duncan (2000, 2002). For a working out of some of these ideas in Britain, see Mort (1987).
11. The planters' ideal of a new space, an enclave in which workers could be moulded according to Western industrial methods, was only very partially achieved. The planters felt hampered by what they considered leakages—trade of rice, coconuts, and toddy and arrack (liquor), back and forth between the plantation and the villages. See Duncan (2002).

12. Wolf (1959: 43) says that such plantation workers lived 'double lives', while Tausig (1980: 92, 103, 113) says they are 'liminal beings'.
13. See Foucault (1979) on the concept of docile bodies. Stewart (1995) explores new world slave plantations in similar terms.
14. The struggle that white male planters waged against their own embodiment in the tropics is the subject of Duncan (2000).
15. See de Certeau's (1984) use of tactics to refer to the workers' resistance and strategies to refer to the planters' attempts at domination. Also see Genovese's (1972) discussion of everyday resistance on slave plantations. Discerning covert resistance from colonial records is extremely difficult. Ramasamy (1992: 100) outlines some forms of resistance on coffee plantations in late 19th-century Malaya, and concludes that 'lack of evidence prevents us from providing a detailed picture of individual forms of resistance among Indian labourers on plantations'.
16. Dutch embassies to the king of Kandy regularly brought European medicines along with pearls, gold, and silver (Uragoda 1987: 69).
17. On the concept of state medicine, see Arnold (1993).

References

Adas, M. (1986). 'From Foot Dragging to Flight: The Evasive History of Peasant Avoidance Protest in South and Southeast Asia', *Journal of Peasant Studies*, 13(1): 64–86.

Administration Reports, Ceylon (1876). Colombo, 122c.

———. (1878). Colombo, 165c–74c.

A Planter (Richard Wade Jenkins). (1886). *Ceylon in the Fifties and the Eighties: A Retrospect and Contrast of the Vicissitudes of the Planting Enterprise During a Period of Thirty Years and of Life and Work in Ceylon*. Colombo: A.M. and J. Ferguson.

Arnold, D. (1993). *Colonizing the Body: State Medicine and Epidemic Disease in Nineteenth Century India*. Berkeley: University of California Press.

———. (1996). *The Problem of Nature: Environment, Culture and European Expansion*. Oxford: Blackwell.

Bandarage, A. (1983). 'The Establishment and Consolidation of the Plantation Economy in Sri Lanka', *Bulletin of Concerned Asian Scholars*, 14(3): 2–22.

———. *Colonialism in Sri Lanka: The Political Economy of the Kandyan Highlands 1833–1886*. Berlin: Mouton.

Ceylon Observer, 4 October 1849.

Chatterjee, P. (2000). 'Two Poets and Death: On Civil and Political Society in the Non-Christian World', in T. Mitchell (ed.), *Questions of Modernity*, pp. 35–48. Minneapolis: University of Minnesota Press.

Courtenay, P. (1980). *Plantation Agriculture*. London: Bell and Hyman.

de Certeau, M. (1984). *The Practice of Everyday Life*. Berkeley: University of California Press.

Digby, W. (1879). *Life of Sir Richard Morgan, Vol. 2*. Madras.
Driver, F. and B. Yeoh (2000). 'Constructing the Tropics: Introduction', *Singapore Journal of Tropical Geography*, 21(1): 1–5.
Duncan, J. (2000). 'The Struggle to be Temperate: Climate and "Moral Masculinity" in Mid-nineteenth Century Ceylon', *Singapore Journal of Tropical Geography*, 21(1): 34–47.
———. (2002). 'Embodying Colonialism? Domination and Resistance in 19th Century Ceylonese Coffee Plantations', *Journal of Historical Geography*, 28(3): 317–38.
———. (2007). *In the Shadows of the Tropics: Climate, Race and Biopower in nineteenth Century Ceylon*. London: Ashgate.
Ferguson, J. (1887). *Ceylon in the Jubilee Year*. London: J. Haddon and Company.
Forrest, D. (1969). 'Hundred Years of Achievement', *The Times of Ceylon Tea Centenary Supplement*, 31 July 1969.
Foucault, M. (1979). 'Docile bodies', in *Discipline and Punish: The Birth of the Prison*, pp. 135–69. New York: Random House.
———. (2000). 'Governmentality', in James D. Faubion (ed.), *The Essential Works of Foucault, 1954–1984, Vol. 3—Power*, pp. 201–22. New York: New Press.
Genovese, M. (1972). *Roll Jordan Roll: The World the Slaves Made*. New York: Random House.
Gough, K. (1981). *Rural Society in Southeast India*. Cambridge: Cambridge University Press.
Gregor, H. (1965). 'The Changing Plantation', *Annals of the Association of American Georgraphers*, 55: 221–38.
Johnson, J. and J. Martin (1846). *The Influence of Tropical Climates on European Constitutions*. New York: London: S. Highley.
Kurian, R. (1989). *State, Capital and Labour in the Plantation Industry in Sri Lanka 1834–1984*. Amsterdam: University of Amsterdam.
Lefebvre, H. (1991). *The Production of Space*. Oxford: Blackwell.
Legg, S. (2005). 'Foucault's Population Geographies: Classifications, Biopolitics and Governmental Spaces', *Population, Space and Place*, 11(3): 137–56.
Livingstone, D. (1991). 'The Moral Discourse of Climate: Historical Considerations on Race, Place, and Virtue', *Journal of Historical Geography*, 17: 413–34.
Massey, D. (2005). *For Space*. London: Sage Publications.
Meyer, E. (1992). '"Enclave" Plantation, "Hemmed-in" Villages and Dualistic Representations in Colonial Ceylon', *Journal of Peasant Studies*, 19(3–4): 199–228.
Mill, J.S. (1962). *Utilitarianism*. Oxford: Blackwell.
Mort, F. (1987). *Dangerous Sexualities: Medico-moral Politics in England Since 1830*. London: Routledge and Kegan Paul.
Papers Laid Before the Legislative Council of Ceylon. (1878).
Poovey, M. (1995). *Making a Social Body: British Cultural Formation, 1830–1864*. Chicago: University of Chicago Press.
Prakash, G. (2000). 'Body Politic in Colonial India', in T. Mitchell (ed.), *Questions of Modernity*, pp. 189–222. London: University of Minnesota Press.

Ramasamy, P. (1992). 'Labour Control and Labour Resistance in the Plantations of Colonial Malaya', in E.V. Daniel, H. Bernstein and T. Brass (eds), *Plantations, Proletarians and Peasants in Colonial Asia*, pp. 91–111. London: Frank Cass.

Schivelbusch, W. (1993). *Tastes of Paradise: A Social History of Spices, Intoxicants and Stimulants*. Vintage: New York.

Scott, D. (2005). 'Colonial Governmentality', in J. Inda, (ed.), *Anthropologies of Modernity: Foucault, Governmentality and Life Politics*, pp. 23–49. Oxford: Blackwell.

———. (1999). *Refashioning Futures: Criticism after Postcoloniality*. Princeton, NJ: Princeton University Press.

Scott, J. (1985). *Weapons of the Weak: Everyday Forms of Peasant Resistance*. New Haven: Yale University Press.

Snodgrass, D.R. (1966). *Ceylon: An Export Economy in Transition*. Homewood, IL: Richard Irwin.

Stewart, L. (1995). 'Louisiana Subjects: Power, Space and the Slave Body', *Ecumene*, 2(3): 227–45.

Stoler, A. (1986). 'Plantation Politics and Protest on Sumatra's East Coast', *Journal of Peasant Studies*, 13(2): 124–43.

Tausig, M. (1980). *The Devil and Commodity Fetishism in South America*. Chapel Hill: University of North Carolina Press.

Uragoda, C. (1987). *A History of Medicine in Sri Lanka: From the Earliest Times to 1948*. Colombo: Middleway Limited.

Van Den Driesen, I.H. (1957a). 'Land sales policy and some aspects of the problem of tenure, 1836–86 Part 1', *University of Ceylon Review*, 14(2): 6–25.

———. (1957b). 'Land Sales Policy and Some Aspects of the Problem of Tenure, 1836–86, Part 2', *University of Ceylon Review*, 15(2): 36–52.

Webb, J. (2002). *Tropical Pioneers: Human Agency and Ecological Change in the Highlands of Sri Lanka, 1800–1900*. Athens, OH: Ohio University Press.

Wolf, E. (1959). 'Specific Aspects of Plantation Systems in the New World', in V. Rubin (ed.), *Plantation Systems of the New World*, pp. 136–46. Washington, DC: Pan American Union.

4
The Distance of a Shout

Sharon Bell

We lived on the medieval coast
south of warrior kingdoms
during the ancient age of the winds
as they drove all things before them.

Monks from the north came
down our streams floating—that was
the year no one ate river fish.

There was no book of the forest,
no book of the sea, but these
are the places people died.

Handwriting occurred on waves,
on leaves, the scripts of smoke,
a sign on a bridge along the Mahaweli River.

A gradual acceptance of this new language.

(Michael Ondaatje, 'The Distance of a Shout',
in Ondaatje 1998: 6)

Perhaps it is the demands, the anxiety, and the uncertainty that leave indelible yet hidden markings on the ethnographer who undertakes field-work in a foreign society. These markings are rendered more complex over time as lives unfold unpredictably in two separate but inextricably intertwined places. This chapter explores these complexities and the play of distance and time with geopolitical reality. The context is my 30-year relationship with Sri Lanka, which began in 1976 with my first 'fieldwork' sojourn in a rural village south-west of Colombo. The relationship has been maintained through the close friendships formed at that time with 'significant others'—the individuals who have enabled continuing intellectual and scholarly engagement with Sri Lanka,[1] the playing out of continuing obligations to my rural hosts, and through the renewed connections and engagement generated by sporadic, and often insultingly short, return visits. But over the three decades of engagement with Sri Lanka, the 'foreign researcher's' interest and involvement, framed by spatial and cultural distance, has also been regularly tested.

The period since the mid-1970s have been turbulent years for Sri Lanka. Ethnic conflict between the majority Sinhalese and minority Tamil populations experienced as 'flashpoints' since independence grew into a civil war that continued through the decades of the 1980s and 1990s. An insurgency movement generated what has become known as a 'time of terror' in the late 1980s.[2] And, shortly after the signing of a ceasefire agreement in 2002, which is widely believed to have brought about a 'state of no war' rather than a state of genuine peace, a devastating tsunami hit the south and east coasts of Sri Lanka, killing thousands, leaving many more displaced, and destroying infrastructure. Over the past two decades, as Sri Lanka oscillated in and out of civil war, and more recently following the carnage and social upheaval of the 2004 tsunami, the import of this distance has also had another dimension. As the 'outsider', the 'other', the researcher's experience has been tempered by the knowledge that her homeground is territory that is safe—the 'immersion', even the heightened concern, is temporary and superficial.

In this chapter the evolving nature of my lived experience with Sri Lanka is explored through auto-ethnography—a reflection on the processes of a foreign researcher negotiating relationships and struggling to find a legitimate voice. The chapter also explores the changing defence of that voice: defences that have had to be moulded to the changing socio-political environment, and defences that have matured with time. The structure of the chapter is built around the most critical 'signposts' of my Sri Lankan journey: incorporation into 'the field' and exposure to ethnic conflict in the 1970s; the emotional and intellectual distance experienced through the decades of the civil war and 'time of terror' that enveloped Sri Lanka in the 1980s and 1990s; and the equally devastating impact of the 2004 tsunami.

This reflection is supported by a conceptual framework proposed by Professor Ghassan Hage (2002). He has developed this framework in the context of his study of migration, in particular of globally dispersed Lebanese families. This framework provides a tool for exploring the notion of shifting geopolitical *affective and symbolic distance*. In doing so it moves beyond the current important interest in migration, movement, and transience[3] to acknowledge that relations are not simply dictated by space, nor borders, nor by the conventions of 'belonging' to a given society or group within society. This chapter explores my earliest fieldwork experience as a time of *incorporation* into a rural community. In tandem with incorporation, the experience of being an 'insider' is also seen as generating *communal indebtedness* to members of a materially disadvantaged community. The development of *intense relations* both in the village, but also with critical friends, colleagues, academics, and political activists during this time is contrasted with the later experience of *intense exclusion*, both during the 'time of terror' and more recently after the tsunami. It is hoped that this discussion will generate further under-standing of the complex question of the place and potential role of the oft-maligned foreign researcher in the postcolonial environment:

> ...to go beyond a solipsistic dwelling on one's own experience in the field which is hardly sufficient. The point is not, simply, to position oneself within the text... but to engage in a critical reflection on one's relationships with others, as circumscribed by institutional practices and by history, both within and outside the academy. (Young and Meneley 2005: 7)

That said, auto-ethnography risks slipping into a confessional mode of discourse and narcissistic reconstitution. Exposure of the fieldwork markings presents a rather difficult task for a number of reasons. Ethnographers have never been entirely at ease with including the 'self' in frame. As Shaffir and Stebbins (1991: 1–2) note:

> The process of leading a way of life over an extended period that is often both novel and strange exposes the researcher to situations and experiences that usually are accompanied by an intense concern with whether the research is conducted and managed properly. Researcher fieldwork accounts typically deal with such matters as how the hurdles blocking entry were cultivated and maintained during the course of study; the emotional pains of this work are rarely mentioned.

The essential conundrum of the ethnographic experience, that it is intensely personal and individualistic, and yet designed (certainly in its modernist form) to produce at least generalisable, at best verifiable, data and analysis, is one that has generated heated debate over the past three decades.[4] Dumont (1978: 7) has noted the paradoxical consequences that the more 'empathetic involvement' and the more that 'involved sympathy' emerge during the fieldwork experience, the more 'disciplined detachment' is found in the published reports 'under the pretext of objectivity'.

The ethnographic experience is also defined by what is expected/accepted within the academic discourse, creating a geopolitical fiction—the fieldwork site, in this case the village, as the source of knowledge and understanding. Even when we do include/explore 'empathetic involvement' in our scholarship, it is invariably restricted to relationships with the appropriate 'subjects' of our study (in this case rural women). Yet our knowledge of another place/society is gained through numerous experiences and a variety of sources. Undertaking research in a rural village provided me with information and data. Close relationships with a handful of village women generated a modicum of understanding. Critical friends, largely urban (extra-village) relationships with university colleagues and political activists provided me with a broader understanding of the socio-political map of my community of incorporation and constant dialogue regarding my modus operandi and my place as a foreign researcher. It is the latter relationships, those based on critical dialogue but grounded in common interests, values and intellectual traditions, that have been sustained over a lifetime. Those with my 'host village' are, in comparison, a polite form—in an essentially hierarchical relationship I offer patronage, as other wealthy/powerful members of Sri Lankan society do, to their supporters, clients, and the needy. I may do so in the context of a moral rather than instrumentalist relationship, but this does not alter the fact that I do not share the same, or similar, life experiences, values or aspirations as my village friends.

Incorporation

When I left Australia and went 'to the field' in Sri Lanka for the first time for two years in 1976 my modus operandi was, I suspect, little different from my colleagues—I was learning, with minimal prior preparation or direction, to be an ethnographer. I spent several months learning the Sinhala language, I 'chose' a village in which to live and work in the (then understudied) south-west lowlands of Sri Lanka, I 'found' a family who was happy to accommodate me, and later I 'negotiated' a house where I could live relatively independently. As long as the local police and the *Grama Sevaka* (village headman in the bureaucratic rather than democratic sense) agreed, there was neither formal nor informal negotiation with the community I was to study. I was there to observe, to learn, to 'write a book about the women', and then to 'make some films'. I was entering/being included in a society, which, although very different from my own, for the most part, followed the rules of 'civility' that I took for granted.

In fact, despite the political tightrope I trod amongst my Marxist colleagues in Colombo, the village I had chosen was delighted to have a foreign visitor in their midst. From the point of view of the 'significant others' within the village, the women I came to know as friends and 'relatives', I was there to amuse, as someone on whom to practise rudimentary English, to show a keen interest in the women and the everyday (not expected of foreigners who invariably sought out the exotic), as a potential source of then scarce foreign 'luxury' items (like blocks of Kraft cheddar cheese, batteries, matches, and soap), to talk about the deserts of Australia, to explain why my country is not peopled by ghosts and demons as Sri Lanka is, and, of course, the photos (the copious images that I was to produce in a land, at that time, without disposable cameras).[5] I was also to find out, many years later, that the small number of 'significant others', those to whom I became close in the village, expected much more—my hosts' simple hospitality and countless small, kind deeds would result in lifelong social obligations.[6]

When I look back, and it is important to emphasise that I am playing with memories and the capricious processes of recollection,[7] I am taken by the fact that people bothered to devote time to my incessant questioning and welcomed me into every event, every celebration, and every crisis. For, in the villagers' eyes, I was just a young female without status, except as the 'other':

> After it became apparent to people in the village that I was a semi-permanent guest it was easy for them to rationalise this by saying that I must have been Sinhalese in a previous life. Nonetheless I was not Sinhalese. In the village I was [and am] always known as *sudu nona* (the white lady). In many superficial ways I lived as the other women of the village did. I looked after my own house and did my own cooking. I ate rice and curry and bathed at a well. I was not conspicuously wealthy although I possessed the technical trappings of camera and tape recorder. Ultimately though I was very different—often a source of amusement, sometimes concern and sometimes pity.
>
> In the villagers' eyes I was young, female, and although married,[8] much of the time I was alone, and childless, which made me an anomaly. Personally I knew that in many crucial respects I was far removed from the life of the village. Although my research grant was not large, I never suffered the economic uncertainty that plagued most of those with whom I lived. Although I followed national politics at election time, I knew my future career was not dependent on the success of a particular party at the

> polls. Although I was told that my world was now populated by a variety of supernatural beings, many of them malign, I never experienced the real fear of possession nor the anxiety associated with displeasing the dead. (Bell 1986: 5–6)

Most people in the village did not, and do not, know my name; yet they were, and are, intensely interested in when and what I have eaten, my weight (then too thin, now sufficiently plump to be worthy of comment), my children (why did it take so long, and why were you so old when you had them?), my mother (is she still alive?), and my horoscope (you still do not know exactly what time you were born, it cannot be, contact your mother and find out immediately!). There remains little interest in what I do (I simply work at 'the university'), but a huge amount of interest in my comings and goings: then from the village to Colombo, more recently to and from Australia. My incessant mobility remains noteworthy for a woman.

Then, as now, beneath the ethnographic façade lay the impurities of the fieldwork experience: 'finding' a village was hellishly difficult (I had absolutely no idea as to how to go about this crucial task when I landed in Sri Lanka);[9] gaining any sort of independence of movement was frowned upon (especially by middle-class villagers who were busily protecting the virginity of their daughters); any hint of privacy impossible (young women should never be alone); surviving without electricity or running water, not so much arduous as unbelievably time consuming; the 'wet' (south-west monsoon)— experienced only once as it was too wet, too thunder-storm dark, too hot to do anything productive. There were no telephones to alleviate intense loneliness and anxiety, except through a complex process at the local post office, requiring all the skills at one's disposal to negotiate a remarkable postcolonial bureaucratic legacy. No wonder there were constant bad moods (on my part), impatience when I should have been grateful for the watchful gaze of my neighbours, frustration at being fed yet again despite pleas that I had just eaten, lack of interest in sickly warm soft drink and stale packaged cake demanded by the rules of Sinhalese 'short visit' hospitality (the purchase of which was likely to have impacted severely on my hosts' finances), and, of course, despair that the 'real work', the ethnography, was not progressing at the pace I (or my academic supervisor) had imagined it should. Add to this an unavoidable entanglement with a postcolonial bureaucracy that had carefully honed the skill of putting foreigners in their rightful place: the endless delays in processing applications and approvals; the ability to render invisible the foreigner in the corner of a government office or archive; the ubiquitous mites (one began to believe deliberately cultivated) in rattan office chairs that left the victim's thighs covered in itchy welts that took weeks to disappear. But the greatest challenge came from the broader context for which this foreign researcher was not at all prepared—a cosmopolitan urban intelligentsia who incessantly questioned the 'right' of the foreigner to be a researcher in their country, who questioned premises and assumptions, and exposed ignorance. The need for close relationships with academic/urban colleagues was as often a source of discomfort as reassurance.

None of these dimensions of the field experience appears in the written or visual documentation of that time. As with my colleagues, these 'impurities' were relegated to field diaries, to letters home, or simply mentally stored for later reference. The eruption of post-1977 election ethnic violence was intriguing, but pragmatically more significant for its disruptive impact on my fieldwork.[10] It is not surprising then that I was unable to see the decline of the people and society I liked to think I was a member of into a state of civil/ethnic war. Nor is it surprising that I was insensitive to the formative nature of the relationships with colleagues involved in the national socio-political struggle.

Yet these experiences and 'markings' from the field have shaped my life. From the first fieldwork experience, I was acutely aware that my Sri Lankan friends and neighbours were giving me the gift of their knowledge, and doing so generously, even though they had never read Mauss on reciprocity.[11] From the time of my first fieldwork I experienced what Ghassan Hage (2002: 204) identifies as *communal indebtedness*:

> Feelings of indebtedness are not restricted to one communal formation. One can belong with equal or varying intensity to several communities. Furthermore, the gift of social life is not offered to individuals only in the process of being born in a specific community. One can incur the debt of communality by voluntarily becoming part of a community that accepts one in its midst.

It might be assumed that incorporation into 'the field', another society and community, and the concomitant communal indebtedness is determined by spatial and temporal dimensions—where you are in relation to your community of incorporation, and how long you have been present or absent. More useful in deconstructing this relationship of geopolitical distance/closeness is Hage's articulation of *affective and symbolic distance*. As he elaborates:

> We all go through our daily lives knowing and/or feeling that some things leave in and on us a much deeper impression than others, that certain realities are experienced more intensely than others. Intensity as I will describe it here is not primarily physical, although it is also that. It is primarily affective. An intensely experienced reality is not the same as a 'hard hitting' reality. Intensity has more to do with the extent to which a reality is involving and affecting.... An intense reality is primarily an intense *relation* where the person's engagement in reality contribute [*sic*] to construct its intensity. (Hage: 193–94, emphasis added)

Reflection on my sense of belonging to the distant (from Australia) community of Sri Lanka reveals the critical importance of this affective and symbolic distance. The defining moments of *intense exclusion*, later transformed by me into *intense relation*, driven by feelings of *communal indebtedness*, have been defined not by geographical distance conceived as Euclidean space, but by geopolitical distance in terms of relationality and connection—the first during the period of the ethnic conflict, and most particularly during what has become known as the 'time of terror'—the late 1980s, and then after the December 2004 tsunami.

Ethnic Conflict: Intense Relation

To contextualise the first period, the ethnic conflict and the resultant 'time of terror', it is salutary to note that my earliest impressions of Sri Lanka in the late 1970s were signposted (now unsurprisingly) with discussions about violence, murder, and torture in the context of everyday discourse. One of my earliest recorded experiences in Sri Lanka was to walk along the beach in a waterfront Colombo suburb with a young companion who recounted tales of babies being killed by their mothers, young girls committing suicide over young love, bodies being washed ashore during the (1971) insurrection, and people being drowned 'all described with gory detail'.[12] Later in the village south of Colombo in which I lived for two years I was told stories of a handful of violent, apparently unpremeditated, murders (invariably brutal, hacking to death of a neighbour). And one memorable evening, following a funeral, the three teenage girls in the family with whom I was staying provided a graphic account of the stages of the burning that the body would be progressing through, given the time elapsed since the lighting of the pyre.... As I choked on my rice and curry, I was coolly told that the skull would now be exploding.[13] At this time I also became familiar with the 'urban myths' (in some senses an inappropriate label in a predominantly rural country, but strangely applicable to the manner in which verbal communication fuelled widespread ethnic hostility within the densely populated south-west) that related, enlarged and reinvented incidents (real or imagined) of Tamil perpetrated violence and torture (dismembered bodies packed and despatched on busy train services as fish to the market).

What was clear, even at the time of my first fieldwork in Sri Lanka, was that in the aftermath of the 1977 national election political violence had the potential to spiral out of control, and that a significant part of that violence was directly or indirectly state sponsored. During this period, when post-election violence broke out throughout many parts of Sri Lanka, primarily instigated by Sinhalese (and much of it aimed at Tamils), the then new (United National Party) government found it easier to give free reign to such 'bloodletting' than to face the real issues that may have fuelled the violence—the systemic economic and social problems the country was facing in its post-independence phase of nation building. Perera (1998: 20) asserts that:

> Immediately after its massive electoral victory in 1977, the newly installed UNP government decreed that police officers were entitled to leave. Usually, in the pre and post election contexts such leave is cancelled in order to maintain law and order given the known potential for violence. Taking complete advantage of the new government's apparent invitation to engage in violence UNP thugs [many of them] roamed electorates setting fire to and looting properties of supporters of the opposition. In a sense, this was the first step taken by the UNP to redirect political violence in a new and dangerous direction with state sponsorship.

In retrospect, it is difficult to know whether such aspects of my first fieldwork experience were significant or whether they have gained significance as political violence has become such a dominant feature of Sri Lankan society. For in the decade after these early days of *incorporation*, the first phase of my *intense relation* with Sri Lanka, a political environment perhaps characteristic of the local level of the rural community, became entrenched at the national level. This was an environment in which the violent settling of old scores was condoned, political jealousies and caste rivalries condemned individuals, and local level factional disputes were inflamed and reinvented as part of broader political movements.[14]

In the two decades following my fieldwork (1980s and 1990s) Sri Lanka transformed into a country where ethnic conflict dominated local and national politics, and political assassination became commonplace. Successive governments proved incapable of restoring peace, and the norms of civil society were eroded.[15] The 'war' in the north and east that pitted the Sinhala majority[16] against Tamil nationalists was a shocking conflict that claimed over 65,000 lives over 20 years.[17] It was also a war that provided the justification for political repression, extraordinary police and defence force powers, media censorship, and during the late 1980s, generated the reign of terror and counter-terror by Sinhala extremists in the south of the island that left a further 40,000 dead and thousands of others disappeared (Perera 1998: 44). But for the rest of the world it was a conflict that was not strategically important enough to warrant too much attention—on the strategic scale, tea is less important than oil.

Over the past two decades numerous writers[18] have explored the conundrum of this underbelly of violence, and indeed the resonance of violence within, and often perpetrated by, a nominally predominantly Buddhist society. Fonseka (1990: 109) argues that:

> The rage for murder in the country has been generated and fuelled by several inter-related conflicts: between ethnic groups (primarily Sinhala and Tamil but also historically with Muslims and Malayalis); between India and Sri Lanka; between the haves and the have nots; and between political parties and alliances cutting across ethnic groups, religious affiliations and social classes.

Perera (1998: 1) observes that:

> Sri Lanka in recent times has become synonymous with political violence and terror.... In fact, Sri Lanka's claim to be a paradise in the Indian Ocean has been overtaken by the harsh reality of being a case study in conflict formation and mis-management, where the much talked about paradise is clearly lost.

Tambiah (1992: 181) contends that it is because the political parties have by and large 'failed to build reliable, systematic integrating structures between themselves and the local level' that the national political elections generate 'a cycle of soaring expectations and bitter disappointment' as ruling parties change position and fail to deliver on their promises. It is, therefore, no accident that Sri Lankan national elections have frequently served as occasions for manifesting as well as generating ethnic and insurrectionary violence.

Post-election violence has become the norm since independence, as have 'ethnic riots', the most destructive of which took place in 1958, 1977, 1981, and 1983.[19] But it was the signing of the 'Peace Accord' between India and Sri Lanka in July 1987 that became a flashpoint for terror and intimidation on a scale never before experienced in this one time island paradise.

This terror was primarily driven by the Deshapremi Janatha Viyaapaaraya (the Patriotic People's Movement, a front for the Janatha Vimukthi Peramuna or the People's Liberation Front), with the state responding with equal terror and intimidation. This was a period during which state terrorism, state-sponsored gangs of killers operating with seeming impunity, and armed death squads of 'patriots' eliminated the possibility of any type of democratic activity. Indeed, in 1989, with an estimated murder rate of 100 per 100,000 of its population, Sri Lanka became 'the bloodiest place on earth' (Fonseka 1990: 109).

A Time of Terror: Intense Exclusion

From 1988 to 1990, the violence in Sri Lanka was so widespread that it became known as the *bhisana kalaya*—the time of terror. During this period I simply had the choice not to 'engage' physically and to distance myself intellectually and emotionally. I was, for some time, able to maintain the distance of safety, civility, and humanity. I was aware that many of my friends were at risk, that many had fled the country, and that those who remained were hidden in a network of 'safe houses'. But in 1988, one of my 'Colombo friends', Vijaya Kumaratunga, screen idol and emerging political leader, was assassinated. The report of the Special Presidential Commission of Inquiry (1997: 9) concluded that:

> The assassination of Vijaya Kumaratunga was a cruel and shocking act of violence directed against a man, a family and the peace loving people of this country. He was ascending as a charismatic political leader at National level with a firm commitment to socialist ideals and National reconciliation... On the 16th February 1988, shortly after 12 noon he stepped outside his house at No. 22/4 Polhengoda Road, Narahenpita in the company of his small son and daughter. He was unarmed and had in his hand a drawing book of his child. An assassin who came on a motor cycle ridden by an accomplice shot him at close range. The assassin did not make any attempt to disguise himself.

Thus, the Commission found that readily identifiable hired killers in front of a number of witnesses had gunned down Kumaratunga.

Kumaratunga's death was the event that for me rendered the political personal and made me painfully aware of my intense exclusion. Having said that, there is no doubt that his life and death is a cultural window that prompts reflection and warrants analysis. The irony, as someone who once repudiated the value of anthropologists focusing their gaze on myths, rituals, and cultural symbolism, in favour of the everyday, the pragmatic, the material, is not lost on me. Vijaya Kumaratunga, it may be argued, was 'not a victim but a symbol'.[20] Each year on the occasion of the anniversary of his death there are numerous commemorative newspaper articles, and the government broadcaster *Rupavahini* compiles a documentary celebrating his life and times. I ask myself, have I been caught up in Sri Lanka's collective infatuation with this one time screen idol? Was I, as a strident young feminist, dismissive of a man I knew to be charming, but also an egotistical womaniser? Why, so many years since his assassination, does he remain so much a part of my Sri Lankan experience? Why do I/we continue to struggle to make meaning?

> The rich and purposeful life of this much loved actor, humanist and politician was snatched away by a band of bloodthirsty barbarians on February 16, 1988 putting millions of fans and the whole country in eternal grief.... A true humanist, Vijaya was a sensitive artiste and politician who loved peace and despised violence and killings. He realised that the have nots were being exploited by the rich and powerful due to some fault in the socio-economic and political structure...It is only a handful of people who become immortal after death. Veteran actor Vijaya Kumaratungsa was one among such prodigious people. (*Sunday Observer Magazine* 1999)

What is obvious is that Kumaratunga's life and death have assumed a symbolic significance that outstrips his mortal achievements.

Mindful that we were less easily seduced by 'fame' in the 1970s and 1980s than in the 21st century, I will set aside the notion of collective (and personal) infatuation. What then did/does Kumaratunga represent that has ensured the collective mourning of his death and his increasing symbolic significance? One might speculate that he represents a time of trust that, if it did not actually exist in Sri Lanka, certainly is believed to have existed—a state of relative civil peace. Kumaratunga was perhaps perceived to be capable of restoring (the concept of) a society based on trust; a society in which, just as in his films, essential good triumphs over evil. Perera (1998) contends that Sinhala rural society has been represented in most local discourses at the popular and scholarly level, as well as in numerous ethnographies as constituted by cohesive social units. Such descriptions 'disregard the serious cleavages and animosities that were well enmeshed in these communities':

> It is difficult to trust strangers when people had lived through a situation in which they could not even trust members of their own community. Security forces compelled people to supply lists of others who were deemed to be anti-government. On its own side the JVP also maintained death lists compiled with the help of local people. The collapse of trust may be graphically illustrated by evoking the *goni billo* during the period of terror. The *goni billo* were masked men who assisted the army to identify people who were arrested to be later interrogated, tortured and murdered. They became 'the disappeared'. For the local community, the identity of the *goni billo*—were they friends, relatives or neighbours—made everyday relations fraught with apprehension and distrust. (Perera 1998: 79)

Kumaratunga also presented as an inspired, and inspiring, young politician who was, and is, popularly believed to have had the capacity to radically reshape his country's destiny; he represented promise in a time of desperation. The fact that his political potency was never really put to the test in the formal role of government, or even opposition, means that his reputation remains untainted. He was never forced to make the pragmatic—or worse still—politically expedient, decisions that all those (including his widow) in political leadership positions in parliamentary democracies face. Indeed, political leaders over the past two decades have proven themselves impotent to address the long-running ethnic conflict, as well as the unaddressed systemic issues of education, economic development, unemployment, and governance appropriate to a multi-ethnic society.

I was to find out later that Kumaratunga's murder was just one in a spate of political assassinations in Sri Lanka that continued until 1990. Hundreds of politicians, government officials, intellectuals, academics, and students were murdered, while thousands more fled to other countries or moved into networks of 'safe houses'. An anonymous report in 1988 documents the death of Vijaya Kumaratunga as one of 270 political murders reported to Parliament for the period 20 December 1987 to 15 October 1988. At this time, those under threat were listed as members of the then ruling party, the United National Party (UNP); all members of local government bodies; members of the Armed Forces; all members of the left and progressive circles who supported the Peace Accord and contested the Provincial Council elections (based on the concept of the devolution of power); and activists of the Independent Students' Union, the All Lanka Peasants' Congress and other human rights, and mass organisations that supported the Peace Accord. As the campaign of terror grew in scale and intensity the targets of this campaign became increasingly broad:

> There is an aura of vindictiveness that marks many of these killings… on several occasions when attacks have been launched on homes there has been no regard for innocent bystanders. Old persons, infants, children, stray visitors, all have fallen in the hail of random bullets. Victims have been burnt to death, stabbed, hacked, decapitated. The common practice at present is to shoot and then to stab. The 'patriots' also introduced the infamous 'lamp-post' killing to the south of Sri Lanka. They often leave behind posters or leaflets acknowledging their hand in the killing and stating reasons as to why, in their opinion, the person deserved such a fate. (Anon. 1988)

It was in this climate of terror and fear that numerous acts of terror were perpetrated at the local level to 'settle old scores':

> The worst form of terror was what came to be known as *ussanyanava* (abductions). The possibility of nightly visitations from either the Tigers, the JVP, the army, the police, or para-military vigilante groups, any of whom could walk into a house and abduct a person with impunity, was a reality that almost everyone lived with. The Emergency Laws and the Prevention of Terrorism Act meant that anyone could be arrested and held without trial for an extended period of time. The mass graves now being uncovered (1994) clearly show that many of those abducted by police, army and para-military groups were summarily killed.... No wonder then that a society that had been avidly interested in politics, where in every home, in private or public gatherings, in the press, in journals, in buses or trains, the main subject of conversation had been politics, by the late 1980s, suddenly went silent. No one dared to talk; no one expressed a political opinion, not even among friends. (Obeyesekere 1999: 45–46)

The complexity and intrigue surrounding political alliances between the state, law enforcement agencies, political parties, and individual politicians at this time is difficult to unravel. The *bhisana kalaya* created an environment in which ordinary people as well as their leaders could take extreme steps to vent their anger and frustration, not just against old enemies, but also against colleagues and neighbours.[21]More recently it has become not uncommon for members of the UNP government, who during this time were also targets of political violence, to be named as those directly responsible:

> The President said the bodies of a majority of youth killed during that period were missing and their grief stricken parents went from one army camp to another in search of them in vain. The UNP, she said, was afraid of upcoming youth leaders even from its own ranks so it was bent on eliminating them. One youth leader the UNP most feared was the late Mr Vijaya

> Kumaratunga. So the UNP used every possible trick to prevent him from winning a parliamentary seat. The President said the commission which probed the Vijaya Kumaratunga assassination had concluded that the late President Premadasa was responsible for planning his murder with the then JVP leadership. (*Daily News*, 3 March 1999)

The ongoing violence in Sri Lanka, awakened in me a sense of ethnographic impotence and professionally paralysing *intense exclusion*.[22] At another level it was a simple emotional journey that others have captured more eloquently than I—the vain attempt to come to terms with a friend's death: 'First it was somebody's somebody. Then it was a friend's friend. Then it was a friend. It goes on and on. I am overwhelmed with sadness...'[23]

A decade previously in the village, I had often wished I had some practical skills or knowledge that would actually help the people who so generously shared their lives with me. I naively wished I had studied medicine or agriculture; even veterinary science would have been useful. Now I felt guilty—the familiar sense of *communal indebtedness*. I had done very little to engage with the ongoing conflict in Sri Lanka. Although I had made the mandatory return to the village in 1985 to show off my two sons (I was now a 'real' woman),[24] as they were so young I had taken a deliberate decision not to put their lives or mine at risk by travelling to Sri Lanka during the late 1980s. I did not re-engage in a serious way with Sri Lanka until the ground was relatively safe after a change in government that brought Kumaratunga's widow Chandrika Bandaranaike Kumaratunga to power in 1994. In the period since, the culture of violence and its tragic manifestations have been the centre of my intellectual and emotional engagement with Sri Lanka. I now ask myself, to what degree is my intellectual and academic interest an attempt to create an *intense relation* with a politic in which I did not directly participate?

If so, I must claim a degree of success as I am now regarded as having a certain degree of expertise, which does not sit entirely comfortably with me.[25] The news of the assassination of Dr Neelan Thiruchelvam (a moderate Tamil politician and an international human rights activist) who was killed by a suicide bomber whilst travelling to work was a reminder of my ambiguous relationship with my community of incorporation—fluctuating between *intense relation* and *intense exclusion*. It was not that the death of Dr Thiruchelvam was unusual—his murder was one of a series of assassinations of moderate Tamil political leaders and rival militant leaders eliminated by the LTTE in recent years, even since the 2002 ceasefire agreement. It was rather the manner in which it was communicated to me via e-mail, as I had returned to Australia a few days previously: 'The news of the death of our mutual friend... sending shocks, tremors, convulsions into our systems.'

This statement resonated, as whilst I had met Dr Thiruchelvam, it would be inappropriate to describe him as a 'friend' in the literal sense. The communication and use of the word 'friend' I think was to imply 'comrade', someone of like mind. Nor could I claim to have experienced the same 'shocks, tremors and convulsions'. I certainly felt shocked, I felt deeply saddened, and I felt depressed by the loss of such an individual who was playing a critical role in the process of political reconciliation. But I could not claim to experience the same, or even similar, loss of his real friends, nor the impact of uncertainty (even fear) that my Sri Lankan colleagues must feel with the passing of every such murder.

This difference, the view from outside, from safe ground, in some ways parallels the issues explored in Sasanka Perera's essay 'On Feeling and Not Feeling Others' Pain', in which he examines the question of our ability to 'experience' others' pain, especially extreme pain such as that experienced under torture:[26]

> There is a vast difference between understanding the reality of torture, that is understanding the reality that torture exists, and actually knowing what it is like. On some occasions, individuals whose testimonies we read in the discourse of human rights would be able to describe the methods used in torture. But the listeners or readers of such descriptions will not feel the pain residing behind those descriptions unless they have also undergone similar experiences. Thus language has merely been successful in describing the fact that people are in pain, not what it is like. (Perera 1999: 51)

Every time I return from Sri Lanka I am asked whether I experienced fear, whether there was any immediate threat. My response has always been negative, 'of course not': one quickly (all too quickly) adjusts to the military presence, the check points, even the body searches. What I am moved to say is, that as someone who is privileged to be able to choose the geopolitical space with which she will engage, that experience is also tempered by the knowledge that one's community of birth is territory that is safe, a society following the norms of civil peace—the 'immersion', the heightened concern, the *intense relation* is something that can be managed, even manipulated. My relationship with my community of incorporation allows me to create and extend the *intense relation.* When I choose, geopolitical intensity overrides geographical distance.

When the tsunami hit Sri Lanka in 2004, I hoped, along with other optimists, that this devastating event may have fractured the established dynamics of the ethnic conflict:

> My dear friends,
>
> I won't bore you with the chronology of my reactions over the past week as my experience pales in comparison to your own which is so immediate! Nonetheless I am moved to write as I am overwhelmed by deep sadness and plagued by the ambiguity of being an insider/outsider. Perversely I wish I could be there with you to share your sadness and find ways to comfort you in your distress. Selfishly my family and I say thank goodness the tsunami did not strike a week earlier when I was there with you....
>
> In response I found myself recanting familiar place names in a sense to hold on to what was once a different reality. Or was it to hypnotise, to dull the senses? Mullativu, Nilaveli, Kalkudah, Matara, Polhena, Galle… realisation that these once familiar haunts are now places that if they still exist I would not recognise. That many of the people who made them the places they were are no longer....
>
> …These were the places, the sites of the unique, dare I confess, exotic, experiences that frame me and my relationship with you. They were the places that the foreign anthropologist writes large in the fashion of: I was there, I did that, my experience was truly out of the ordinary (and it was!). They were places where once the greatest threat came from mosquitoes or snakes or the heat. Where danger was defined in the more remote reaches by the need to enter the coastal jungle to defecate—but even then there was a friend in tow to stand guard….
>
> Of course in the East this idyll had already been lost through the decades of war—Mullaitivu long since a jungle for human tigers and land mines, not straying '*sudus*'. Another cruel irony: the Sri Lankan tsunami death toll has taken only half the number of lives claimed by the ethnic conflict over the past two decades. The world remains largely oblivious to the latter no less real toll—slow, barely perceptible from the outside, bleeding, versus unabashed, in our faces carnage.
>
> My heart goes out to you. Like other optimists (fools, do I hear you say?) I harbour the vein hope that the enormity of events will sufficiently change the political landscape, that my and your comrades will revalue the cost of a life, any life—how else can I restore my faith in humanity if not in the gods? (Letter from author to Colombo, 5 January 2005)

After the Tsunami

Since the devastating tsunami hit the south and east coasts of Sri Lanka in December 2004 killing over 35,000 and leaving another half a million people homeless, the geopolitical landscape of Sri Lanka has again dramatically and irrevocably changed. There is now a 'joke' that circulates amongst Colombo's intelligentsia: did you know there were three equally devastating tsunami waves? The first was the sea. The second, the invasion of 'relief' forces. The third, the numerous foreign NGOs who are effectively removing what remains of community sustainability, resilience, and capacity building. In many ways this joke, not out of character coming from my old Marxist colleagues (one has to remember that Sri Lanka is still nominally a socialist state), symbolises the frustration, the distance, and the impotence that so many feel 'after the tsunami'. Such jokes trivialise a profound and life-changing experience, and the way the 'other', my community of birth—the West—has responded to this event. Such jokes are also an expression of the complex ways in which we human beings respond to impossible circumstances.

Like so many others in Sri Lanka, and around the world, late December 2004 and much of January 2005 was for me a time of anxiety and uncertainty. But in marked contrast to the 'time of terror', thanks to technology, news of friends came as swiftly as media images to our screens. This generated an impression of a close, *affective relation*. Much of the news was 'good' news, of friends and families who survived. This added reassurance to the ubiquitous, and shocking, media coverage, and the daily increasing death toll.[27] Yet some correspondence, particularly from colleagues working with women's groups, added a sickening, inhuman, incomprehensible dimension—a dimension that was not captured in mainstream media:

> Now the stories of sexual abuse and violence begin to trickle in. We have sent out teams to check on these stories... and will have a full report by Saturday, we hope. Also, there are fears of girls being kidnapped from the camps... because there is still no security provided to the camps to speak of. Although we have petitioned the Women's Ministry today and hope it will change. (E-mail from Colombo, 4 January 2005)

For months I again experienced disempowerment and *intense exclusion*, tempered now by continuing, if not unproblematic, media coverage. Interestingly, this exclusion was compounded, rather than alleviated, by the experience of geographical proximity. Six months after the tsunami the experience of being a 'tsunami tourist', albeit a well-intentioned one, was a journey through a zone of profound discomfort. To find myself back in Sri Lanka, regarded by those who do not know me as just another well-meaning foreigner with so little to offer in the context of so much need, or worse still, with so much to offer but having to compete with all the others engaged in a similar humanitarian mission, was profoundly unsettling.

Notwithstanding the impressions generated by the media, the coastline was not uniformly devastated. Local topography was a decisive card played in this cruel game. Some coastal communities remained intact whilst neighbouring areas were completely devastated. 'Being in the wrong place at the wrong time', something we had learnt to live with through the decades of Tamil Tiger terrorism and Sinhala nationalist retribution, now had new meaning. Everyone, it seems, has a story of disaster or escape, and these small narratives are quickly becoming set pieces to engage the foreigner: 'We were supposed to travel south to visit our in-laws, but we were late and missed the bus'; 'That child went to visit her grandmother for Christmas, if she had remained here she would not have been killed. But her grandmother was old and frail. It might have been her last Christmas. It was their last Christmas.'

As these stories are told and retold, it becomes difficult to know what is real and what in the retelling is a reflection of enduring politics: 'Everyone in this village survived, except those who went to the Christian church for shelter. The priest told them that God would look after them. He [*sic*] didn't. They were all killed.' For the benefit of visitors, complete strangers graciously count the number of family members lost: 'two daughters', 'two sons', 'my mother and mother-in-law', 'every family here is the same'. But that loss, and the accompanying grief, is no longer tangible to the visitor, who did not know these people who are no longer as real, living human beings—who cannot fathom how one goes about grieving when the scale of loss is so great. And that grief, the grief of incomprehensible loss, is compounded by trauma and guilt that is also beyond the reach of the visitor: 'His little girl was missing all night. They thought they had lost her, but in the morning they were reunited'. 'I was minding the children. They were in my care. They were all lost…'

One's gaze seeks to penetrate the now-benign landscape. Is that debris and rubble the norm in a poor community, or was it the wave? There a fibreglass boat ripped in two. Overhead, watermarks that lap at the ceilings of still intact buildings. There, unbelievably, a steel railway line 50 metres from its original position. Everywhere wells now offer residents only saltwater. Hundreds, perhaps thousands, of families are still living in tents and makeshift wooden houses—small huts stamped 'temporary dwelling'—'gift of the people of' Denmark, or Japan or Ireland or Turkey. How temporary these 'microwaves' in the 30 degree heat?

One also, involuntarily, scours the roadside graveyards: a fresh grave there, several more here. Are these 'victims' or just the ordinary, everyday dead? In the war-ravaged east this becomes a profound question. Tsunami damage looks like war damage, or poverty. Orphans are orphans, but the mass of orphans in many institutions are war orphans, and they have been there for years. Why does the world only want to know about the tsunami orphans? As a war orphan, is my case less urgent, less appealing?

In the east the growing military presence might generously be construed as protection and reconstruction, but the military's omnipresence and vigilance speaks of another life-threatening danger that does not come from the sea. How does the visitor understand the recent loss in the context of families that may have been dislocated three or four times by war, each time losing everything? How does one retain the will, the resilience to start again? As a 'tsunami tourist', how does one find the point of meaningful, negotiated, humanitarian contact, of *intense relation* that you have at times enjoyed and at other times deftly constructed?

Like war zones, post-tsunami communities are characterised by the fact that, despite everything, life (on the surface at least) goes on, as it must. Trains run on rebuilt lines. Overcrowded buses thunder down chaotic and inadequate roads, competing now with shining UN and OXFAM four-wheel drives. Children in neat white uniforms go to school, their laughter and childish chatter not revealing those who are now missing from their midst. Small, makeshift shops offer essential goods for sale to even poorer neighbours, as they have always done. The elderly and the unemployed sit on porches watching, but perhaps not seeing, the much more diverse passing parade—so many *sudu*s ('whitefellas' to use the indigenous Australian vernacular).

For those, like myself, who were not there to experience the moment of destruction; for those whose visit post-dates the ensuing days and weeks of fear, despair and hopelessness; for those who have not experienced the overwhelming stench of death and the visible signs of carnage, there is an inevitable lack of connection.[28] Reality does not mirror the indelible media images locked in one's mind. This new reality is an imperfect fit—despite geographic incorporation, it does not translate into the *intense relation* that was expected.

Back in Colombo, at a dinner with friends, I yet again occupy the position of 'other' as I am aware of the powerful cultural shaping of what I, as a foreigner, see and feel, or rather don't see and don't feel, in this landscape. The talk is of spirits of the dead who must now populate those tsunami-ravaged coastal strips. My friends express discomfort about returning to once loved beaches, not just because of physical damage, but because the invisible landscape of the afterlife has also changed. They recollect the unsettling atmosphere at the time of the tsunami—towns filled with dogs inexplicably howling. Their conclusion, the presence of spirits of the dead, is not one I would have naturally drawn, although this was a dimension of the carnage, of which I was culturally aware. In a land where relatives go to great lengths to ensure the transition of the deceased from one world to the next, I in my rusty Sinhala, had (inappropriately?) asked strangers still living by the sea whether they were worried about the spirits of the numerous dead. Of course, they said no they were not, but then quietly, uncomfortably added 'some people may be thinking like that, but they don't say anything.' This was the skill of silence, of speaking only in whispers—a skill finely honed during the 'time of terror'.

I am reminded of Kevin Clements' reflections on the overwhelming significance attached to 9/11 in the West—a terrorist act that is a mere speck in the morass of global, more often than not national, rather than international, terrorism. In this context Clements raises the important question 'for whom do we grieve', 'for whom do we mourn'?[29] Why is it that 20 years and over 65,000 deaths as a result of ethnic conflict in Sri Lanka failed to be worthy of our, the 'other's' collective attention, yet when half that number of the same people, in the same place are killed or 'disappeared' by a big wave, we very publicly grieve and our response is generous? Are the victims of the tsunami less implicated than those of war? Or, following Lederach (2005), are we more capable of extending our empathy, exercising our moral imagination in a way we could not in the context demanded by breaking a culture of violence:

> The moral imagination rises with the capacity to imagine ourselves in relationship, the willingness to embrace complexity without reliance on dualistic polarity, the belief in the creative act, and acceptance of the inherent risk required to break violence and to venture on unknown paths that build constructive change. (ibid.: 5)

Perhaps it is not just that there is a strong feeling of an *affective relation* amongst us coastal dwellers, sometimes Asian beachside tourists, that this might have been us, simply 'in the wrong place at the wrong time' (as some of us were), but that for most of us, our empathy did not involve inherent risk, nor a political stance, nor indeed a creative response.

Postscript

It is unnecessary to say that the definition of 'otherness' is context specific. Just because as a foreign researcher I have been *incorporated* into a rural village, may have been exposed to more facets of 'traditional' culture, and have detailed knowledge of the lives of a number of rural poor women, does not mean that my understanding or expertise equals that of my Sri Lankan counterparts whose life experiences in their own society have obviously been very different to my own. In many ways, despite the long period of time involved, the sum total of my experiences 'in the field' remains, in relative terms, a thin level of exposure very different from colleagues who were born, educated and subtly inducted into the mores of their own language, literature, religion, and society.[30] Nonetheless, the fact that I see through a different cultural lens can be advantageous—I ask different questions (some that perhaps shouldn't be asked), I interpret answers differently, I give different weight to the outcomes of analysis, and I am appalled by a culture of violence that many of my colleagues now accept as the norm. This difference, together with my capacity as an outsider to 'imagine myself in relationship' (Lederach 2005) with a wide range of people (perhaps a wider range than if I was more sensitive to social nuances of class, caste, and ethnicity) underpins my potential to contribute. It is my 'otherness' that is simultaneously a strength and weakness—an 'otherness' far more complex than implied by the simplistic label 'foreign researcher'.

On the other hand, I cannot deny that much of my Sri Lankan experience is shaped by the legacy of colonialism and my own society's positioning as a Western state,[31] and, therefore, my identity within that context. As *sudu nona* I am (generally) accorded deference and respect. I am socially accepted where, were I from a different ethnic background or non-Western state, I might be excluded. My 'intellectual tradition' is firmly located on the dominant Euro-American axis, as is my cultural baggage.[32] But in untangling this dynamic of identity it is important to recognise the differential privilege that I enjoy. A significant part of my 'otherness' is due to two critical elements: the freedom to exercise choice and my relative mobility. Both of these factors are fundamental to my engagement with Sri Lanka, particularly at times of political unrest. Unlike many of my colleagues, I am free to divorce myself from intractable social and political problems, and even physically leave, or not engage, if I feel at risk. This is *incorporation* from an extraordinarily privileged position; any pretext to equality is shallow.

When experiencing a state of *intense relation*, such as when I am in Sri Lanka or, indeed, interacting with the Sri Lankan community in Australia, I do not see myself as a 'foreign researcher'; rather I am a member of a community into which I have been *incorporated* as professional colleague, friend, and 'relative'. In each of these roles I have accumulated a mantle of *communal indebtedness* that shapes my engagement with my Sri Lankan colleagues and friends. Nonetheless, I remain *sudu nona* and that ambiguity of positionality—of simultaneously being self and other, of being at times included and at others excluded, by agency, circumstance, or intellectual construct—is a terrain worthy of nuanced analysis. I am left reflecting on my limited understanding as the 'other' of another country's complex socio-political map, and of the unpredictable playing out over a lifetime of *communal indebtedness* and the profound impact of the conditions of civil peace and civil war—perhaps wanting/needing to shout but only generating a whisper, daring to reject this new language.

Notes

1. I am particularly indebted to colleagues attached to the Social Scientists' Association, Colombo; the University of Colombo; and the University Grants Commission.
2. There was an earlier insurgency in 1971 that had many of the same hallmarks, and ostensibly driven by the same Marxist 'youth movement'—the Janatha Vimukthi Peramuna (JVP)—but the more recent was triggered by very different circumstances, defending very different (Sinhala chauvinist) values. The JVP is now a legitimate political party.
3. See for instance Clifford 1997.
4. See Okely and Callaway (eds) (1992) *Anthropology and Autobiography*.
5. Remarkably well-preserved old Polaroids carefully wrapped in plastic sleeves are still pulled out of cupboards to remind me of 'those days'.
6. My neighbour's daughter, once a precocious 4-year-old, 'adopted' my partner and I as surrogate parents after the untimely death of her father. Over three decades we have provided for her education, arranged employment opportunities normally reserved for the Colombo elite, helped find her a husband, and then covered the cost of her marriage. We provide small gifts towards the house she is struggling to build and cover the costs of inevitable 'emergencies'. We are now 'grandparents' to her daughters and look forward to helping meet the needs of the next generation—a small price to pay for a whole village's care and hospitality.
7. Robins (1995: 204) reminds us that memories lack the stability of geological strata, but rather need to be seen in terms of an active past–present relationship.
8. I had married as an undergraduate, but like many students in the early 1970s was caught up in the feminist debate about the questionable role of the nuclear family. On the bookcase of my student share house the O'Neills' book *Open Marriage* (1973) had a prominent place, just as it did in influencing how (some of us) played out our lives and relationships.

9. In those days we were 'prepared' for the field in an avuncular sort of way, with minimal linguistic skills, strong recommendation that we should complete the short course on tropical medicine, instructions to situate (read build/procure/insinuate) ourselves at the epicentre of our chosen society, dispense cargo and even modern drugs with appropriate confidence and authority, and return from the field as experts (Bell 2004: 19).
10. I was not only 'protected' by villagers, but by a wonderfully concerned and supportive Australian High Commissioner Alexis Borthwick, who, on one memorable occasion as post-election ethnic violence broke out, sent, to the astonishment of my new-found village friends, his black Mercedes to the village to collect me and take me to the relative safety, certainly less isolated environs, of friends in suburban Colombo.
11. Mauss' seminal 1924 *Essai Sur le Don* explores the moral obligations attendant upon giving gifts. The work has generated a wealth of scholarship in anthropology and related disciplines, influencing leading scholars such as Levi-Strauss, Godelier, Derrida, Bourdieu, Polyani, and Strathern. Recently Mauss' concepts have been adopted by scholars conceptualising the knowledge economy such as Gibbons (see Mauss 1990).
12. Diary entry, 23 October 1976.
13. Diary entry, 27 April 1977.
14. As Paul Alexander (1981: 113) has observed in his analysis of the 1971 insurrection:

    > Studies of Sri Lanka, as with other post-colonial societies, have equated politics with the concerns and activities of a small urban-centered elite… political activities amongst the peasantry—at least 70 percent of the population—are seldom mentioned…. Peasants seldom write accounts of their political activities and it is more difficult to gather accurate data on a disaggregated rural movement…. Academics and the local intelligentsia—from Left, Right and Centre—have consistently used models of political action which presuppose that the rural population is an undifferentiated and residual category: an amorphous mass serving as a colourful backdrop for more important events on centre stage.

15. This is reflective of Hobbes's emphasis on the importance of the sovereign's ability to reward and punish. His 'civil society' is constituted and held together by state power (Hobbes 1994: xiii, 3–9). For a discussion, see Ehrenberg (1999).
16. Seventy-four per cent of the population compared to 18 per cent Tamil minority.
17. Amnesty International is concerned that continuing human rights abuses are part of a systematic campaign by the LTTE against other Tamil political groups opposing them (ASA 37/004/2003).
18. Fonseka (1990), Hoole (2001), Jayawardena (1986), Kapferer (1988), Obeyesekere (1984), Perera (1998), Tambiah (1992), and Uyangoda and Biyanwala (1997).

19. Tambiah (1992: 49) provides an even earlier example of complicity of government (in this case, the UNP) in inflaming ethnic conflict:

    Toward the end of March 1958, the National Transport Board sent a fleet of new buses to the north with Sinhalese letters on the license plates, and the Federalists defaced them and substituted Tamil letters. Wriggins relates the sequel as follows: 'Over one hundred and fifty Tamils were arrested. In retaliation in the south, Sinhalese gangs smeared tar over Tamil lettering on stores run by Tamils. The police were slow to restore order' (Wriggins 1960: 267). Manor continues the story thus: 'Within twenty-four hours, things in the capital had got out of hand. Two large groups of defacers, one of them lead by bhikkhus, systematically combed the city, and even managed to obliterate the Tamil section of a sign in three languages on Bandaranaike's official Cadillac which read "left hand drive".' Police were instructed to show restraint and, while guarding Tamil and Indian shops in central Colombo from attack, were lenient about other actions (50), such as the stopping of vehicles with Tamil lettering and the assault of Tamil truck drivers in Sinhalese majority areas. As a result 'some Sinhalese lawbreakers assumed that "our government" did not object to such doings.' (Manor, The Expedient Utopian: Banaranaike and Ceylon, 1989, p. 285) … It was in this atmosphere of the weakening of law enforcement agencies that the riots of 1958 exploded around the time that the Federalists were preparing to hold their annual convention in Vavuniya in the north preparatory to launching a campaign of non-violent protest.

20. This phrase is drawn from the work of Nayanananda Wijaya Kulatilaka, who had been a participant in, and a victim of, the violent 1971 JVP insurrection as a young man. In 1972 he was 'betrayed by a comrade' and was held in remand for almost two years by the CID in Colombo (Growney 1999: 13). During this time, and throughout his lengthy trial, Kulatilaka used his art to express his feelings and to record aspects of the brutality of the environment in which he was confined. His series of pastels on paper depicting the rape of Prema Manamperi at Katharagama, bearing the inscription 'not a victim but a symbol', powerfully express the desire to overcome political and sexual impotence (ibid.: 26). Kulatilaka's view on the collective amnesia (even denial) that surrounds the violence of the 1980s is that people continue to live in fear of speaking out, despite the changed political circumstances and mood.
21. Sri Lankan villages are highly factionalised with bitter disputes occurring over scarce resources. One of the most tragic and widely publicised cases of this playing out of national politics at a local level was that of what has become known as the Embilipitiya massacre. At a court case in February 1999, following the exhumation of mass graves it was revealed that 'the architect and the prime hand behind the brutal massacre was none other than the Principal of Embilipitiya Maha Vidyalaya [Embilipitiya High School] of which 25 victims were students. It also transpired that these poor children had

paid with their lives because of a joke which they played on the son of the Principal Lokugalappatti in the form of a love letter. The principal then went berserk and turned his wrath on the students for this innocent little prank' (*Daily News* 17.2.1999). Lokugalappatti's fabrications 10 years earlier, that the students were members of the JVP, led to the death of the 25 17-year-olds, their mutilated bodies 'dumped like garbage into a mass grave'.

22. The doctoral thesis that I had successfully completed a few years previously in my mind was rendered meaningless—I had written about another time, another political era; it may as well have been another place. I could never bring myself to publish from it.
23. Artist Anoli Perera on the occasion of the assassination of Dr Neelan Thiruchelvam, a moderate Tamil politician and international human rights activist and close friend, who was killed by a suicide bomber whilst travelling to work in Colombo in 1999.
24. In Sri Lanka spinsters are traditionally despised, and barrenness is considered a bad omen.
25. Not least as in 1999 I was able to spend another long period in Sri Lanka (six months). During this time I researched a documentary on Kumaratunga's life and death, *The Actor & the President* (2000) for Australia's multicultural broadcast network, SBS.
26. The late Susan Sontag has explored similar themes more recently (2003, 2004), particularly in relation to the power of photographic images of torture and war.
27. This is also in marked contrast to the 'time of terror' when deaths/murders were either brutally public or were whispers rather than statistics—the process of 'confirmation' of the fate of the thousands of 'disappeared' continues.
28. I had left Sri Lanka the week before the tsunami following one of my regular 'short visits'. These days when Sri Lanka competes with numerous professional obligations, close colleagues say I am 'like a shower of rain' (I suspect a tropical downpour)—a short period of intense engagement and I disappear.
29. Presentation at the Griffith University Multi-Faith Centre UNESCO International Symposium 'Cultivating Wisdom, Harvesting Peace', August 2004.
30. When not interacting with English speakers, I negotiate a linguistically challenging environment in a second language—closer to the level of a 5-year-old than an academic, and with all the hallmarks of the Sinhala language spoken by young village women.
31. Robinson (2003: 273–76) reminds us how much the influence of the colonial past persists, especially with reference to Western academic hegemony and the resultant marginalisation of all other scholarship.
32. Even my physical traits (fair skin, light brown hair that may be considered 'blond') are generally considered desirable, although one colleague does wonder when I will be rid of my 'skin disease' (typically Australian freckles, the trophy of too many hours in the sun).

References

Alexander, P. (1981). 'Shared Fantasies and Elite Politics: The Sri Lankan "Insurrection" of 1971', *Mankind*, 13(2): 113–32.

Amnesty International Index Reference System ASA 37/004/2003. Available online at www.amnesty.org/en/library/info/ASA37/004/2003/en, accessed on 14 September 2005.

Anon. (Unpublished MS). 'Tentative List of Political Assassinations in Southern Sri Lanka, from August 1, 1987 to October 15, 1988'.

Bell, S. (Unpublished MS). 'Women and Wage Labour: The Impact of Capitalism in Southwest Sri Lanka'. Unpublished Ph.D. thesis submitted to University of Sydney, 1986.

———. (2004) 'Writing Research Culture', in V. Mackie and B. Groombridge (eds), *Re-searching Research Agendas: Women, Research and Publication in Higher Education*. Perth: Curtin University of Technology.

Clifford, J. (1997). *Routes: Travel and Translation in the late Twentieth Century*. Cambridge, MA: Harvard University Press.

Daily News. (1999). 3 March.

Dumont, J.P. (1978). *The Headman and I*. Austin, Texas: University of Texas Press.

Ehrenberg, J. (1999). *Civil Society: The Critical History of an Idea*. New York: NYU Press.

Fonseka, C. (1990). *Towards a Peaceful Sri Lanka: Six Introductory Seminars for University Students*. Helsinki: United Nations University, World Institute for Development Economics Research.

Growney, P. (1999). *Nayanananda*. Ratmalana: Print-Inn.

Hage, G. (ed.) (2002). *Arab-Australians: Citizenship and Belonging Today*. Melbourne: Melbourne University Press.

Hobbes, T. (1994). *The Elements of Law*. Oxford: World Classics Edition.

Hoole, R. (2001). *Sri Lanka: The Arrogance of Power, Myths, Decadence and Murder*. Jaffna: University Teachers for Human Rights.

Jayawardena, K. (1986). *Ethnic and Class Conflicts in Sri Lanka*. Dehiwala: Centre for Social Analysis.

Kapferer, B. (1988). *Legends of People, Myths of State: Violence, Intolerance and Political Culture in Sri Lanka and Australia*. Washington, DC: Smithsonian Institution Press.

Lederach, J.P. (2005). *The Moral Imagination: The Art and Soul of Building Peace*. New York: Oxford University Press.

Mauss, M. (1990). *The Gift: The Form and Reason for Exchange in Archaic Societies (1923–24)* (translated by W.D. Halls). London: Routledge.

Manor, J. (1989). *The Expedient Utopian: Bandaranaike and Ceylon*. Cambridge: Cambridge University Press.

Obeyesekere, R. (1999). *Sri Lankan Theatre in a Time of Terror: Political Satire in a Permitted Space*. Colombo: Charles Subasinghe & Sons.

Obeyesekere, G. (1984). *The Institutionalisation of Political Violence and the Dismantling of Democracy in Sri Lanka: Myths and Realities*. Colombo: Centre for Rational Development.

Okely, J. and H. Callaway (eds). (1992). *Anthropology and Autobiography* (ASA Monographs 29). London: Routledge.

Ondaatje, M. (1998). *Handwriting*. London: Bloomsbury.

O'Neill, N. and G. O'Neill. (1973). *Open Marriage: A New Lifestyle for Couples*. London: Avon.

Perera, S. (1998). *Political Violence in Sri Lanka: Dynamics, Consequences and Issues of Democratization*. Colombo: Centre for Women's Research.

———. (1999). *The World According to Me: An Interpretation of the Ordinary, the Common, and the Mundane*. Colombo: International Centre for Ethnic Studies.

Robins, T. (1995). 'Remembering the Future: The Cultural Study of Memory', in B. Adam and S. Allan (eds), *Theorizing Culture: An Interdisciplinary Critique after Postmodernism*. London: UCL Press.

Robinson, J. (2003). 'Postcolonialising Geography: Tactics and Pitfalls', *Singapore Journal of Tropical Geography,* 24(3): 273–89.

Shaffir, W.B. and R.A. Stebbins (eds). (1991). *Experiencing Fieldwork: An Inside View of Qualitative Research.* Newbury Park, CA: Sage Publications.

Sontag, S. (2003). *Regarding the Pain of Others*. New York: Farrar, Straus and Giroux.

———. (2004). 'Regarding the Torture of Others', *New York Times Magazine*, 23 May.

Special Presidential Commission of Inquiry (1997). *Report of the Special Presidential Commission of Inquiry into the Assassination of Mr Vijaya Kumaratunga*. Colombo.

Sunday Observer Magazine (1999). October 10.

Tambiah, S.J. (1992). *Buddhism Betrayed? Religion, Politics and Violence in Sri Lanka*. Chicago: Chicago University Press.

Uyangoda, J. and J. Biyanwila (eds) (1997). *Matters of Violence: Reflections on Social and Political Violence in Sri Lanka*. Colombo: Social Scientists' Association.

Wriggins, H. (1960). *Dilemmas of a New Nation*. Princeton, NJ: Princeton University Press.

Young, D.J. and A. Meneley (eds). (2005). Auto-Ethnographies; The Anthropology of Academic Practices, Broadview Press.

5

Cartographic Violence: Engaging a Sinhala Kind of Geography

Benedikt Korf

On Postcolonialising Geography: Who and What?

In *Anthropologizing Sri Lanka*, Susantha Goonatilake (2001: xiii-xiv) attacks a number of respected anthropologists, Sri Lankan and foreign, and their purported misrepresentation of Sri Lankan history. His controversial book starts from a sociology of science perspective and tries to show how some key informants in Sri Lanka 'fill in the contextual details of a complex reality that is Sri Lanka' so that 'this postcolonial anthropology appears worse than anything colonial anthropology wrought'. Goonatilake is disgruntled about the fact that much scholarship on Sri Lanka is written outside the island-state and that few gatekeepers in Sri Lanka itself have channelled it, mistakenly and falsely in his view, towards a more cosmopolitan, multicultural understanding of Sri Lanka's troubled ethnic relationships. For Goonatilake, a 'high-profile Sinhala nationalist' (Spencer 2007: 71), this is a problem.

While I do not share his political visions nor empathise with the tone of his critique, Goonatilake's book does urge us to reflect on what postcolonial geography means in the Sri Lankan context, especially a 'postcolonial' geography authored by scholars based in the West. James Sidaway (2000: 592) has argued that, since postcolonialism aims to expose and challenge Western imperial practices of survey, mapping and classification, 'any mapping of the postcolonial is a problematic and contradictory project' (ibid.: 592). How, then, can 'postcolonial' geographical scholars based in Europe and North America avoid recolonising

Sri Lanka through the hegemony of elite theory and the production of elite geographical knowledge? As Jenny Robinson (2003) has lucidly discussed, there is no easy escape from the pitfalls of 'postcolonialising' geography.

For Robinson, the postcolonial critic should unveil the parochialism in Euro-American scholarship and learn to provincialise claims to understanding, in particular by reflecting upon the dominance of that elite Euro-American theory. Among the tactics she suggests for a more *cosmopolitan* theorising, two are particularly important in this context: engaging with regional scholarship, and transforming the conditions of the production and circulation of knowledge. How then can we 'postcolonialise our practices' (ibid.: 274)? Among other things, Robinson suggests engaging with regional scholarship by paying closer attention to the writings and researches of regional scholars and their networks (ibid.: 279–80). She also mentions that a region's scholarship may be divided and contested, and that our engagement may entail difficult political choices.

This chapter is an attempt to take Robinson at face value by engaging with Sri Lankan geographers' writings on topics that have also been at the heart of my own research: the question of territoriality and belonging in the north-east of Sri Lanka, or, more precisely, the question of land and conflict, and the demand for a Tamil homeland (for example, Korf 2004, 2005, 2006; Korf and Fünfgeld 2006). This attempt will come in the form of a critique of what I consider two core papers written by Sri Lankan, in this case Sinhalese, geographers teaching at a Sri Lankan university. These geographers developed what I call 'a Sinhala kind of geography' based on the legacy of Sri Lanka's Sinhalese hydraulic civilisation and subsequent geographies of the nation-state. Both papers follow in the footsteps of Goonatilake's intervention as they engage with and criticise Western scholarship on the geographies of Sri Lanka's north-east as part of the political project of Sinhala nationalism.

The two texts invite such a direct engagement, since they differ markedly from Goonatilake's book in the nature of their scholarship. The first text, written by G.H. Peiris (1991), engages with empirical material. He uses both spatial statistics and historical scholarship to refute the political claim for a Tamil homeland.[1] G.H. Peiris, therefore, engages with arguments that, in turn, justify a critical analysis of his work (and he or others may then respond). The second text is a paper written by C.M. Madduma Bandara (2001) that discusses the rational basis and merits of a proposal to redraw the territorial boundaries of provincial administration following the hydraulic logic of river basins (Madduma Bandara 2001).

What makes his text significant for my critique is that Madduma Bandara legitimises this territorial reshuffling with the relative marginalisation of the Sinhala-Buddhist polity within colonial and postcolonial Sri Lankan politics. In principle, both writings gesture towards a space for academic debate and deliberation, which is effectively foreclosed by Goonatilake's writings.

The chapter is simply an elaboration of a critique—a critique that is made through engaging and taking seriously two important papers written by Sri Lankan geographers. Nothing more, nothing less. Through this critique, I will show how these papers act as, and become, discursive formations of a Sinhala-Buddhist nationalism and wield a considerable power in Sinhala nationalism. The chapter proceeds in the following manner: first, it will briefly reproduce the main arguments in the two texts and subsequently subject them to a critique. The critique will first analyse the internal consistency of their arguments and the political conclusions drawn from their writings, and then discuss how these arguments play into the politics of Sinhala nationalism in Sri Lanka. I will argue that the two texts produce a Sinhala kind of geography with a kind of cartographic violence at its disposal. This cartographic violence is signalled in spatial representations that play politically into the hydraulic imperialism of Sinhala nationalism.

Readers may note that I have selected two Sinhalese geographers for my critical engagement. It is important to clarify my own position here: I seek to critique the ways Peiris and Madduma Bandara challenge the concept of a Tamil homeland and other demands for devolution of the north and east in Sri Lanka as part of Sinhalese nationalism. One could equally deconstruct the writings of Tamil scholars who attempt to justify a Tamil homeland and Tamil nationalism through 'historical', ethnic, or other such means. As Kristian Stokke (1998) notes, Sinhalese and Tamil nationalisms can be considered as mirror images of one another, and have been instrumental for the elite in both ethnic constituencies to mobilise and rally political support (see also Kleinfeld 2006; Thangarajah 2003).

Kandyan Geographers doing Sri Lankan Geography

G.H. Peiris is Professor Emeritus of Geography at the University of Peradeniya and was a Fellow at the International Centre for Ethnic Studies (ICES) in Kandy until recently. In the 1980s and 1990s, he published several articles in which he: *(a)* renounced the scientific validity of the historical foundations of the Tamil representatives' claim for a separate homeland (Peiris 1991); and *(b)* where he highlighted the 'scientific inaccuracies' within studies conducted by international scholars that drew attention to the Sinhalese nationalist inflection of settlement schemes in the north, east and north-central provinces (Peiris 1994). Central to my analysis is the 1991 (1985) paper where Peiris places the scientific justifications for the political demand of a Tamil homeland 'under critical scrutiny' (Peiris 1991).

Peiris screens out three central claims propagated by Tamil politicians to provide historical justification for the Tamil homeland demand as these have been voiced in political pamphlets, such as the party conventions of the Federal Party in 1951, and the Tamil United Liberation Front (TULF) manifesto of 1977. These three claims are:

1. Tamils have always formed a distinct nation with its own territory in Sri Lanka, which they lost only after Portuguese colonial occupation.
2. The British arbitrarily unified two nations, the Sinhalese kingdom and the Tamil kingdom, through the creation of the colonial state.
3. After independence, state-aided colonisation brought Sinhalese settlers into the north and east, thus encroaching on the traditional homeland of the Tamils, and furthermore that this state-aided colonisation has benefited the Sinhalese more than Tamils (ibid.: 14).

In Peiris' view, all three claims are scientifically unsubstantiated, but central for him is the refutation of the third proposition.

From an analysis of ancient times until the 12th century, the glorious past of a Sinhalese kingdom whose capital city was located at Anuradhapura, Peiris concludes that the first proposition 'does not confirm to any of the scholarly interpretations of known facts of history' (ibid.: 17). Only after the 12th century did the kingdom of Jaffna yield considerable power over the north of Sri Lanka with a subsequent 'Tamilisation' of the north and east.

These modern ethnic frontiers are then discussed in more detail: 'the spatial dimension of the processes of Tamilisation, a precise understanding of population patterns, frontiers of settlements, and the geographical limits of cultural transformation' (ibid.: 19). The paper suggests that though Sinhalese peasants continued to cultivate some land in areas, now under the territorial delimitation of the north and east, the 19th century was a process of gradual recession of Sinhalese occupancy, due to epidemics,

FIGURE 5.1

G.H. Peiris's Representation of Ancient Hydraulic Territories and Settlement Frontiers in Sri Lanka

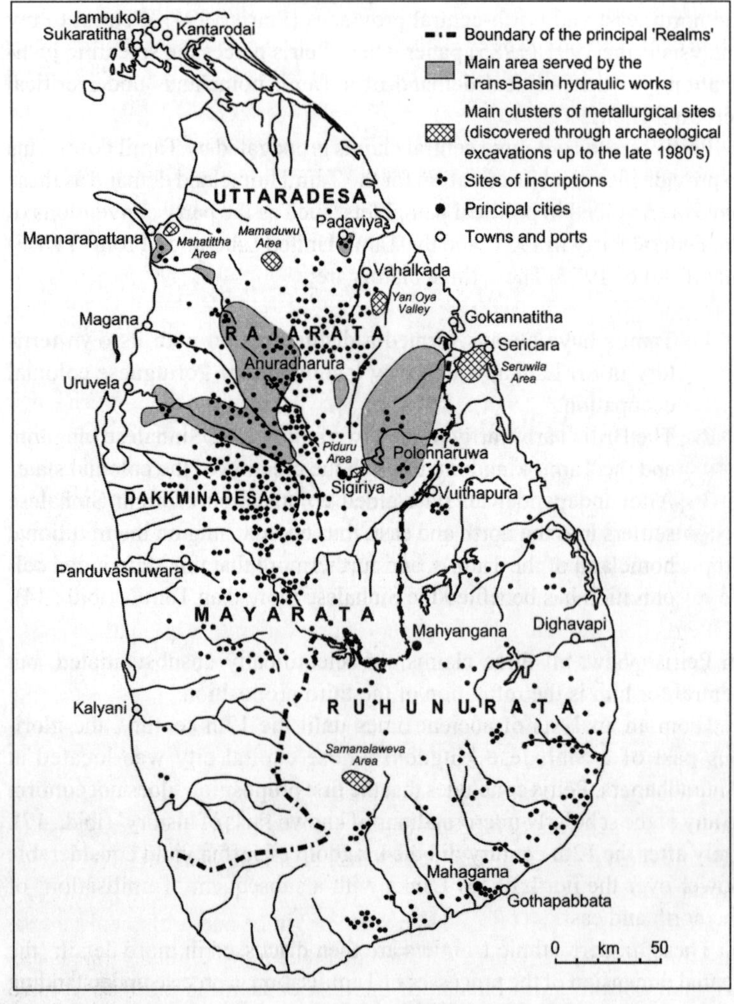

Source: Reproduced from Peiris (1996: 15), Cartographic layout: Sandra Maher.

famines, and cultural assimilation by other ethnic groups, while there was a continuing expansion of the non-Sinhalese population in several areas of the dry zone.

Peiris uses a spatial representation of population data to underline his proposition that the process of Tamilisation, that is, the advance of Tamil settlements at the expense of Sinhalese, had not penetrated significantly into the interior of the north-east province. He finds Sinhalese depopulation being earmarked by the names of 'numerous abandoned village tanks marked on our source maps in the uninhabited tracts' (Peiris 1991: 20). This form of mapping allows him to conclude that 'the demand by one ethnic group for exclusive proprietary rights over Provinces and Districts which encompass extensive tracts of territory which it had never occupied [namely the inland territories]... appears in its true light as one which lacks *rational* basis' (ibid.: 24, emphasis added).

After the analysis of the pre-independence population patterns, the paper analyses the third proposition of Tamil nationalism: that Sinhalese immigration through state-supported colonisation schemes had changed the ethnic composition of the population of these areas, making Tamils a minority in places that were populated largely by them before this process began. The eastern districts of Trincomalee and Amparai (the former southern part of Batticaloa) have been central to this claim as they have experienced significant changes in the ethnic population ratios with a significant increase in the Sinhalese population numbers and relative proportions. Tamil nationalists considered this to be an attempt to make Tamils a minority in their own homeland.

Peiris does not dispute the general observation that population ratios have changed in favour of the Sinhalese, but focuses on spatial statistics of territorial *occupation*—which ethnic group has settled in which specific locality. His point is that, while the numbers of Sinhalese may have been rising in those districts, these Sinhalese did not drive Tamils away from their territory, but largely settled on formerly uninhabited or sparsely inhabited areas. Peiris demonstrates the validity of his argument by considering most of the grievance cases that Tamil nationalists have used to substantiate his proposition.

His first case is Gal Oya, a large-scale irrigation and settlement scheme in Amparai district, where substantial numbers of Sinhalese peasants originating from areas outside of the district (and the north-east) have been settling from the 1950s onwards. The paper concludes that those localities were 'an exclusive Sinhalese area in *pre*-Gal Oya times' (ibid.: 27, emphasis added). The second case is Trincomalee district with the provincial capital of the north-east and a strategically important natural harbour. Trincomalee has also seen a sharp rise in the Sinhalese population

FIGURE 5.2
G.H. Peiris's Representation of Ethnic Settlement Pattern According to the 1981 Census

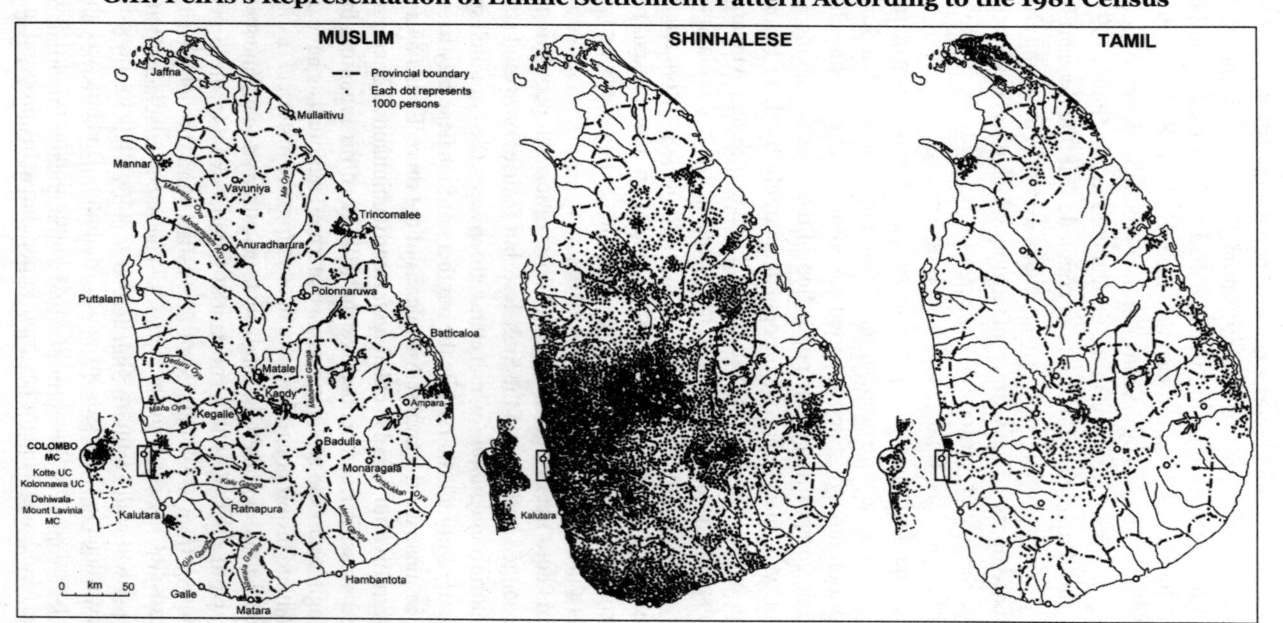

Source: Reproduced from Peiris (1991), Cartographic layout: Sandra Maher.

ratio since the beginning of the 20th century. Peiris argues that this rise needs to be contrasted with the ongoing process of decay in the Sinhalese settlement areas of the interior part of the district in the 19th century and a parallel increase in Tamil population. Only based on this account could population changes in the pre- and post-independence period of the 20th century be adequately understood. He (Peiris 1991: 29) concludes that, first, Tamils and Muslims were the overwhelming majority of district population; second, that Tamils and Muslims had only recently settled in interior parts of the district; third, that the declining share of Tamil population in the late colonial period was largely due to the development of Trincomalee town (and not agricultural settlements); and fourth, that Sinhalese *purana* (traditional) settlements continued to exist in the interior parts of Trincomalee, and that in the post-independence period, the influx of people was largely to Trincomalee town, which, in turn, became ethnically more heterogeneous.

The paper also engages with the disputed Kantalai and Morawewa colonisation schemes (interestingly, not the Allai Extension Scheme in Seruvila, Muthur, and Eachchilampattai divisions), all of which were launched in the 1950s in Trincomalee district. Peiris suggests that Sinhalese settlers have not *replaced* (in the sense of driving out) Tamil and Muslim peasants living in the area before, but settled on largely uninhabited or sparsely populated territories, populated, if at all, by Sinhalese: in the case of Morawewa, this scheme has been located in an area which had been predominantly inhabited by Sinhalese before. The Kantalai scheme, on the other hand, has 'resulted in an increase of the Sinhalese population in an area where there was a non-Sinhalese majority up to the early 1950s' (ibid.: 29), but in a sparsely populated area. In the Tambalagama and Vendrasanpura units of the scheme where Tamils and Muslims live, no land had been allocated to the Sinhalese. Therefore, these irrigation schemes have not driven out Tamils or Muslims from their land as Tamil nationalism's third proposition had suggested.

While Peiris's concern was to deconstruct the historical justifications of the Tamil homeland demand, another Sinhalese geographer from the University of Peradeniya, C.M. Madduma Bandara, developed propositions for a scientifically sound reordering of provincial administrative boundaries. This proposal was first suggested in the report of the Sri Lankan Land Commission that was appointed by President J.R. Jayewardena in the 1980s, of which Madduma Bandara was chairman. The report was published in 1987 (Madduma Bandara et al. 1990). Since then, Madduma Bandara has tried to popularise his proposal at various occasions. In the inaugural address at the Peradeniya University Lecture Series (PULSE) on 24 January 2001, he presented his ideas of 'alternative boundary' mapping (Madduma Bandara et al., 2001). This paper interests me precisely because it attempts to *naturalise* the highly disputed issue of provincial boundary-making in Sri Lanka, and to separate provincial boundaries from ethnic boundaries.

Madduma Bandara's paper argues as follows. First, the current delineation of regional boundaries was a manifestation of the imprints of colonial lines 'on our map'. The government's devolution proposal (from 2000) followed the spatial logic of colonial administrative boundaries that were drawn to 'satisfy the strategic and exploitative needs of an alien maritime power… [although these] colonially defined provinces… are… irrational and unreasonable' (ibid.: 1–2). The paper, therefore, suggests an alternative, 'rational' regional framework, which is more 'development-oriented'—a 'scientific' approach of boundary mapping based on hydraulic watersheds or river basins (ibid.: 1). The paper argues that a scientific approach avoids the pitfalls of politics and 'searches for compromise solutions, to please pressure groups' (ibid.).

The paper maps out the (harmful) colonial legacy of administrative boundaries as lost opportunities of post-independence Sri Lanka: 'If not for colonial interventions, …how can one [otherwise] explain the existence of four land-locked provinces out of a total of nine?' (ibid.: 9). The paper suggests that the current spatiality of provincial boundaries as stretched along the coast mirrors the interests of colonial powers that once controlled these coastal regions, and only subsequently gained supremacy in the heartland of the Kandyan kingdom. As a result, the current provinces that formed the core of the Kandyan kingdom have no access to the ocean. Madduma Bandara concludes: 'The implementation of the proposed political package [the devolution proposal of 2000] will only facilitate the perpetuation of this unholy colonial legacy' (ibid.).

The paper sets out the scientific reconstruction of boundaries by emphasising that 'it is well known among *planners*' (ibid.: 20, emphasis added) that in Sri Lanka, land was intimately linked with water. The problem, the paper identifies, is that current administrative boundaries, because they are an imprint of colonial rule, largely ignore this linkage: river basins cross regional boundaries. The 2000 devolution proposal, the paper argues, further adds to this confusion, because control over inter-provincial rivers is vested with the centre, but the land under these schemes comes under regional administration. This could invite conflicts between upstream and downstream users, and could create violence over water use because conflict was inbuilt in the spatial separation of natural river flows and administrative boundaries.

In contrast to the current administrative template for conflict, the proposal suggests a regional demarcation based on river basins.

> There is no problem about the clarity of the proposed boundaries, since they are all watersheds... given modern rapid survey and… technology, [boundary identification on the ground] could be completed within a few days… none of the new regions is land-locked [as they have been during colonial rule and continued to be thereafter], and all have an outlet to the Indian Ocean (Madduma Bandara et al., 2001: 21–24).

Madduma Bandara's proposal would solve the problems left by the colonial legacy: it would make boundaries clear (so to avoid conflict over its delineation), it would open up all provinces to the sea (rectifying

FIGURE 5.3
C.M. Madduma Bandara's Proposal of Naturalising Regional Boundaries Compared to the Original Provincial Boundaries

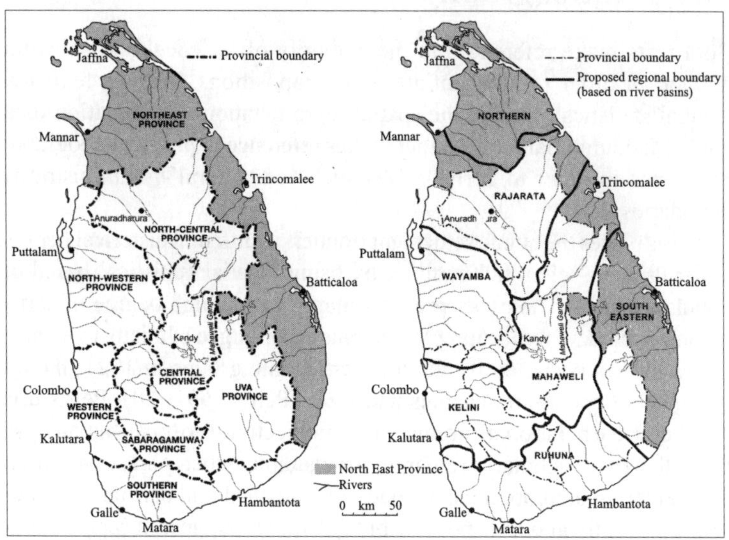

Source: Reproduced from Madduma Bandara (2001: 22). Cartographic layout: Sandra Maher.

the colonial injustice that left some provinces land-locked), and it would follow modern technologies and reasoning.

Cartographic Violence and Hydraulic Imperialism

Both texts display what I will call a 'Sinhala kind of geography' as they use the reference to 'science' in order to substantiate political claims of Sinhala nationalism. This Sinhala kind of geography works through three methodological strategies: spatial statistics, the physical geography imagination and cartographic violence. These methodological mechanisms play politically into a Sinhala nationalist current of thought that can be subsumed as hydraulic imperialism. In my view, this geography requires a critique—a critique of its rhetoric, its discourses and its politics, in particular its political embeddedness in a genealogy of political and historical discourses of Sinhala nationalism as hydraulic imperialism.

The Rhetoric of Spatial Statistics and Physical Geography

Both texts make references to the authority of 'science' and scientific method in order to substantiate their propositions. Peiris's text uses 'spatial statistics', that is, the spatial representation of population data, while Madduma Bandara's paper makes reference to physical geography as science in order to derive 'objective'—or 'natural'—administrative boundaries.

Peiris places the ethnic settlement frontiers at different historical periods under critical 'scientific' scrutiny by using 'spatial statistics' based on population data. The paper presents maps 'with a high degree of cartographic accuracy' for locating settlements according to ethnicity to identify the territories occupied by the different ethnic groups in 1921, though it neglects population densities and sizes (Peiris 1991: 20). Peiris uses the rhetoric of 'rational' argument and objectivity to give his analysis the authority of scholarly research, for example, when phrases are used, such as 'from a comprehensive body of statistical and cartographic evidence presently at our disposal' (ibid.: 29). This suggests a separation of subjective, political perceptions and opinions from 'scientific' scrutiny of the 'facts'. The study uses statistics and cartography as rhetorical tools for establishing truth claims: numbers are 'objective', thus one can derive a rational explanation, which is contrasted to political perceptions (which are then 'proven' to be false).

Madduma Bandara's text equally refers to 'rational' arguments for the demarcation of regional boundaries following the hydraulic logic of river basin morphology. The text elaborates on the negative and harmful leftovers of colonial rule and the shortcomings of Sri Lankan politics as a contrasting foil to rational, scientific solutions of administrative boundary mapping: 'The propositions taken by different groups are often based on myths and misconceptions. *Unlike in science*, in politics a lie that had been repeated hundred times can become the gospel truth' (Madduma Bandara et al., 2001: 13, emphasis added). The text claims authority by drawing upon science, in this case, physical geography (or hydrology), rather than petty politics, ideology or simply opinions. This is the 'physical geography imagination': scientific objectivity that allows its author to delineate objectively verifiable boundaries; to make truth claims. As Madduma Bandara explains: 'There is no problem about the clarity of the proposed boundaries, since they are all watersheds' (ibid.: 21).

Cartographic Violence?

Peiris's spatial statistics emphasise the territorial *occupation*, the question of who settled at which place at a particular time. The principle of occupation does not problematise *how many* people settled at a particular place. The emphasis on territorial occupation of different ethnic groups prior to the start of the colonisation schemes in the dry zones plays down the quantitative change in ethnic population numbers and ratios in a particular district as a result of in-migration of Sinhalese settlers. The paper argues that the spatial statistics demonstrated that Sinhalese settler inflows to Trincomalee and Amparai districts had not driven out or displaced Tamil or Muslim indigenous people from land they had formerly occupied. Rather, Sinhalese settlers came to cultivate land that was either uninhabited or where few Sinhalese *purana* peasants had formerly lived. This argument sidelines anxieties among the Tamil minority that the changes in ethnic ratios in some districts (that is, the relative numbers of each ethnic group) influenced the electoral landscape of Sri Lanka (thereby disadvantaging Tamil parties) and undermined the territorial claims of the Tamil homeland demand as it diluted the Tamil majority, making them gradually a minority in their own territories (see, for example, Balasundarampillai 2002; Sampanthan 1985 on Trincomalee).

Furthermore, the paper draws conclusions that are not confined to the statistical or empirical material, but are used to construct value-based political arguments that masquerade as normative assessments precisely because they claim to be grounded in fact. Peiris's paper concludes with just such a *normative* argument:

> In a densely peopled country like Sri Lanka, where the prevailing pressure of population on land is intense, 9% of its population claiming exclusive rights over 29% of its territory is in itself somewhat unfair. Moreover, the acute scarcity of resources for agriculture from which Sri Lanka suffers implies that the country cannot afford to have uninhabited 'buffer zones' between concentrations of different ethnic groups. Nor can such uninhabited and underutilized tracts of territory be reserved untouched as future *lebensraum* for any one ethnic group of the country. (Peiris 1991: 34, emphasis original)

The text starts with 'scientific' (empirical) analyses and ends with normative statements. It jumps from an 'is'—the empirical spatial statistics—to an 'ought', namely, that one ethnic group *should* not claim all those lands in the north and east as its own (especially pertinent in this sense is resource scarcity elsewhere). This is not just a *normative* claim, but also irreducibly political. It is not the kind of claim that can be derived logically from the preceding empirical analysis; it is a political statement thus open to political deliberation and criticism.

Madduma Bandara's paper is contextualised in the rhetoric of Sinhala nationalism. It is written, for example, that Sri Lanka could be a flourishing jewel being one of the few countries worldwide 'with an unbroken recorded history' (Madduma Bandara et al., 2001: 5) had it not been invaded by South Indians (the Tamils) and by the European colonisers who sowed the seed of inter-ethnic antagonisms. The text mentions in passing that the 'Sinhala people… always constituted the hard-rock base of the nation' (ibid.). The text appeals its readership that without the 'petty political interests that nurture mediocrity and inefficiency' (ibid.), Sri Lanka could have regained its position after independence instead of succumbing to poverty and social conflict. While proponents of the devolution package of 2000 suggested devolution as a panacea for peace and inter-ethnic harmony, Madduma Bandara notes that the Sinhalese people 'for whom Sri Lanka is their only ethnic and cultural homeland in the world [while the Tamils also have Tamil Nadu in India], seem to have *received only passing consideration*' (ibid.: 11, emphasis added).

These comments tacitly transport an image of the Sinhalese majority population as being victims of both colonialism and current politics. The text seems to argue that recent devolution proposals perpetuated the discrimination of the Sinhalese people—a discrimination that they had suffered already under colonial rule. Recent political proposals and a policy of ethnically defined provincial boundaries endangered the break-up of the unitary state and triggered national disintegration—a template for further escalation. The paper alerts the reader that 'present day political pundits have rescinded to a position where they seem to be only worried about the acceptance of their proposals by armed terrorist groups [that is, the LTTE]… and other fanatic pressure groups' (Madduma Bandara et al.,: 12–13).

The paper provides detailed descriptions of the seven regions proposed, and their endogenous development potential, their cohesion and viability. Critical in the proposal for the ethnic conflict and its territorialisation are the districts in the eastern province. Trincomalee district, which is considered of strategic importance due to its harbour and due to its location between the north and east, would be cut into two pieces, one belonging to the Mahaweli region, the other to Rajarata region. Both are also central in the analysis of the proposal. Rajarata, 'freed from its earlier land-locked nature' (ibid: 29) can diversify its economic activities using coastal and marine resources. Anuradhapura, a former stronghold of Kandyan kings, is suggested as a possible capital for Sri Lanka. The boundary mapping corresponds with a Sinhala nationalist desire to control the riverbanks of the major rivers, like the Mahaweli. It would also limit the influence of Tamils to the northern region, which would be made smaller in terms of territorial space. It would confine the influence of Tamils administratively to the north, because the east would be divided among three different regions, each without a Tamil majority.

I would argue, then, that this proposal to redraw administrative boundaries according to river basins does not amount to a rationalist solution, but a nationalist one to exert spatial control over the island-space. The discourse of 'natural boundary' is highly political: the proposal constitutes a 'rational', a scientific, argument to achieve supremacy of a central state (which would be dominated by the Sinhalese constituency). Such a proposal is likely to increase the cartographic anxieties of the Tamil and Muslim minorities. This type of 'rationalist' solution is not geared towards inter-ethnic accommodation, but instead Sinhalese domination, which would be unacceptable for Tamils (and Muslims) in a future solution to the ethnic conflict. Natural science and rational scientific argument is used to legitimise such a political project.[2]

The interventions of Peiris and Madduma Bandara effectively play out a kind of cartographic violence. The two texts deploy 'science' and 'geography' to substantiate Sinhala nationalist positions in a kind of epistemic struggle over who holds the 'truth' and who holds an entitlement to which territorial spaces. They use spatial statistics and 'the physical geography imagination' to undermine the Tamil homeland demand and to substantiate the territorial politics of Sinhala nationalism. These contestations over territorial claims have been one central grievance in the deterioration of Tamil–Sinhala relations since the 1950s.

Hydraulic Imperialism

In order to understand the political significance of these two texts, we need to contextualise them historically. When Peiris' paper was first presented at ICES in 1985, Sri Lanka had just experienced the anti-Tamil riots of 1983, Tamil militantism was on the rise, and Sri Lanka was sliding into 'civil war'. It was the time of the Timpu Conference where Tamil politicians negotiated with the United National Party (UNP) regime on political concessions. It was one of the last attempts of the old guard of Tamil parliamentarians to effect major concessions from the Sinhalese majority as they were more and more losing support among the Tamil youth who found themselves attracted by Tamil militantism. At the Timpu Conference, R. Sampanthan, a Tamil United Liberation Front (TULF) M.P. from Trincomalee, summarised the main concerns of Tamil politicians regarding the colonisation schemes in the north-east (Sampanthan 1985). He emphasised the changes in ethnic population ratios in Trincomalee. Peiris's text can be read as a response to those statements, as an attempt to show their being lacking in scientific validity. Both Sampanthan's statement at Timpu and Peiris's ICES seminar presentation were dated back to August 1985.

Madduma Bandara's intervention first came in 1987 as part of the report of the Land Reform Commission. Again, during this time period, negotiations were ongoing over constitutional amendments granting higher autonomy to the north-eastern province. Central in these negotiations was the sharing of power between the centre and the north-eastern province, specifically the distribution of administrative power between centre and the province to allocate state land in colonisation schemes (Bastian 1995). Again, in 2000, the Sri Lankan government passed a devolution package in order to accommodate some of the Tamil grievances. Madduma Bandara's intervention in the inaugural lecture at the University of Peradeniya in

2001 directly addressed this as flawed, an imprint of the colonial past and petty politics. This signals that Madduma Bandara's interventions were intended to intervene in the political spaces of negotiations at quite specific times.

The two interventions can be contextualised in a much longer genealogy of a postcolonial Sinhala nationalist discourse around hydraulic civilisation, ancient past and an innocent peasantry. The discourse on Sri Lanka's (or Ceylon's) ancient historical past as a hydraulic civilisation and society started already when Ceylon was still a British colony. The colonial officer R.L. Brohier, for example, compiled a widely acclaimed volume on Ancient Irrigation Works in Ceylon (1934) in which he surveyed the ancient small-scale tank irrigation systems that were formerly neglected by the colonial rulers. The (Sinhalese) Minister of Agriculture, D.S. Senanayake, later to become the first Prime Minister of post-independence Sri Lanka, linked agriculture with patriotism (1999 [1935]) by proposing a national irrigation systems development that aspired to food self-sufficiency. This placed the paddy farmer at the core of a peasant ideology (Moore 1985), which has influenced post-independence populist politics in Sri Lanka for a long time.

Post-independence land colonisation policies in dry zone Sri Lanka implemented this peasant ideology as a response to colonial land use policies. The British colonial administration, aiming at facilitating the acquisition of land for (private investors') plantation development, had declared all land not permanently cultivated or demonstrably under private ownership to be owned by the Crown (Lands Encroachment Ordinance No. 12 of 1840, also known as Waste Lands Ordinance). This denied a large part of the rural population, especially in the wetlands, legal and physical access to grazing land and land for shifting cultivation (*chena*). Since that time, almost 80 per cent of the overall land area in Sri Lanka is considered to be state land. Since the establishment of the 1928 Land Commission, the 1935 Land Development Ordinance and specifically after Sri Lanka gained independence in 1948, successive Sri Lankan governments have alienated state land under various titles for private, corporate or state use, especially though to rectify colonial policies and grant access to land for the rural peasantry (Bastian 1995; Brow and Weeramunda 1992; Farmer 1957; Herring 1983; Moore 1985; Peiris 1996; Singh 1989).

The peasant ideology became a political instrument to achieve a 'post-colonial' justice of sorts for the Sinhalese peasantry. 'Sinhalese' nation building was inter-alia implemented through the rebuilding of the Sinhala hydraulic civilisation: large-scale irrigation and colonisation projects in the dry zone of Sri Lanka promised technological progress, development and a reawakening of the ancient past. These settlement schemes helped territorialise Sinhala-Buddhist ambitions for a 'pure' state-to-come. The peasant ideology and a political discourse on food self-sufficiency after independence coincided with the aggressive colonisation of geographical areas that were at the hinterland of Tamil and Muslim settlements in the north-east (Brow 1988; Manogaran 1987; Moore 1989; Peebles 1990; Tennakoon 1988; Thangarajah 2003). Arguably, Tamil homeland ideology—narratives of Eelam—emerged as a response to this potent Sinhala-Buddhist state (to-come) building (Shastri 1990; Tambiah 1986, 1992; Thangarajah 2003).[3]

State colonisation turned into hydraulic imperialism through the Accelerated Mahaweli Scheme, a large-scale irrigation scheme that sought to colonise large tracts of land in the north and east, and the north-central provinces. This accelerated settlement policy coincided with an escalation of inter-ethnic tensions towards the end of the 1970s and early 1980s. Some Sinhalese politicians openly used nationalist rhetoric to position the Accelerated Mahaweli Scheme as the rebirth of an ancient hydraulic Sinhalese past (Tennakoon 1988). Sinhalese peasants became military frontiersmen in a battle for territorial control in the north and east (Thangarajah 2003), a battle that soon turned into civil war in 1983 (although this was only one of many factors for the escalation of violence in the 1970s and 1980s). In turn, this colonisation policy, its Sinhala-nationalist rhetoric and the 1983 experience nurtured cartographic anxieties among the ethnic minorities, whose livelihoods were largely located in the north and east—the Tamils and Muslims.

The significance of Peiris and Madduma Bandara's interventions lies in their attempt to rationalise and objectify Sinhala nationalism, its hydraulic imperialism and its discourse of the Sinhala hydraulic heritage. By putting the question of Tamil homeland and boundary mapping into the realm of 'science', the two texts lift it atop political controversy and ethnic antagonisms, and make the claims of Sinhala nationalism appear as both (scientific) necessary and natural.

Persuasive Cartography and a Sinhala Kind of Geography

In *Postcolonial Insecurities*, Sankara Krishna (1999) has argued that the modernist effort to construct nation-states on the basis of singular notions of sovereignty and identity has come to a dead end in South Asia because it has nurtured insurgent violence. In the case of India, Krishna (1996) has shown how anxieties around questions of national identity and survival are particularly acute in postcolonial society. These anxieties can be represented in cartographic manifestations—cartographic anxieties: 'Cartography becomes nothing less than the social and political production of nationality itself' (ibid.: 194). While in the Indian case, national identity revolves around the cartographic (and territorial) boundaries of the nation, in Sri Lanka, the question is about who 'owns' the island, whether it is defined as a homogeneous or heterogeneous cultural entity and how regional boundaries may be drawn to create ethnically homogeneous political entities.

The map has often been implicated as a tool for objectifying, marking and inscribing territories and boundaries (Rose 1999). However, subjectivity in map making is inescapable, which also implicates maps as persuasive communication devices designed consciously or otherwise to support particular hypotheses or political agendas (Black 1997; Harley 1992; Huggan 1989; Tyner 1982). Denis Cosgrove (2007: 203f) provides us with an illuminating example of 'persuasive cartography': in 1941, in the middle of World War II and German geopolitical 'propaganda' mapping, Hans Speier (1941: 313) published a paper where he explains how propagandists exploit the symbolic power of maps to 'turn geography into a kind of magic'. He concludes:

> The only techniques which enable the propagandist to present the whole by means of nonverbal symbols are statistical and cartographic in nature.… [T]he propagandist who uses them borrows the prestige of science and *at the same time violates its spirit*. (ibid.: 330, emphasis added)

Peiris and Madduma Bandara's 'persuasive' cartography as the 'science' of map-making has turned into a kind of cartographic violence. The geographical imaginations pertinent in their 'Sinhala geography' entail an epistemic violence that makes the map an instrument of the 'work of purification' (Spencer 2003: 26). Purification, Bruno Latour (1993) writes, is the cultural work of maintaining the fictitious separation of nature and society. The impossible work of purification in Sri Lankan politics is the attempt to 'maintain the illusion that "the nation is the same people living in the same place"' (Spencer 2003: 27), that is, that Sri Lanka is a Sinhala-Buddhist island. Peiris and Madduma Bandara's cartographic violence is the practice of 'purifying' the Sri Lankan map and its geographical imaginations, effectively creating a Sinhala kind of geography *as a scientific necessity*. Such map-making—the production of a 'pure' Sri Lanka—is a kind of 'epistemic violence' (Spivak 1990). Epistemic violence provides the grounds for multiple forms of hegemony and violence. It is not confined to the continuation of (post) colonialism in forms of Western domination in global knowledge production and economic liberalisation. It also emerges as a continuation of postcolonial legacies in nationalist agendas in Sri Lanka; it is a part of the structural or cultural violence of a politics of (ethnic) exclusion.

Jacques Derrida (2005: 93) writes that the 'strongest is never strong enough to be master all the time, unless he transforms force into right.' Force is never enough unless it becomes right—and one way of converting force into right is through establishing epistemic hegemony and thus establishing the definitional and legitimising powers for, in this case, a Sinhala kind of geography. The potential epistemic violence of the two texts lies in their merging of an 'ought' and an 'is'—by demonstrating 'scientifically' or 'rationally', they show 'how things are' and derive from this how they *ought* to be. This helps Sinhala nationalism to narrate the story of the 'pure' island and legitimise those political steps that help achieve this ideal state-to-come—the topography of a Sinhala-Buddhist nation (Korf 2006).

But—and this is an important 'but'—even if 'scientifically' all the *empirical* facts in the two papers were (it) accurate as the two authors attempt to persuade us, this still would not indicate what a political solution *ought* to look like. Debating such political 'oughts' should be subject to *uncoerced* deliberation to open political debate. What is our role then as postcolonial geographers in the delicate politics of epistemic violence? Robinson's (2003) move towards provincialising geography and the production of a more cosmopolitan theorising is suggestive here. In the intricate connections of postcolonial nationalisms, regional scholarship—that is, scholars located in places of the 'south'—often plays a powerful and influential political role in legitimating the politics of nationalist exclusion. These same writings are at times relatively neglected in the international circuits of academic publishing or disregarded for scholarly weakness or political extremism. This is problematic. Provincialising international and postcolonial academic practice requires taking those scholars, such as Peiris, Madduma Bandara or Susantha Goonatilake, seriously. It means engaging them in scholarly dispute. As Jonathan Spencer (2007: 71) notes: 'Reading Goonatilake's splenetic attacks... it is hard not to think we must be doing something right to warrant this level of attention.'

Notes

1. In another paper Peiris (1994) has criticised work on colonisation in the north and east and the role of the Accelerated Mahaweli Scheme in promoting Sinhalese colonisation written by international scholars like Peebles (1990), Shastri (1990 and Manogaran (1987), by seeking to rationally refute their arguments. By showing some numbers employed in those writings to be dubious, his paper claims their whole argument is flawed (and, thus, their proposition that state-aided colonisation was discriminating against Tamils and Muslims).
2. The rationalisation of regional boundaries based on river basins is questionable on 'scientific' grounds as well: 'naturalising' political boundaries essentialises regions as containers, containers of river flows and of economic flows, as if those flows were necessarily to coincide with and remain confined within administrative boundaries.
3. Muslim political identity developed at a later stage in the 1980s and only emerged when Muslims felt increasingly squeezed between the lines in the civil war of the north and east (O'Sullivan 1999). Muslims developed their own ethnic political representation and started to demand their own homeland, as the territorialised space of Muslimness (Korf 2006).

References

Balasundarampillai, P. (2002). *Trincomalee: Geo-politics, Ethnic Dimension and Development Potential*. Thirunelvey, Sri Lanka: Sociological Society, University of Jaffna.

Bastian, S. (1995). *Control over Land: The Devolution Debate*. Colombo: International Centre for Ethnic Studies (ICES).

Black, J. (1997). *Maps and Politics*. London: Reaktion Books.

Brohier, R.L. (1934). *Ancient Irrigation Works in Ceylon*. Colombo: Ceylon Government Press.

Brow, J. (1988). 'In Pursuit of Hegemony: Representations of Authority and Justice in a Sri Lankan Village', *American Ethnology*, 15(2): 311–27.

Brow, J. and J. Weeramunda (1992). *Agrarian Change in Sri Lanka*. New Delhi: Sage Publications.

Cosgrove, D. (2007). 'Epistemology, Geography, and Cartography: Matthew Edney on Brian Harley's Cartographic Theories', *Annals of the Association of American Geographers*, 97(1): 202–09.

Derrida, J. (2005). *Rogues: Two Essays on Reason*. Stanford, CA: Stanford University Press.

Farmer, B.H. (1957). *Pioneer Peasant Colonization in Ceylon*. London: Oxford University Press.

Goonatilake, S. (2001). *Anthropologizing Sri Lanka: A European Misadventure*. Bloomington, IN: Indiana University Press.

Harley, J.B. (1992). 'Deconstructing the Map', in T. Barnes and J. Duncan (eds), *Writing Worlds: Discourse, Text and Metaphor in the Representation of Language*, pp. 231–47. London: Routlegde.

Herring, R.J. (1983). *Land to the Tiller: The Political Economy of Agrarian Reform in South Asia*. New Haven, CT: Yale University Press.

Huggan, G. (1989). 'Decolonizing the Map: Post-colonialism, Post-structuralism and the Cartographic Connection', *Ariel*, 20(4): 115–31.

Kleinfeld, M. (2006). 'Destabilizing the Identity–Territory Nexus: Rights-based Discourse in Sri Lanka's New Political Economy', *GeoJournal*, 64(4): 287–95.

Korf, B. (2004). 'War, Livelihoods and Vulnerability in Sri Lanka', *Development and Change*, 35(2): 275–95.

———. (2005). 'Rethinking the Greed–Grievance Nexus: Property Rights and the Political Economy of War in Sri Lanka', *Journal of Peace Research*, 42(2): 201–17.

———. (2006). 'Who is the Rogue? Discourse, Power and Spatial Politics in Sri Lanka', *Political Geography*, 25(3): 279–97.

Korf, B. and H. Fünfgeld (2006). 'War and the Commons: Assessing the Changing Politics of Violence, Access and Entitlements in Sri Lanka', *Geoforum*, 37(3): 391–403.

Krishna, S. (1996). 'Cartographic Anxiety: Mapping the Body Politic in India', in M.J. Shapiro and H.R. Alker (eds), *Challenging Boundaries: Global Flows, Territorial Identities*, pp. 193–214. Minneapolis, MN: University of Minneapolis Press.

———. (1999). *Postcolonial Insecurities: India, Sri Lanka, and the Question of Nationhood*. New Delhi: Oxford University Press.

Latour, B. (1993). *We Have Never Been Modern*. Hemel Hempstead: Harvester Wheatsheaf.

Madduma Bandara, C.M. et al. (1990). *Report of the Land Commission—1987*. Sessional Paper No. III. Colombo: Department of Government Printing.

———. (2001). 'Redefining the Regions of Sri Lanka: A National Need of Our Time'. Inaugural Address at the Peradeniya University Lecture Series (PULSE), Peradeniya, 24 January.

Manogaran, C. (1987). *Ethnic Conflict and Reconciliation in Sri Lanka*. Honolulu, HI: University of Hawaii Press.

Moore, M. (1985). *The State and Peasant Politics in Sri Lanka*. Cambridge: Cambridge University Press.

———. (1989). 'The Ideological History of the Sri Lankan 'Peasantry', *Modern Asian Studies*, 23(1): 179–207.

O'Sullivan, M. (1999). 'Conflict as Catalyst: The Changing Politics of the Sri Lankan Muslims', in S. Gamage and I.B. Watson (eds), *Conflict and Community in Contemporary Sri Lanka*, pp. 253–78. New Delhi: Sage Publications.

Peebles, P. (1990). 'Colonization and Ethnic Conflict in the Dry Zone of Sri Lanka', *Journal of Asian Studies*, 49(1): 30–55.

Peiris, G.H. (1991). 'An Appraisal of the Concept of a Traditional Tamil Homeland in Sri Lanka', *Ethnic Studies Report*, 9(1): 13–39.

———. (1994). 'Irrigation, Land Distribution and Ethnic Conflict in Sri Lanka: An Evaluation of Criticisms, With Special Reference to the Mahaweli Programme', *Ethnic Studies Report*, 12(1): 43–88.

———. (1996). *Development and Change in Sri Lanka: Geographical Perspectives*. Kandy: Sri Lanka: International Centre for Ethnic Studies (ICES).

Robinson, J. (2003). 'Postcolonialising Geography: Tactics and Pitfalls', *Singapore Journal of Tropical Geography*, 24(3): 273–89.

Rose, N. (1999). *Powers of Freedom*. London: Cambridge University Press.

Sampanthan, R. (1985). 'Statement made by Mr. R. Sampanthan, Member of TULF Delegation at the Timpu Conference', in Tamil United Liberation Front (eds), *Devolution of Power in Sri Lanka: Main Documents, August 1983 to October 1987*. Colombo: TULF Publication.

Senanayake, D.S. (1999 [1935]). *Agriculture and Patriotism*. Colombo: Associated Newspapers of Ceylond.

Sidaway, J.D. (2000). 'Postcolonial Geographies: An Exploratory Essay', *Progress in Human Geography*, 24(4): 591–612.

Shastri, A. (1990). 'The Material Basis for Separatism: The Tamil Eelam Movement of Sri Lanka', *Journal of Asian Studies*, 49(1): 56–77.

Singh, K. (1989). *Land Reforms in South Asia*. New Delhi: South Asian Publishers.

Speier, H. (1941). 'Magic Geography', *Social Research*, 8: 310–30.

Spencer, J. (2003). 'A Nation "Living in Different Places': Notes on the Impossible Work of Purification in Postcolonial Sri Lanka', *Contributions to Indian Sociology* (n.s.), 37(1&2): 25–47.

———. (2007). *Anthropology, Politics and the State*. Cambridge: Cambridge University Press.

Spivak, G. (1990). *The Post-colonial Critic: Interviews, Strategies, Dialogues*. New York: Routledge.

Stokke, K. (1998). 'Sinhalese and Tamil Nationalism as Post-colonial Political Projects from "Above", 1948–1983', *Political Geography*, 17(1): 83–113.

Tambiah, S. (1986). *Sri Lanka: Ethnic Fratricide and the Dismantling of Democracy*. Chicago: Chicago University Press.

———. (1992). *Buddhism Betrayed?* Chicago: Chicago University Press.

Tennakoon, S.N. (1988). 'Rituals of Development: the Accelerated Mahaweli Development Program of Sri Lanka'. *American Ethnology*, 15(2): 295–310.

Thangarajah, Y. (2003). 'Ethnicization of the Devolution Debate and the Militarization of Civil Society in North-eastern Sri Lanka', in M. Mayer, D. Rajasingam-Sennayake and Y. Thangarajah (eds), *Building Local Capacities for Peace: Rethinking Conflict and Development in Sri Lanka*, pp. 15–36. New Delhi: Macmillan.

Tyner, J.A. (1982). 'Persuasive Cartography', *Journal of Geography*, 81(4): 140–44.

6

Geography, Spatial Politics, and Productions of the National in Michael Ondaatje's *Anil's Ghost*

Tariq Jazeel

Published in 2000, *Anil's Ghost* is Michael Ondaatje's fifth novel and his first to be set in Sri Lanka, the country of his birth. Despite previous engagements with his homeland in the memoir *Running in the Family* (1982) and a collection of poems *Handwriting* (1998), this novel nurtures a literary return of sorts for Ondaatje, who, since 1962, has been based in Canada: as one reviewer writes, 'Anil lets [Ondaatje] go back not just physically but spiritually' (Verma 2001: 46). The combination of the novel's volatile and contested subject matter, and Ondaatje's post-*English Patient* domestic status as perhaps one of Sri Lanka's most famous authors living overseas, has inevitably politicised this homecoming. This chapter considers the novel's political intervention by offering an engagement with the text that evokes the importance of space, of geography, to thinking through the vexed politics of Sri Lankan nationhood and identity. Specifically, the chapter focuses on a few key moments in the novel that involve the main protagonist and her encounters with the reclusive former archaeologist, Palipana, in his secluded rural hideaway. In doing so, it evokes not only Ondaatje's well-known obsession with history (see Hutcheon 1985, for example), but also his (perhaps latent) reliance on geography. More generally, and in the context of this volume's attempt to *spatialise politics*, the chapter teases out the historical landscape geographies and landscape experiences that play a central, often neglected, role in Sri Lanka's racialised political conflict. In doing so it offers a reading that intervenes spatially in the contemporary discourse on Sri Lankan politics and identity.

The novel is set in Sri Lanka in the mid-1980s to the early 1990s, at the height of the civil war and in the midst of uprisings from the ultra-left Sinhalese Janatha Vimukthi Peramuna (JVP). Anil Tissera, the novel's main protagonist, is a Sinhalese Sri Lankan born forensic anthropologist who emigrated to London some 15 years prior to the start of the narrative, eventually to settle in Arizona. On this, her first trip back to Sri Lanka, she returns as a United Nation's human rights envoy to forensically investigate charges of government-sponsored killing. Together with government employee and archaeologist, Sarath Diyasena, to whom she is paired, and armed with a skeleton unearthed in a restricted-access government archaeological reserve, she attempts to forensically excavate 'the truth' behind a life cut short, they think, by the government. Harder than scientifically proving that the skeleton belongs to a victim of a government-sponsored murder, is Anil's struggle to find anyone in the government who will actually listen to the evidence. When at last she is able to present her case, she faces another struggle altogether: to leave the country alive having publicly implicated the government.

Throughout the novel, Sarath and Anil enlist the help of three more characters to discover the truth about their skeleton, and it is around these characters that the novel's narrative is built. Gamini is Sarath's estranged brother, a brilliant but overworked and amphetamine-dependent doctor struggling to stay afloat amidst the sea of wounded and dead bodies brought daily to his under-resourced accident and emergency ward. Ananda is an artisan and villager whom Sarath and Anil employ to build a reconstruction of their skeleton's head from the skull they possess. The embodiment of a creative 'national' tradition, Ananda works through the text as intractable counterpoint to the altogether different ways of seeing and knowing figured through Anil's more positivist, forensic anthropological gaze (Jeganathan 2004a: 186). In this reading, however, I focus upon Anil's encounters with Palipana, Sarath's former archaeology professor. Now a reclusive forest-dwelling ascetic nearing the end of his life in an enchanted pocket of rural and arid north-eastern Sri Lanka, he offers Anil and Sarath advice on their investigations when they do not know to whom they can turn. Palipana was one of Sri Lanka's foremost archaeologists. Sinhalese himself, the novel says he was at the centre of a nationalist group who 'wrestled archaeological authority away from the Europeans' (Ondaatje 2000: 79). We are also told that Palipana was eventually discredited by charges that some of his greatest archaeological discoveries were in fact nationalistically motivated fabrications. Ondaatje's character Palipana is quite obviously, and for good reason, based on the real-life early-20th-century government archaeologist, Senerat Paranavitana, whose considerable efforts to inscribe a Sinhala-Buddhist history onto Ceylon's rural landscapes through the painstaking renovation of archaeological ruins I regard in more detail in the next section. It is Anil's encounters with Palipana, her negotiations and experiences of the fabric of his forest home, the 'The Grove of Ascetics', and the novel's depiction of Palipana's bodily presence to the world that this chapter suggests, evoke important insights into the spatial politics of identity and nationhood in Sri Lanka.

Reading Spatially: The Geographies of *Anil's Ghost*

In reading *Anil's Ghost* spatially, this chapter mobilises geography in two intersecting ways. First, and underpinning the analysis in the body of this chapter, I contend that the spatialities and orientations through which the text itself has been constructed are significant. More precisely, *Anil's Ghost* is a diasporic novel, written in Canada, first published in North America and Europe, and only then in Sri Lanka. However, I also choose to situate the novel firmly within the field of Sri Lankan literary production, an increasing portion of which is written overseas today. In doing so, and in keeping with a theme that runs through other chapters in this volume (notably Duncan, Bell and Wickramasinghe), I refuse to contain the spatiality of the nation-state within its territorial borders. To premise that a mode of diasporic Sri Lankan cultural production like *Anil's Ghost* can play a role in shaping the nation-state and national imaginations is to conceptually distance oneself from organicist, seed-like discourses of nationhood and nationalism. Instead, it is to acknowledge that the colonial and post-independent island-state is an historical and ongoing process of relational instantiation within a world in which it is both embedded and indelibly connected. Borrowing particularly from Latin American subaltern studies, this is to evoke the problematic territoriality of the nation-state, choosing cautiously instead the conceptual and representational deterritorialisation of a nation-state whose frontiers remain both permeable, and indeed constituted by, the dynamic process of 'transculturation' (Beverley 1999; Ortiz 1995). Spatially, transculturation is to provisionally think the nation outward; to implicitly interrogate the absolutism that currently characterises either prevailing insular or separatist geographical imaginations. The postcolonial nation-state in this analysis is formed as much through its connections within broader, international modes of knowledge production, representation and narration as it is by political processes that unfold within its own territorial borders.

This should not be taken as an apology for the spatialities and power relationships that underpinned colonialism itself, for colonialism remains but one idiom and episode of transcultural encounter amongst a vast tapestry of dynamic and ongoing relationality. Whilst the precise topologies, political role and power of the diasporic national itself must always be for debate and negotiation, contemporary diasporic geographies themselves offer modes of political *potential* at the very least. As a form of diasporic Sri Lankan literary expression, *Anil's Ghost* is suggestive because it points to the complex processes of memory transformation and the creation of transcultural perspectives on—as well as critiques of—existing social and spatial structures in former homelands. Ondaatje's position in North American and European book markets has unburdened his writing of labels of Burgher or minority literature, and instead his imaginative literature is able to critically engage with the rationalisations of a range of contemporary Sri Lankan nationalisms. Indeed, the increasing volume of Sri Lankan literature written overseas, by the likes of Ondaatje, Romesh Gunesekera, Shyam Selvadurai and Karen Roberts, for example, is characterised by diasporic literary negotiation of the impingements that bear upon the Sri Lankan self.[1] As recent work on diaspora has argued, movement, migration and the very idea of diaspora expression points to a potential that allows the migrant to negotiate belonging and attachment to a country of origin in ways that do not necessarily require the performance of essential or absolute belongings associated with nationalist or raciological thinking (Gilroy 2000; White 1995). Caution must be exercised, however, in the extent to which diaspora is celebrated as an emancipatory concept.[2] The point of departure in this chapter, moreover, is that *Anil's Ghost* be considered no less Sri Lankan because of its author's outer-nationality, its deterritorialisation. And in this context it becomes useful to highlight the ways by which this type of writing out of place can achieve more than just mere description from a distance of worlds left behind. Distance, and the ability to look back at and across it, can in fact open new doors and find new angles through which to enter the social, political and spatial reality of those worlds (Rushdie 1991: 13–18). And pursuant to literary studies' approaches to deciphering the narration of the nation (Bhabha 1990), this is to treat Sri Lanka as much as a textual subject, formed through diverse and discrepant modes of representation, as it is material and spatially incarnate, or territorial object (Ismail 2005).

These connections between the textual and the material feed into the second way that geography is mobilised in this chapter, which more directly lays the foundations for the reading that follows. In particular, in this chapter, I explore the fictive spaces through which the novel's narrative is built, and specifically how Ondaatje's writing of these spaces enables an engagement with the complex ways that material Sri Lankan landscapes themselves have been textually constructed and inscribed with meaning through colonial encounter. In a recent essay on *Anil's Ghost*, Antoinette Burton (2004) draws attention to Ondaatje's classically postcolonial and post-structural juxtaposition of the tensions between positivist, normative approaches to historical truth, as embodied by Anil and her deeply held commitment to the bones-as-truth thesis, and acknowledgement of the cultivation of historical 'truths' in South-Asia that are highly contingent on the way knowledge of the past is handled and authorised, evoked, as Burton suggests, by the character of Palipana. In reading the novel's negotiation of the tensions between two competing regimes of 'the truth', Burton raises important political questions around the ways that history and historical facts have been recovered from hidden depths, and how a historical imagination has been mobilised in the discourse on Sri Lanka's cultural politics of identity.

Such critical engagements with the politics and social effects of truth and historical fact in contemporary Sri Lankan society are not new within Sri Lankan studies (Gunawardana 1990, 1995; Perera 1999: 103–34; Scott 1995). However, in what follows, I pick these themes up from a geographical perspective by arguing that space is central to and inseparable from critical perspectives on the construction and handling of the historical imagination in Sri Lanka. In particular, a spatial reading of *Anil's Ghost* draws attention to the spatial politics embedded in the histories implicated in Palipana's turbulent biography and the ways that they come to affect Anil so deeply. By using *Anil's Ghost* as a segue into Pradeep Jeganathan's work on the colonial conquest and authorship of 'ancient' Anuradhapura (1995), this chapter adopts a postcolonial and post-structural reading of the textuality of meaningful landscape history and subsequent modes of landscape experience. It focuses attention on the *production of* meaningful space through the ongoing pursuit, and the subsequent authorship of historical 'truth'. Furthermore, I draw attention to the co-constitutive relations between these types of spatiality and social relations/identities by teasing out the politics of the landscape experiences embedded in *Anil's Ghost*.

Whilst reading, *Anil's Ghost* spatially involves engaging the spaces in and through which the narrative unfolds, it also implores attentiveness to the complex ways that narrative produces and invests those material spatialities with powers of agency that act upon subjects. Space emerges not merely as a container, stage or neutral backdrop against or in which political struggles unfold. Instead, it becomes the very currency and diction of the struggles and politics of personhood that fictive characters negotiate.[3] The use of spatial metaphor in Ondaatje's previous work has been well-explored, particularly the racial and conceptual hybridities that emerge in his mobilisation of notions of cartography, topography, and boundary (Silva 2002). Here, however, I pursue an analysis more attentive to the material political effects of spaces that have themselves been textually constructed and inscribed with meaning. I explore how Ondaatje's fictive spaces mobilise a politics located in real landscape, and specifically bodily experience of that landscape; and subsequently how this type of landscape geography connects to particular inflections of the national. Thinking geographically about *Anil's Ghost* and (one of) its fictive spaces proposes that Sri Lanka's racialised politics of difference is inseparable from a spatial politics. In this sense, the literary landscape—'The Grove of Ascetics'—is rendered transparent as one of the spatial forms and fantasies through which a culture and its hegemony make its presence (Carter 1987: xxii). For the Grove—fictively depicted as a clearing in the dry shrub forest dotted with boulders and other stone remnants of a 6th century Buddhist monastery as well as contemporary wood structures that have effectively fused the past with the present—comes to stand for so many other 'ancient'/'ruined' places and landscapes in rural central and southern Sri Lanka. Reading *Anil's Ghost* spatially shows the central role that these familiar landscapes play in producing the racialised contours of the modern Sri Lankan nation-state, it explores the micro-spatialisations of race as they are experienced in everyday life. Importantly, then, it is the tensions and connections between both levels of geography sketched in this section, the diasporic as a space of intervention or possible (re)formation, and the textuality of material space itself, that enable this particular engagement with spatial politics in Sri Lanka. It is the figure of the diasporic—Anil—that enables this critical, textual intervention.

Spatial Politics: Landscape, Nationhood, and Post-structural Geography

Landscape Experience

A central theme running through the novel is Anil's reconnection with the country of her birth. Upon her arrival in Sri Lanka, it becomes clear that she does not want to belong; she continually denies traces of her Sri Lankan heritage and she obfuscates childhood memories in ways that seem fuelled by a sense of shame at the country's path through bloodshed. Throughout the novel, however, Anil gradually reconnects with Sri Lanka, sensuously at first and then cerebrally as she at last admits to herself and to others that she is Sri Lankan. Her public assertion of Sri Lankan-ness comes towards the end of the novel in a one-sided government hearing amongst an overwhelmingly Sinhala audience. Here, she accuses the government of state-sponsored murder based on her forensic evidence, 'I think you murdered hundreds of us,' she clearly asserts (Ondaatje 2000: 272). And now her return is complete. Ironically, of course, as the narrative proceeds it is this affirmation in a hall packed with government officials that endangers her own life. In this sense, Ondaatje articulates the sense of uneasiness that many diasporic Sri Lankans feel in negotiating their own senses of belonging. I want to focus, however, more specifically on Anil's *process* of reconnection, particularly on the sensuous and bodily connections with landscape that facilitate her eventual cerebral articulation of Sri Lankan-ness, because these narrative processes, I suggest, speak of landscape geographies that continue to reproduce Sri Lanka's exclusive topographies.

Anil's process of reconnection is drawn through the novel. The process of re-remembering the Sri Lanka that part of her still has a deep affection for happens gradually, and it happens as much through her enchantment and physical reconnection with the country's rural landscapes as it does through any self-conscious search for her own cultural identity. However, her transition from disavowal to reconnection is marked by a ravaging bout of illness that renders her feverish, incapacitated and delirious for some two days. This moment marks an important hinge in the narrative. From this moment onwards Anil's physical reconnection with Sri Lanka's rural landscapes proceeds with some gusto, offering a clue that her eventual emergent Sri Lankan-ness is as affective as it is cerebral.

It is after her illness that Anil and Sarath visit Palipana in his ruinous 6th century Buddhist monastery hidden deep in the northern dry zone shrub forests, 'The Grove of Ascetics'. Of Palipana, we are told that originally he took only his books, writing tablets and his niece to look after him in this fragile 'leaf-hall' home. We learn that, as his sight faded, he became one with his weather-beaten home, he 'too now was governed by the elements,' (ibid.: 84). Anil soon becomes spellbound with the simple life that Palipana leads in this enchanted pocket of rural Sri Lanka. She begins to forge connections with the tranquillity and poetics of surrendering to Sri Lanka's rural landscapes. Anil senses and admires that the now-blind Palipana is attuned to his environment, somehow woven into the fabric of this place:

> She imagined he could hear the one bird in the forest distance. She imagined he could hear Sarath's sandals pacing, the scrape of his match, the sound of his beedi a few yards away. She was sure he could hear all that, the light wind, the other fragments of noise that passed by his thin face, that glassy brown boniness of his own skull. And all the while the blunt eyes looked out, piercing whatever caught them. (Ondaatje 2000: 87)

Anil proceeds to attune herself similarly to this enchanting environment through an accumulation of sensations. Whilst taking a bath in the ruinous but still usable nearby well when Sarath, Palipana and the girl are sleeping, her actions assume near sacred significance:

> Once more she dropped the bucket into the water and jerked it up and poured it over her hair and shoulders so the water billowed within the thin cloth onto her belly and legs. She understood how wells could become sacred. She would give every earring she owned for an hour by a well. She repeated the mantra of gestures again and again. When she had finished she unwrapped the wet cloth and stood naked in the wind and the last of the sunlight, then put on the dry sarong. (ibid.: 89)

Her experiences with Palipana in the 'The Grove of Ascetics' change her. She begins to feel more attuned to the place in the same way that she perceives both Palipana and Sarath are. Eventually, the novel's narrative voice suggests that she manages to weave her own body into this place; like Sarath and Palipana, she begins to feel a deep corporeal connection to the Grove.

> Anil kept thinking of Palipana's sightlessness in this landscape of dark green and gray. The stone steps and rock nestled against rock. These bones of an old settlement. It felt to Anil as if her pulse had fallen asleep, that she was moving like the slowest animal in the world through grass. She was picking up intricacies of what was around them. Palipana's mind was probably crowded with such things, in his potent sightlessness. I will not want to leave this place, she thought, remembering that Sarath had said the same thing to her. (ibid.: 97)

Just being there—dwelling—in this enchanted rural landscape that to Anil feels somehow beyond sacred, ultimately helps her discover a Sri Lanka to which she longs to belong.

The Politics of Landscape Experience

Scratching beneath the surface of Anil's encounters with Palipana in this place suggests how Ondaatje's novel more broadly evokes a spatial politics of Sri Lankan nationhood and identity through the considered use of Palipana and his home, 'The Grove of Ascetics'. As stressed earlier, Palipana is the fictional incarnation of the early-20th century head of Ceylon's Archaeological Survey Department, Senerat Paranavitana. Landscape experience in much of south and central rural Sri Lanka has strong connections with the cultivation of racialised, territorialised identifications, and Ceylon's Archaeological Survey Department has been largely responsible for the inscription of meaning in Sri Lanka's rural landscapes over the last 150 years or so. As Pradeep Jeganathan (1995) has shown in his work on another of Sri Lanka's 'ruined' landscapes, Anuradhapura, the ancientness and Sinhalese historiographical narratives within which it has come to be discursively positioned in contemporary Sri Lankan society are inseparable from mid- to late 19th century historical, archaeological and aesthetic practices of colonial and Orientalist authority. In short Anuradhapura's own ancientness is a modern—that is to say, colonial—production:

> The authoritative epistemology of Anuradhapura, that is the field of power and knowledge it is located in today, was created in a radical rupture in the nineteenth century. And hence, Anuradhapura is as old as that rupture. (ibid.: 108)

Just as Jeganathan's work has effectively shown the modern production of Anuradhapura's ancientness, he has also demonstrated how the establishment of Ceylon's Archaeological Commission in 1868 resulted from colonial fixations and dilemmas about what to do with Anuradhapura and the ruinous remains of old settlement 'discovered' there (ibid.: 123–24). The question of Anuradhapura—how to author Ceylonese antiquity and maintain British political authority in the colony—called into existence Ceylon's (post)colonial disciplinary 'archaeological formation'.[4] Importantly, for this reading of *Anil's Ghost*, this disciplinary archaeological formation set in motion events across the colony that eventually led to a significant and gradual process of re-imagining many more rural landscapes—a process in which Senerat Paranavitana came to play a key role in the first few decades of the 20th century. A process that Ondaatje's character Palipana thus becomes heavily implicated in.

It was in the late 19th century that the eminent London-trained Orientalist Dr P. Goldschmidt led exploratory fieldwork on behalf of the Archaeological Survey Department. His team mapped and photographed numerous cave and rock inscriptions in the colony's arid and inhospitable marginal forests, then deemed an impediment to progress. His reports indicate that following the excavations at Anuradhapura, the North-Central Province was amongst the first of those regions to be explored in this systematic way (Goldschmidt, n. d.), and, not insignificantly, these were those forests located near Ondaatje's fictional 'Grove of Ascetics'. Back in Colombo, Goldschmidt painstakingly translated and recorded these inscriptions in the hope of producing a *Corpus Inscriptionum Zeilanicorum*, in the process identifying numerous ruinous sites across the colony that were formerly inhabited by Buddhist monks and warranted further exploration, attention and possible restoration; sites that warranted the kind of archaeological industry that had been going on at Anuradhapura since 1875. Goldschmidt's efforts must be understood in the more general context of the South Asian imperial historian's scholarly obsession, from the 17th century through the early 19th, with finding texts that could be treated as evidence of South Asia's own 'authentic' histories (Jeganathan 1995: 110–11). Whereas Goldschmidt's work was shaped by that Orientalist desire to seek out and translate South Asia's own text-based histories, his work and findings were also part of an emergent and unfolding discourse of historical and rooted Ceylonese 'nation-ness' that pervaded colonial administration and management through the mid- to late 19th century. This was a wilful colonial history writing that fed into, and is continuous through and after, the 'restoration' of Anuradhapura. Even well before the restoration of Anuradhapura, even before Goldschmidt's explorations, various colonial office departments were particularly enthralled by the prospect of 'discovering' Ceylon's past. One invited forestry expert, for example, remarked in 1833:

> More than 1000 years ago Ceylon must have been inhabited by a large and powerful nation, who built large cities, temples, and palaces of which the remains are so common in the forest of the North-Central province and elsewhere. Frequently one finds in the depths of the densest forests, and hidden in amongst the undergrowth, the massive ruins of ancient temples and palaces, overgrown with trees, and undistinguishable from the rest of the forest. (Vincent 1833)

Also, in the mid- to late 19th century the comparative science of religion was percolating through empire. 'Buddhism' as a reified, normative category and religion was emerging in the Western imagination, and in Ceylon a Buddhist religious community was also crystallising whilst at the same time being marked as Sinhalese (Scott 1999: Ch. 2).[5] That 'ancient' yet 'large and powerful nation, who built large cities, temples and palaces' referred to by the visiting colonial officer F. D'A. Vincent, thus, normatively emerged by the end of the 19th century as 'racially' Sinhalese and 'religiously' Buddhist. By the end of the 19th century racial theories and debates unfolding in the *Journal of the Royal Asiatic Society of Ceylon* began also to hierarchically position the Sinhala 'race' over the Tamil (Angell 1998; Jeganathan 1995). Translation of the 5th century Buddhist chronicle, *The Mahavamsa*, which appeared to 'prove' that the Tamil presence in Ceylon was due to 'invasion' from South India, was gradually and progressively being married with the apparently evidentiary status of the 'ruins' being unmasked and restored across the colony by the archaeological formation.

Of course, the 19th century translation of the *Mahavamsa* bears a lasting and not to be overlooked impression on contemporary foundational narratives of the Sri Lankan nation (*see* the introductory chapter). If the translation of the *Mahavamsa* is a pivotal process in what Jeganathan (1995: 109–18) terms the modern nation's 'historiographic formation', its lasting political effects, he argues, also lies in the violent transformations of the text and the subjugation of indigenous knowledges—'notions of incalculable, non-linear time and "fantastic miracles"', for example—wrought through the very act of colonial translation itself. One particular effect being that legendary second-century B.C.E. battles between the now designated 'Sinhala' hero king Dutthugamini and the 'Tamil' usurper Elara, rendered in 5th century poetic diction were being translated as racialised fact by British Orientalists. Importantly, the *Mahavamsa* famously depicts an epic battle in which Dutthugamani defeats Elara to regain Sinhalese control of a kingdom whose seat of power was in Anuradhapura. The colonial archaeological formation, of which Anuradhapura's excavation/restoration and Dr Goldschmidt's late 19th century archaeological and epigraphical discoveries were part, lent 'scientific' proof that these fables actually occurred. In other words, the 'archaeological formation' was beginning to verify the textualised 'historiographic formation'. Archaeology offered the spatial correlates for this positivist history writing; it supplied the colonial nation's state. But crucially, through this period most of Ceylon's considerable historiographic knowledge production complex—the translation of texts and inscriptions; archaeological excavation, measurement and subsequent restoration of ruins; and displaying practices—happened either in the colonial capital Colombo (in which a new museum was built in 1877), or in the vast laboratory/museum-like archaeological sites at places such as Anuradhapura (Jeganathan 1995: 123; Perera 1998). The significance of this spacing of the historiographic industry lies in the symbolic framing, containment and regulation of one 'culture' by the dominant other (Perera 1998: 88). The colony's historic 'culture' was 'stored' and 'analysed' in museum and archaeological site respectively.

It was the early 20th century appointment of state archaeologist Senerat Paranavitana, however, that marked a turning point in the historiographic knowledge production complex, and subsequently in Sri Lankan historical geography. Although this chapter does not claim to write anything like Paranavitana's biography, it is important to emphasise the heady vortex of rapidly cementing, colonially produced, authoritative knowledges within which his professional career was forged in Ceylon. First, his passage to the Archaeological Survey Department was consistent with the period in which Sinhala and Tamil 'race' thinking had become persuasive communitarian narratives filtering through late colonial public culture. Second, being a practising Buddhist, he was profoundly effected by the comparative science of religion that had helped spawn protestant modes of Buddhism in early 20th century Ceylon. Third, as noted previously, he navigated a social landscape, in which the Orientalist translation of the *Mahavamsa* had already rendered the colonial island-state through a linear, historiographic formation comprised of 'Sinhala glory and then Tamil destruction, Sinhala reconquest and Tamil desecration, repeating, re-cycling' (Jeganathan 2004a: 192). And fourth, he was appointed Director of the Archaeological Survey Department following the Donoughmore Commission's promulgation of a policy of the 'indigenisation' of the colonial government.

Paranavitana's administrative reports suggest that his religious faith convinced him of the need to continue to 'prove' the truth of the *Mahavamsa* through the scientific tools at his disposal: Archaeology and Epigraphy. His reports suggest that his own early brand of Sinhala nationalism was not necessarily motivated by 'racial' or 'religious' bigotry, but instead by an unbending desire to prove to the world and—perhaps more importantly—to himself, the truth of Ceylon's Sinhala-Buddhist historiographic formation. In this sense there is a great deal of continuity between early colonial archaeological praxis and Paranavitana's late colonial variant. Frequently, for example, he would take an almost forensic interest in individual inscriptions because of, as he wrote, their 'evidence for the veracity of the Mahavamsa' (Paranavitana 1934). For Paranavitana, it seems the jury was still out on this text, but as the colonially educated, objective scientist, he was able to test its reliability.

Alongside these continuities, however, the 1930s and 1940s saw Paranavitana initiate a new approach to archaeological praxis that effectively re-inscribed Ceylon's rural landscapes with the Sinhala-centred historical frameworks outlined in colonial translations of the *Mahavamsa*. Paranavitana wrestled archaeological interest away from the museum display cabinets in the colonial capital Colombo, and back into Ceylon's rural landscapes where countless valuable finds were previously made only to be removed by colonial 'explorers'. Speaking some 35 years after his appointment, his eventual successor identified the tide change in archaeological praxis that Senerat Paranavitana was instrumental in shaping:

> Time was when people thought that the functions of Archaeology were limited to the exhibition of objects in museums. The position today is different. Any one with the faintest idea of Archaeology knows today that objects removed from their place of find have lost much of their value.... The accepted principle now is to leave objects in their original places. (Godakumara 1967)

The effect was to de-centre Ceylon's archaeological industry; to take it out of Colombo and the Anuradhapura complex, and back into the colony's forgotten landscapes. Paranavitana's team embarked upon a colony-wide programme of restoration and epigraphical translation in situ, which included considerable further work in the inhospitable, arid regions around the North-Central and Southern Province where at the time, despite the restoration work at well-established archaeological complexes like Anuradhapura of which Jeganathan writes, the colonial imagination still tussled with moral and economic dilemmas between regressive, unruly 'nature', and progressive, civilising 'culture' and 'agriculture'. Paranavitana's approach effectively breathed life back into the dead archaeological artefacts in the museum cabinets, charging their corresponding landscapes with the profound new senses of time and history that had emerged from the restorative work at 'ruined' city complexes like Anuradhapura, and from the translations of the *Mahavamsa*.

Careful analysis of his reports reveals the political effect of this new type of archaeological praxis in late colonial Ceylon. In 1934, Paranavitana set about archaeological restoration and epigraphical work at a site called Situlpahuwa located in the arid south-east Rohanarata region, which today lies within the boundaries of Sri Lanka's most famous National Park, Yala. Recognising the site from its description in the *Mahavamsa*, Paranavitarna's account of a 2,200-year-old inscription found here is telling, the tone amplifying the racialised politics that inhered in translations of the document's poetic renditions of Sinhala history:

> An inscription under the drip ledge of a cave at Koravakgala, near Situlpavuva in the Magam Pattu, mentions a general... named Mita, of

> King Devanampiya Abhaya. It is possible to identify the King Abhaya of this record with Dutthugamini Abhaya, *the national hero of the Sinhalese, and his ten legendary warriors who helped Dutthugamini to conquer the Tamils*. (ibid, emphasis added)

His words equate Sinhala history with what he suggests was a legitimate, pre-modern Sinhala 'nation', grounding a contemporary, imagined Sinhalese 'national' community in both antiquity and place, and configuring this particular pocket of rural Ceylon as a landscape central to Sinhalese struggles with a dangerous Tamil other. It is not insignificant that today Yala National Park, within which this site is located, is replete with the Sinhala-Buddhist historical resonance that Paranavitana has helped to inscribe (Jazeel 2005).

All over the colony, similar such forgotten landscapes designated 'regressive' or 'unruly' by colonial administration were being reinvented by similar modes of archaeological praxis: the discovery and in situ translation of pre-modern, Sinhala Buddhist archaeological and epigraphical remains in the midst of inhospitable, fever-infested or miasmic landscapes. Precolonial Sinhala history and memory were beginning to reside in these previously neglected landscapes, and Paranavitana's Archaeological Survey was allowing this igneous history to speak for itself. Elsewhere, already existing colonial archaeological restoration sites like the Anuradhapura complex were just as significantly being infused with the body politic of an increasingly nativised, archaeological and epigraphical industry. Paranavitana's Archaeological Survey Department was de-colonising landscape through archaeological praxis, but it was simultaneously re-colonising landscape because it could only act in the raced language and idiom of the Sinhala-centred historiographic formation that the colonial archaeological formation and Orientalist translation had produced. Colonial Office administrative reports record countless inscriptions translated by Paranavitana, including testaments that cave dwellings were bequeathed to the Buddhist monkhood by various sovereign kings across different regions. These in particular offered ownership claims that emphatically demonstrated that Crown land never actually was *terra nullis*. At the same time, however, these anti-colonial claims also precluded Tamil, Muslim or Burgher claims to any sort of rooted attachment to soil.

Ondaatje's Palipana then is inalienably connected to this dense complex of authorial spatial history, and evoking this historical landscape geography through him enables us to open out and re-read Anil's experiences and bodily encounters in 'The Grove of Ascetics' amidst the 6th century Sinhala-Buddhist ruins where, like Palipana, she learns to mindfully and affectively pick up the intricacies of the world around her. Through these textual encounters and negotiations, Ondaatje's novel offers critical insights into how this type of historical geography acts in the present, on how the types of movement through space enacted through Anil and Palipana help us to understand the ongoing cultivation of an exclusive politics of identity and nationhood in Sri Lanka that is inseparable from its mid- to late-colonial history.

To pursue these insights we must return to ruins. In his book *The Presence of the Past*, the anthropologist Steven Kemper (1991) explores the powerful ways by which the archaeological restoration of Sinhala ruins across Sri Lanka has contributed to what he refers to as 'enacting Sinhala nationalism'. He suggests how the careful scientific practice of restoring ancient piles of rubble to what archaeologists believe was once their original state makes it difficult to separate what is 'legitimately ancient' from what is a modern reconstruction. This process infuses the present with an architectural and religious historical past, rendering landscape history not just visible, but importantly open to the realm of human experience. There is a troubling tension in Kemper's work, for his analysis easily confuses the modern (colonial) production of ancientness as discussed earlier, with a notion of the 'legitimately ancient' that is recovered through the restoration of place, and which seamlessly becomes 'Buddhist sacred place' (for a fuller critique, Jeganathan 1995: 107–08). In other words, the implication in Kemper is that archaeological effort does have the capacity to unlock (positivist) histories embedded in stone, and this occurs under the sign of 'restoration' (ibid.). In similar ways, in the passages from *Anil's Ghost* quoted previously, the novel's narrative voice offers us a glimpse of her commitment to this uncomplicated, positivist historiographic formation: 'Anil kept thinking of Palipana's sightlessness in this landscape of dark green and gray. The stone steps and rock nestled against rock. *These bones of an old settlement*' (Ondaatje 2000: 97, emphasis added). That historical truth so unproblematically presents itself to Anil through the evidentiary nature of ruins is unsurprising given her vocation as forensic anthropologist. For in her professional life, she depends upon such positivist reconstruction of the truth about the past.

Despite this tension in Steven Kemper's work on the *The Presence of the Past*, he usefully opens a space for thinking about the confluence of material geography and subjectivity in the spatial politics of nationalism. In his own words, in the experiential moment the 'blurring of past and present is the very thing that gives sacred places that palpable sense of their sacredness' (Kemper 1991: 136). The point worth emphasising here is that in Sri Lanka's rural landscapes, in and around its ruin sites such as Ondaatje's 'Grove of Ascetics', the transcendent poesis of experience, so often designated sacred, is inseparable from the archaeological and historiographic formations thus far teased out in this paper. Subjects feel connections with the Sinhala history that has been inscribed in the landscape and its surrounds: '[Anil] understood how wells could become sacred. She would give every earring she owned for an hour by the well. She repeated the mantra of gestures again and again' (Ondaatje 2000: 89). The nature of the sacredness that Anil's gestural mantras evoke is now clear. Experiences of, and connections with, a palpable sense of sacredness at such sites are not uncommon, and the political implication is that such commonplace landscape experiences connect the subject with a 'glorious', 'heroic' and exclusive Sinhala past to which these ruins point. It is also significant that these experiences take place in the midst of what is popularly regarded as Sri Lankan 'nature', as it is but a short pre-reflective step for these embodied experiences to be objectified as expressions of reality located in the very soil of the land. In this sense, the link between Anil's emergent sense of Sri Lankan-ness ('I think you murdered hundreds of *us*' [ibid.: 272, emphasis added]) and her transformative, embodied experiences in 'The Grove of Ascetics' are hugely significant; her well-bath and other experiences in the Grove, for example, can now be read in ways that foreground the ongoing constitution of subjectivities and social relations through this type of everyday, sacred landscape experience. The ancientness and sacred aesthetics produced variously by colonial archaeological restoration and historiographic formation emerge, as Pradeep Jeganathan (1995: 128–30) suggests, as commodity to be consumed.

Of course, Anil's transcendent landscape experiences in the Grove do not transform her into an apologist for militant Sinhala-Buddhist nationalism.[6] In fact, as a result of her experiences in the Grove, Anil eventually articulates a stringent humanist critique of Sinhala-Buddhist chauvinism, perhaps betraying Ondaatje's own commitment to the humanist paradigm that has underpinned much of his prior work (Kella 2000).[7] Furthermore, it is not insignificant that Anil eventually accuses the government of murdering hundreds of *us*, for this suggests her inability to think beyond Sri Lankan-ness scaled as (inter)national identification, perhaps also betraying the markings of a particular type of 'cosmopolitan' diasporic Sri Lankan national. In teasing out Anil's experiences in the Grove, however, this chapter suggests that the novel mobilises ways of thinking about how subjectivities are rendered in relation to place, and how geography as ground is positioned to signify an exclusive spatial politics of identity and nationhood in Sri Lanka.

In this respect it is important to draw attention to the type of body mobilised through Palipana himself. His is a Buddhist body, whose 'potent sightlessness' is significant, particularly with respect to the Buddhist philosophy and discourse of the body mobilised through the landscape geographies thus far evoked. The over-determination of meaning in landscapes such as 'The Grove of Ascetics', the ways that its histories have been inscribed and subsequently naturalised, strongly suggest that sacred experiences encountered there are bestowed through Buddhism. Religious philosophy is mobilised in the experiential moment, particularly for the Buddhist, as the latent Buddhist nature of these landscapes maps bodies in ways that give rise to a transcendent poetics in which nature and culture are felt to merge, for in Buddhist philosophy there is no nature/culture dialectic. It appears then that the Grove has offered Palipana the perfect aid to spiritual effort, his seclusion here has given him insights into the nature of a universal Buddhist reality.[8] This is a place where, from Anil's perspective at least, Palipana is close to a return to an unfeeling point of balance within the natural world. It does not matter that he has lost the use of his eyes, for his Buddhist body still has the use of its five other senses: sound, touch, taste, smell and mind. For many, the poetics of experience in and through similar types of Sri Lankan landscape offers ways of glimpsing this Buddhist reality, and in a country that has written Buddhism into its constitution, this is neither coincidental nor can it be divorced from the politics of nationhood. For, to connect with this Buddhist reality is to mobilise Sinhalese historical narratives, which, as emphasised, also configure Tamils as invaders in a national space that is Sinhala by 'nature'.

Post-structural Geography

This chapter has engaged a few encounters in *Anil's Ghost* to enable a post-structural geographical critique of how the national is produced, and, importantly, to interrogate what apparently *true* senses of the national are produced *as* in Sri Lanka. These are themes that are central to Ondaatje's probing novel. Palipana, the novel tells us, was discredited in the latter stages of his career. Scholars found no evidence to corroborate his greatest epigraphical work that explained the political tides and royal eddies of the island in the 6th century. His translations seemed to have ended a generation of debates amongst Sri Lankan historians, and they were confirmed by his reputation for meticulous research. But, quite simply, the texts Palipana claimed to translate did not exist, throwing into doubt the credibility of his life's work.

> Now it seemed to others that he had choreographed the arc of his career in order to attempt this one trick on the world. Though perhaps it was more than a trick, less of a falsehood in his own mind; perhaps for him it was not a false step but the step to another reality, the last stage of a long truthful dance. (Ondaatje 2000: 81)

The braiding of Palipana's own life and religious beliefs with his professional and academic work was in fact comparable to the construction of a carefully choreographed fiction of sorts. The political significance of this important juncture in the narrative, of course, lies in the implication that he had by this time already helped to write and spatialise large chunks of Sri Lankan history, as had his real-life counterpart Senerat Paranavitana; and, it bears repeating, these are histories that have configured Tamils as 'invaders' to an island constructed historically as Sinhala-Buddhist by 'nature'.

What then are the boundaries between historical truth and fanciful narrative in the construction of the modern nation-state? This is the question that *Anil's Ghost* poses, backing post-structural claims within the humanities and social sciences that if nations are constructed as inventions, or artefacts, then their existence is predicated upon an apparatus of cultural fictions (Shannon-Peckham 1996: 67; Bhabha 1990). The cultivation of racialised Sri Lankan subjectivities locked in hierarchised dependent relations to one another emerges from the spatialisation of authorised narrations of a Sri Lankan nation. Ondaatje's inclination to place under scrutiny the textuality of reality is not new, as Linda Hutcheon (1995) has noted in her reading of *Running in the Family* (Thieme 1991). Post-structuralism is indeed central to Hutcheon's own engagement of this text when she reads Ondaatje's historiography as carefully choreographed poetic construct. Even if events seem to speak for themselves, history is made by the writer, she asserts, recognising Ondaatje's interest in drawing attention to narrative as a way to impose meaning and form on the chaos of historical event. As I have shown in this chapter, *Anil's Ghost* draws attention to the geographies of nation and narration; to the way that selective discourses and historical narratives are spatialised in ways that powerfully cultivate the meaning and form of the national.

If any more evidence were required for Ondaatje's exposition of the textuality of geographical reality, it is worth drawing attention to a thought-provoking one and a half-page vignette on the Sri Lankan National Atlas in *Anil's Ghost*, which appears well before readers are introduced to Palipana. Sitting somewhat dislocated from the narrative thread of the novel, written in italics, it begins:

> *The National Atlas of Sri Lanka has seventy-three versions of the island—each template revealing only one aspect, one obsession: rainfall, winds, surface water of lakes, rarer bodies of water locked deep within the earth.*
>
> *The old portraits show the produce and former kingdoms of the country; contemporary portraits show levels of wealth, poverty and literacy.* (Ondaatje 2000: 39)

Why 73? What is the basis for selecting 73 different mappings of the island to authorise a Sri Lankan geography? Each, of course, is just one obsession. Just 40 pages later we learn of Palipana's own obsession that was eventually revealed to be the work of his overactive and wishful imagination; the poetic fabrication of a nation's historiography.

The National Atlas of Sri Lanka is an official historical geography authorised by the state in 1988, just five years after the riots and the outbreak of civil war. Its section on 'Ancient Cities and Settlements' informs that although the presence of humankind in Sri Lanka probably dates from around 75,000 years ago, Sri Lanka's 'Historical Epoch' begins only from 250 years B.C.E. This transition is marked by the conversion of King Devanampiya Tissa to Buddhism by the son and emissary of the Indian Emperor Asoka. At once, in this official document Sri Lanka's pre-Buddhist history is relegated to the rather inconsequential realm of 'Pre-history'. Such claims to historical and geographical truth regulate the terms of Sri Lankan reality, and, as I have shown, as systems of regulation they are enmeshed in relations of power, domination and spatiality that cultivate the still point of subjectivity, of experience, of identity, of difference. Through the power of word and map Sinhala-Buddhism stakes its authorial claim on the historiography of the nation-state. As Ondaatje might say, 'just another obsession'.

Conclusion

Like most authors, Ondaatje seems well aware of the burden of representation. In an interview in a British newspaper in 2000, just prior to the novel's publication, he was at pains to stress that he was wary of tackling Sri Lanka's political crisis. The novel is just his take on a few characters, a personal tunnelling into the war, not *the* statement, just his statement

(Jaggi 2000). His wariness to 'speak for' certainly emerges from the precarious politics that surround diasporic vision. For, to dogmatically assert the authority of a diasporic intervention, to 'speak for', is—even in fiction—to reproduce the power relations and geographies of colonial regimes that so violently and devastatingly spoke for and simultaneously dispossessed. Furthermore, and echoing the dilemmas the foreign Sri Lankan studies scholar must negotiate (Bell in this volume), Ondaatje seems well aware of the spatialities of relative privilege and security that many (but by no means all) diasporic nationals can enjoy (Jeganathan 2004a). The ability of the diaspora figure to extricate oneself from spaces of violence come the end of an 'intervention' does not go unnoticed by the characters that Anil leaves behind:

> 'American movies, English books—remember how they all end?' Gamani had asked that night. 'The American or Englishman gets on a plane and leaves. The camera leaves with him. He looks out of the window at Mombassa or Vietnam or Jakarta, someplace he can look through the clouds. The tired hero…the war, to all purposes is over.' (Ondaatje's *Anil's Ghost*, quoted in Jeganathan 2004a: 187)

Ondaatje's novel may not be an attempt to tackle the political crisis, but its characters, its narrative, and, above all, the novel's textual spaces do offer intriguing doors and angles through which to enter Sri Lanka's social, political and spatial reality.

Anil's Ghost is thus an important if tentative statement that offers much to the critical Sri Lankan studies scholar today who seeks, instead of 'speaking for', to 'speak to' (Spivak 1988) Sri Lanka; particularly speaking to questions of *how* the passions of Sri Lankan identity and nationhood are historically and textually produced (Ismail 2001). Engaging critically with the novel's textual spaces exposes one of the modern Sri Lankan nation-state's most taken-for-granted structures and spaces—its landscape geographies—as a geographical production. As Pradeep Jeganathan's (1995: 105) work on the colonial authorship of Anuradhapura has shown, authoritative forms of knowledge not only produce discursive objects, but non-discursive objects also; that is to say, authoritative knowledge produces material geographies, landscape itself. More than this, as I have argued here, in such materialities is embedded significant political agency. This reading has intervened in debates around Sri Lanka's cultural politics of difference, specifically by interrogating the materiality and power of 'The Grove of Ascetics' and other such Sri Lankan landscapes. It has questioned what is a commonly perceived ontological distinction between apparently innocent historical Sri Lankan landscape geographies and the country's more troublesome racialised realities, and in doing so it has suggested that Sri Lanka's cultural politics is inherently spatial, not just in terms of the familiar territorial and separatist claims and counter-claims of Sinhala and Tamil nationalists, but also in the commonplace subjectivities and experiences of everyday life *in* and *through* place. I have sought to draw the messy, complex, yet critically productive lines of connection between the historical and cultural productions of meaningful yet taken-for-granted spatiality, subjectivity and the ongoing cultivation of a racialised politics of difference in Sri Lanka. For these are lines that yield potentially insightful interventions into the political discourse on the 'truths' of Sinhala identity and nationhood that are locked in Sri Lankan soil, stone and tree. As Michel Foucault (1980: 118) argued in his *Power/Knowledge* interviews:

> I believe that the problem does not consist in drawing a line between that in a discourse which falls under the category of scientificity, or truth, and that which comes under some other category, but in seeing historically how effects of truth are produced within discourses which in themselves are neither true nor false.

Whilst the realities of race, nation and subjectivity have fuelled Sri Lanka's civil unrest, they are concepts whose roots variously can be traced through 19th century racial theory, Orientalist scholarship and their spatialisation through colonial and anti-colonial archaeological praxis. The very status of race, nation and subjectivity as common currencies of difference in contemporary Sri Lanka testify to how successfully they have been naturalised and woven into the fabric of everyday, real space. To move beyond them is a postcolonial challenge that demands the re-imagining of some of the most obstinate takens-for-granted.

Notes

1. For work that explores these diasporic literary negotiations, see Jazeel (2003) and Burnett (1997). It is important to stress, however, that a diasporic authorial position is not the only condition that allows such literary insights into the effects of nationalisms in Sri Lanka. For an example of domestic literature that achieves similar critical negotiations, see Pradeep Jeganathan (2004b).
2. See Note 1. As a diasporic spatiality and sensibility emancipates subjects from nationalist or raciological identifications, it may just as easily re-inscribe other exclusions, along the axes of class, gender or sexuality, for example. For a

timely reminder of the dangers of uncritical valorisations of diaspora, see Brah and Coombes (2000).

3. For more on geographical engagements with imaginative literature, see Jo Sharp (2000), and Marc Brosseau (1994).
4. The term is borrowed from Jeganathan (1995), who uses it to refer to the institution of a dense cluster of archaeological practices.
5. On Buddh*ism* and the Western imagination, see Peter Bishop (1993).
6. Although some scholars have suggested that Ondaatje's novel unwittingly re-inscribes Sinhala-Buddhist hegemony. For a lively exchange on these interpretative tensions, see Ismail (2000), and Coomaraswamy (2000).
7. As an aside, it is worth adding that throughout the novel the narrative does not distinguish between political/mob violence committed by the LTTE, the JVP or the government. In the humanist analysis, political violence is a universal.
8. For more on Buddhist nature and the dissolution of nature/culture dialectics, see Guruge (1984), de Silva (1998), and Batchelor and Brown (1992).

References

Angell, M. (1998). 'Understanding the Aryan Theory', in M. Tiruchelvam and C.S. Datthathreya (eds), *Culture and Politics of Identity in Sri Lanka*, pp. 41–72. Colombo: International Centre for Ethnic Studies.

Batchelor, M. and K. Brown (eds). (1992). *Buddhism and Ecology*, Delhi: Motilal Banarsidas.

Beverley, J. (1999). *Subalternity and Representation: Arguments in Cultural Theory*. Durham and London: Duke University Press.

Bhabha, H. (1990). 'Introduction: Narrating the Nation', in H. Bhabba (ed.). *Nation and Narration*, pp. 1–7. London and New York: Routledge.

Bishop, P. (1993). *Dreams of Power: Tibetan Buddhism and the Western Imagination*. London: Athlone Press.

Brah, A. and A. Coombes (eds). (2000). *Hybridity and its Discontents*. London and New York: Routledge.

Brosseau, M. (1994). 'Geography's Literature', *Progress in Human Geography*, 18(3): 333–53.

Burnett, P. (1997). 'The Captives and the Lion's Claw: Reading Romesh Gunesekera's "Monkfish Moon"', *Journal of Commonwealth Literature*, 32(2): 3–16.

Burton, A. (2004). 'Archive of Bones: *Anil's Ghost* and the Ends of History', *Journal of Commonwealth Literature*, 39(1): 39–56.

Carter, P. (1987). *The Road to Botany Bay: An Essay in Spatial History*. London and Boston: Faber and Faber.

Coomaraswamy, R. (2000). 'In Defense of Humanistic Way of Knowiñg', *Pravāda*, 6(9 and 10): 29–30.

de Silva, P. (1998). *Environmental Philosophy and Ethics in Buddhism*. London and New York: MacMillan Press.

Foucault, M. (1980). *Power/Knowledge: Selected Interviews and Other Writings, 1972–1977* (edited by Colin Gordon). New York and London: Pantheon Books.

Gilroy, P. (2000). *Between Camps: Nations, Cultures and the Allure of Race*. London: Penguin Books.

Godakumara, C.E. (1967). 'Administration Report of the Archaeological Commissioner for the Financial Year 1964–65'. The Department of National Archives, Sri Lanka, January 1967.

Goldschmidt, P. (no date). 'Report on Inscriptions Found in the North Central Province and in the Hambantota District'. The National Archives, London (TNA) CO57/70, circa 1877.

Gunawardana, R.A.L.H. (1990). '"The People of the Lion": The Sinhala Identity and Ideology in History and Historiography', in J. Spencer (ed), *Sri Lanka: History and Roots of Conflict*, pp. 45–86. New York: Routledge.

———. (1995). *Historiography in a Time of Conflict: Construction of the Past in Contemporary Sri Lanka*. Colombo: Social Scientists' Association.

Guruge, A. (1984). *Buddhism: The Religion and its Culture*. Colombo: The World Fellowship of Buddhistso.

Hutcheon, L. (1985). 'Running in the Family: The Postmodernist Challenge', in S. Solecki (ed.), *Spider Blues: Essays on Michael Ondaatje*, pp. 301–15. Montreal: Vehiculé Press.

Ismail, Q. (2000). 'Anil's Ghost: A Flippant Gesture', *Pravāda*, 6(9 and 10): 24–28.

———. (2001). 'Situations: Speaking to Sri Lanka', *Interventions*, 3(2): 296–308.

———. (2005). *Abiding by Sri Lanka: On Peace, Place and Postcoloniality*. Minneapolis, MN: University of Minnesota Press.

Jaggi, M. (2000). 'The Soul of a Migrant', *Guardian*, 29 April.

Jazeel, T. (2003). 'Unpicking Sri Lankan "Island-ness" in Romesh Gunesekera's *Reef*', *Journal of Historical Geography*, 29(4): 582–98.

———. (2005). 'Nature, Nationhood and the Poetics of Meaning in Yala (Ruhuna) National Park, Sri Lanka', *Cultural Geographies*, 12(2): 199–228.

Jeganathan, P. (1995). 'Authorizing History, Ordering Land: The Conquest of Anuradhapura', in P. Jeganathan and Q. Ismail (eds), *Unmaking the Nation: The Politics of Identity and History in Modern Sri Lanka*, pp. 106–36. Colombo: Social Scientists' Association.

———. (2004a). 'Disco-*very*: Anthropology, Nationalist Thought, Thamotharampillai Shanaathanan, and an Uncertain Descent into the Ordinary', in N. Whitehead (ed.), *Violence*, pp. 185–202. Santa Fe, NM: School of American Research Press.

———. (2004b). *At the Water's Edge*. New York: South Focus Press.

Kella, E. (2000). 'Beloved Communities: Solidarity and Difference in Fiction by Michael Ondaatje, Toni Morrison and Joy Kogawa'. Unpublished Ph.D. dissertation, University of Uppsala, Sweden.

Kemper, S. (1991). *The Presence of the Past: Chronicles, Politics and Culture in Sinhala Life*. Ithaca, NY, and London: Cornell University Press.

Ondaatje, M. (2000). *Anil's Ghost*. New York: Vintage.

Ortiz, F. (1995). *Cuban Counterpoint: Tobacco and Sugar* (translated by Harriet de Onís). Durham and London: Duke University Press.

Paranavitana, S. (1934). 'Annual Report of the Archaeological Survey of Ceylon for 1934, by Senerat Parnavitarna Esq.', The National Archives, CO 57/241. London, UK.

Perera, N. (1998). *Society and Space: Colonialism, Nationalism and Postcolonial Identity in Sri Lanka*. Boulder, CO: Westview Press.

Perera, S. (1999). *The World According to Me: An Interpretation of the Ordinary, the Common, and the Mundane*. Colombo: International Centre for Ethnic Studies.

Rushdie, S. (1991). *Imaginary Homelands: Essays and Criticism 1981–1991*. London: Granta Books.

Scott, D. (1995). 'Dehistoricizing History', in P. Jeganathan and Q. Ismail (eds), *Unmaking the Nation: The Politics of Identity and Gistory in Modern Sri Lanka*, pp. 10–25. Colombo: Social Scientists' Association.

Scott, D. (1999). *Refashioning Futures: Criticism after Postcoloniality*. Princeton, NJ: Princeton University Press.

Shannon-Peckham, R. (1996). 'Between East and West: The Border Writings of Yeorgios Vizyinos', *Ecumene*, 1(1): 65–76.

Sharp, J. (2000). 'Towards a Critical Analysis of Fictive Geographies', *Area*, 32(3): 327–34.

Silva, N. (2002). 'The Anxieties of Hybridity: Michael Ondaatje's "Running in the Family",' *Journal of Commonwealth Literature*, 37(2): 71–83.

Spivak, G. (1988). 'Can the Subaltern Speak?' in C. Nelson and L. Grossberg (eds), *Marxism and the Interpretation of Culture*, pp. 271–316. Chicago: University of Illinois Press.

The National Atlas of Sri Lanka (1988). Colombo: Survey Department.

Thieme, J. (1991). '"Historical Relations": Modes of Discourse in Michael Ondaatje's *Running in the Family*', in C.A. Howells and Lynette Hunter (eds), *Narrative Strategies in Canadian Literature: Feminism and Post-Colonialism*, pp. 40–48. Milton Keynes and Philadelphia, PA: Open University Press.

White, P. (1995). 'Geography, Literature and Migration', in Russel King, John Connell and Paul White (eds), *Writing Across Worlds: Literature and Migration*, pp. 1–19. London: Routledge.

Verma, A. (2001). 'Love in a Time of War', *India Currents*, 15(9): 46.

Vincent, F.D.'A. (1833). 'Extracts from the "Forest Administration of Ceylon. Report on the Conservation and Administration of the Crown Forests in Ceylon", by F.D'A. Vincent Esq. (of the Indian Forestry Service), 1883', National Archives, CO 57/88. London, UK.

7

Meeting Places? Centre and Periphery in Civil Society Peace Work

Camilla Orjuela

Introduction

The sporadic chatter in the hall ceases as the young actors and dancers enter the stage. The members of Centre for Performing Arts (CPA) begin their impressively choreographed version of the famous play *Ashoka*. Boys and girls dressed magnificently—sometimes as many as 50 on stage at a time—have come to Colombo from different parts of Sri Lanka. The girls performing Kandyan dance are from Avissawela in the south, while those doing the Bharatanatyam scenes have travelled from the war-affected north. This performance is indeed not only about offering the audience breathtaking entertainment, it is also a way to provide a meeting place for youth from different sides of an ethnic divide that has been carved out by over 20 years of war. Just as the typically Sinhalese Kandyan dance and the Tamil Bharatanatyam share the same stage, so do youth who would otherwise not have had a chance to meet.

Identity politics play a central role in many contemporary violent conflicts. Conflicts over access to power and resources are often fought under nationalist or ethnic banners. In the process, the boundaries between the 'self' and the 'other', the friend and the enemy, are deeply engraved by the tools of history writing and territorial claims. Experiences of violence nurture distrust and the propagation of images of the other as a vicious enemy against whom military means need to be used. Security becomes linked to group-homogeneity predicated upon difference and separation from others, chiefly those representing the 'enemy' (Jabri 1996; Kaldor 2006; Pieterse 1997). Efforts to bring an end to contemporary identity-based wars need to involve the provision of security to people as well as political solutions allowing for power sharing between groups (often in the form of devolution of power to territories claimed by minorities). To achieve this, however, peace researchers and policy makers have increasingly recognised that there is also a need to bridge cemented self/other distinctions, to foster inter-ethnic understanding and trust, and promote inclusive identities that challenge ethnic polarisation.

That ethnic division to a large extent has a geographical dimension is clear, not least from the case of Sri Lanka. The Tamil separatist movement challenges the centralised Sinhalese-dominated state. It attempts to create a new, alternative 'centre' in the north-east, and to assert the Tamils as a people with its own homeland and right to self-determination rather than as a minority in the Sinhalese-dominated Sri Lanka. The civil war between the Sri Lankan government and the Liberation Tigers of Tamil Eelam (LTTE) has augmented ethnic divisions by geographical separation. The war zone—particularly the LTTE-controlled parts of the country and the Jaffna peninsula in the north—has been largely inaccessible during long periods of time and thus isolated from the rest of the country. Displacement has tended to generate mono-ethnic settlements. The images of the 'other' as vicious enemy and the incompatible views of what the conflict is about held by people from different ethnic groups (and nurtured by ethnically divided media reporting) are reinforced by physical and territorial separation.

As the mistrust and divides between people constitute one obstacle (of several) to peaceful conflict resolution, efforts to support peace increasingly concentrate on bridging these divides and providing space for dialogue. In Sri Lanka, as in many other war zones around the world, a range of non-governmental actors have engaged in activities aiming to promote inter-ethnic understanding and popular support for an end to the war. This type of work—for instance, peace education, exchange programmes, rallies and media campaigns—has expanded since the mid-1990s along with the interest of international development agencies to provide funding.

This chapter takes a critical look at the attempts by civil society actors to provide meeting places and bridge ethnic divides in the context of ethnic conflict in Sri Lanka. It argues that far from offering inclusive and alternative views of identity, the peace movement mirrors the ethnic and spatial divides that characterise Sri Lankan society. Although peace work does provide space for meetings and interaction across ethnic divides, it simultaneously reinforces divides between centre and periphery structured along ethnic, geographical and class lines. Peace work thus risks underpinning the persistence of a colonial spatial imagination that takes for granted Colombo as centre, and the north-east, as well as areas in the south of the country, as periphery.[1]

Ethnic Polarisation and Peace Building

Politicisation of ethnic identity and the claim to power on the basis of a particular identity is a central feature in many contemporary violent conflicts (Kaldor 2006). Identity-based struggles have become increasingly common in a globalised world, which continues to be organised in nation-states, inconsistently based on the idea of a people's right to self-determination. Ethnic identity has become:

> ...a weapon of revenge against centuries of discrimination and new forms of exploitation; it serves as an instrument for applying pressure in the political market; and it is a response to needs for personal and collective identity in highly complex societies. (Melucci 1996: 386)

In violent struggles—whether waged against a dominating state or against rebel groups—the construction of exclusionist identities is vital. The discourse of inclusion and exclusion creates a distinction between friend and enemy that allows little room for uncertainties or ambivalent identities; unity requires strict boundaries between 'self' and 'other' (Jabri 1996: 7). In the quest for unity, ordinary people (marked with clear identity labels) risk becoming pawns in the game of identity politics. Attacks on civilians and symbolic assaults on, for instance, places of worship are part of a strategy to instigate fear, forge clear-cut divisions between friend and enemy, and assert the claim over territory by so-called ethnic cleansing. The consequence of such warfare is not surprisingly a confirmation of enemy images through lived experience, and increased polarisation and separation between groups.

Security guarantees and just distribution of resources and power are essential ingredients in attempts to bring about peace in such conflicts. Along with this, however, efforts to counter mistrust and images of the other as enemy are necessary among top-level leaders to make negotiations and political problem solving possible, and among ordinary people to secure popular support for peace initiatives and avoid local conflicts that could spread and make havoc of such initiatives. Civil society actors (NGOs, religious and other respected leaders, grassroots organisations, etc.) have in many conflict zones taken on a role promoting trust-building between conflicting parties and ordinary people divided by ethnic conflict. Civil society is sometimes pointed to as a space where inclusive, non-extremist identities can be nurtured. Civil society actors have been singled out as those who could mobilise people for peace, bridge ethnic divisions, oppose extreme nationalism, and pave the way for a new, multicultural society (Lederach 1997; Richmond and Carey 2005; Rupesinghe and Anderlini 1998).

Mary Kaldor (2006) talks about 'islands of civility'—local people who, in the midst of war, struggle against the politics of exclusivism and keep alive civic multicultural values. These are people and groups who refuse to accept the politics of war, and who keep contacts across the divides and keep the option of ambivalent identities open (for example, in the case of the Hutus and Tutsis in Rwanda who chose to call themselves Hutsis [2006: 11]). These 'islands', Kaldor argues, represent a potential solution to conflicts, and should be strengthened by outsiders who want to contribute to peace. Jay Rothman (1997) offers a similar idea in his ARIA[2] framework for resolving identity-based conflicts. According to his model, conflicting parties proceed from antagonism to resonance, from a callous self-versus-other situation (the 'other' as enemy) to cooperation and a common identification as 'we' ('we are in this conflict together'). The first phase of Rothman's conflict resolution process (Antagonism) gives the parties a chance to express their anger and frustration, and to give their interpretation of the conflict. Blaming the other side, polarisation between the sides, and ascribing and projecting bad traits to the enemy is common at this stage. However, the antagonism thereafter grows into understanding of the other side, and the discovering of shared experiences and interests (Resonance). It is in this process that identities built on enemy images can be transformed into more peaceful ones. Instead of building the self-image on a struggle against evil adversaries (us–them), interdependence is recognised (us–you), and a self-image as peacemaker can be fostered (ibid.: 39). Although identification is still irretrievably linked to a binarised 'other' who is defined as different from the 'self', the self–other relationship is re-framed, and a more inclusive position is made possible.

Similar ideas underlie many approaches to conflict resolution, not least those applied by civil society actors. However, they can often be criticised for building on a static and acontextual view of identity. 'Identity conflicts are about who we really are,' says Rothman (ibid.: xiii), and thereby, risks hiding the fluctuating and relational nature of identity. Identity should be understood not as a noun (something you have), but as a process, a striving for 'identification'. Identification is a constant process of defining and redefining, of constructing and belonging to a 'we' as opposed to those who are different (Hall 1990). An unreflected assumption that there are homogeneous groups with clear-cut identities which can enter into dialogue can thus enforce the wartime logic of fixed identities.

Moreover, the conflict resolution's emphasis on dialogue between two parties risks ignoring (or at best underestimating) the issue of power. Bipolarity between equal parties representing their respective identity groups is often assumed, and power asymmetries (regarding for instance resources, legitimacy or political representation) are hidden. A dilemma with peacemaking is that the strivings for 'peace' and for 'justice' tend to end up at loggerheads. Identity-based civil wars often originate in marginalisation or suppression of a group that consequently takes up arms to fight for justice, claiming rights to power on basis of their identity ('we are a people with the right to self-determination'). Mobilisation around an ethnic identity is thus a 'weapon of the weak', which can be utilised against a dominant power. 'Peace', articulated as an 'end to the violence' (which might mean a return to status quo), will chiefly be in the interests of the most powerful. And in this formulation 'peace work', which primarily focuses on fostering understanding and nurturing inclusive identities can be seen as taking the side of the dominant group. Alternative identities, inclusiveness and discourses of multiculturalism (or Kaldor's 'islands of civility') can thus serve to hide the dominance of the powerful over the weak, to perpetuate unequal power relations in a 'multicultural' society. A downplaying of ethnic identity can thus be a way to disarm the weaker party struggling against suppression. Unsurprisingly, 'understanding' between groups is not enough to change unequal relationships. On the contrary, an emphasis on shared identities implies a universality that veils power. As expressed by Ernesto Laclau (1996: 50): 'The universal is no more than a particular which at some moment has become dominant.' Thus, efforts made in peace work to emphasis an identity as 'human beings' might only be an attempt by the hegemony to enclose the particulars, the dominant hoping to be universal (Hall 1991: 68).

Ethnic Polarisation in Sri Lanka: The Postcolonial Spatiality of Violent Conflict

The centralised nature of the state is at the core of the conflict in Sri Lanka. During colonial times, Sri Lanka (then Ceylon) was made into one administrative entity by the British, and economic and political power was centralised in Colombo. 'Combining the name and the territory, it was the British who finally produced Ceylon,' Nihal Perera (1999: 24) notes. The perception of Sri Lanka as one 'natural' political unit and the importance of the unitary character of the state were developed after independence as part of a Sinhalese nationalist discourse. The building of an all-inclusive Sri Lankan identity linked to the independent state failed, as the Sinhalese majority group came to dominate the state, both politically and culturally (the most notable demonstration of this was the Sinhala-only language politics from 1956). Post-independence history in Sri Lanka has been characterised by marginalisation experienced by the minority ethnic groups, as well as by the Sinhalese masses in marginal areas. Colombo and the Western Province developed into the economic and political centre of the island, with a large distance prevailing between this centre and the less developed, less powerful periphery of the rest of the island. A little more than 50 per cent of the GNP is generated in the Western Province (inhabited by 29 per cent of the population), while Uva, North-Central and North-Eastern Provinces together produce less than 5 per cent (Ministry of Finance and Planning 2005: 29). The north-east is estimated to have the highest levels of poverty and lack of access to basic services, as it has been triply affected by years of neglect by the centralised state, the war-inflicted destruction, displacement and impediments to economic activity, and more recently the grave impacts of the tsunami (Sarvananthan 2006; World Bank 2005). The estate sector in central Sri Lanka and rural areas in the so-called 'deep south' also suffer from high levels of poverty.

A welfare state with a large public sector and extensive education system developed in the 1950s, promising upward mobility to the rural masses. However, subsequent cuts in the public sector made it difficult to meet the aspirations for a better life held by a relatively well-educated rural youth. Violent socialist rebellions emanating from the 'deep south' in the early 1970s and the 1980s resulted from this form of social and economic marginalisation. Similarly, the Tamil separatist struggle can also be seen as a reaction from the periphery to the centralisation of power in Colombo. In spite of cries for regional devolution of power and appeals for federal solutions to the north-east conflict, the tendency towards increased centralisation has continued (*Polity* 2005). While Sri Lanka formally has a relatively decentralised structure, in practice, the centre—Colombo—has taken over much of the functions of the provincial councils, and local government institutions lack resources. Large parts of the war-affected north-east are without elected representatives in their local bodies due to an inability to hold elections. The colonial relations between an administrative and economic centre (Colombo) and periphery thus persist more than 50 years after independence. Economic development emanates from the Colombo area, and only partly 'trickles out' to the rest of the country, while political leaders distribute benefits to the peripheries through patron–client-like relationships.

As Catherine Nash (2002: 220) writes, 'The imaginative geographies of colonialism both persist and are reworked in the name of globalisation.' In Sri Lanka market liberalisation in the late 1970s and the processes linked to globalisation have contributed to the growth of a new urban (that is, Colombo-based) middle class. This class, employed, for instance, in NGOs and the private sector, is English-speaking and linked up with the global world. While the new urban middle-class nurtures cosmopolitan identities, increasingly marginalised rural elite groups tend to be those who maintain strong nationalist ideas and mobilise against the perceived threat to Sinhalese culture and Buddhism, or against the suppression of the Tamil people by the Sinhalese-dominated state (Hettige 1998). From the perspective of the marginalised, the others (defined either on the basis of ethnicity or class) appear to be privileged, while one's own group is neglected, marginalised, and distant from the centre.

Ethnic polarisation has grown in the wake of political conflict and war experiences. Although people from different ethnic groups in many places live relatively mixed together (except in the northern war zone), segregation and polarisation has taken place, most visibly between Sinhalese and Tamils. The Sinhala-only policy of 1956 introduced a segregation of the education system along language lines, and removed the common language, English, and the school as a space where children and youth communicated and met across ethnic divides. The Sinhalese/Tamil polarisation has been clearly demonstrated in the media, which has largely been used to promote the views of the two main parties in the conflict. That government soldiers have 'sacrificed their lives' while 'terrorists have been eliminated' in the formulation of the Sinhala media is illustrative. The media has thus fed into the conflict and served to legitimise violence, for example, by picturing atrocities as inevitable reactions to previous violent acts by the other side (Kandiah 2001).

The violence has incited yet more segregation. Anti-Tamil riots, especially the widespread bloodshed in 1983, prompted many Tamils to flee areas where they were a minority—to the north or abroad. Ethnic cleansing made the guerrilla-controlled north and Jaffna purely Tamil; the Sinhalese who used to live there had long since left, while tens of thousands of Muslims were forced by the LTTE to hurriedly leave in 1990. In mixed areas, the war has disrupted inter-village and inter-ethnic economic links. 'The trend has been for displaced peoples to move, reside, and receive assistance (or not) in mono-ethnic settlements, which has accentuated the ethnic polarizations occurring because of the war' (Forut 2001: 16). Unwarranted cross-ethnic contact has, in tense areas, often been looked upon with suspicion, and those who engage in it have been assumed to be informers. The emergency situation has given ethnic markers a significant function in daily life. Tamils have been singled out as suspected 'terrorists' by their language, names and looks, while ID checks and passes verify their identity. Tamilness has become a burden, something to hide.

People's experiences of ill treatment and loss have reinforced a view of the 'other' as a cruel enemy worth fighting. The following story told by a man who had travelled from Trincomalee to Colombo to obtain a passport for his mother illustrates this well:

> I was caught by the police and locked up at the police station as an LTTE suspect. I am a government servant, and only came to get the passport. I was crying inside, and my mother was on the outside. I had all kinds of IDs, and the bank ID too. I tried to contact someone who could get me out, and in the end managed to get a Sinhalese acquaintance to come. After that I started thinking that if I am ever again taken by the police without reason, and I am released, I will go to the LTTE! I have never had any relations with the LTTE before. But if I am taken by the police again, I will be willing to leave my family, and take up arms and fight with the LTTE.[3]

Similar mechanisms of loss that subsequently prompt desires for revenge and produce otherness have been experienced by the Sinhalese, as expressed by a woman who lost her husband as a soldier: 'My two sons now want to join the army to fight the LTTE who killed their father.'[4]

However, the ethnic polarisation has not been definitive and clear-cut, but contextually determined. The tradition of cross-cultural mixing has still been strong in many places, where people from different ethnic groups interact, live in mixed settlements, visit each other, make friends, or even intermarry. In mixed areas in the parts of the country spared from warfare it has been common to take part in each other's religious festivals, weddings and funerals. Families of different ethnicities send each other food items as gestures of friendship during various celebrations, and economic relations are often intertwined (although sometimes unequal). The National Youth Survey, carried out in 1999–2000, revealed that young people had few friends from other ethnic groups (the Sinhalese 5 per cent, Tamils 14 per cent and Muslims 22 per cent), although 40 per cent of the sample stated that they were interested in contacts with other cultures. Forty per cent of the Sinhalese, 35 per cent of the Tamils and 30 per cent of the Muslims saw no problems in marrying outside their ethnic group. From this survey data, Marcus Mayer (2002: 211–14) concludes that: 'There is no strong ethnic antagonism among Sri Lankan youth, rather indifference and lack of interaction.'

Images of the other as vicious enemy have often not been ascribed to the other ethnic group as such. The polarisation has more to do with a deep divide in the understanding of what the conflict is about, and the view of the LTTE and the Sri Lankan government as evil-minded 'terrorists' or 'suppressors' respectively. In schools, little is taught that explains the political and economic roots, and contemporary developments of the ethnic conflict. Instead, a history of heroic Sinhalese kings, defeating 'filthy' and invading Tamils is often taught in government-controlled areas, while the righteousness of the Tamil struggle against state suppression is taught in LTTE-controlled areas. Alternative interpretations and perspectives have not been recognised. Ignorance about what the war is about is widespread; something that can serve as a breeding ground for rumours and fear. There has been a widespread feeling among Tamils that the government does not care about the plight of their civilians, something that is confirmed each time the government shells civilian targets in the north (Balasingham 2001: 308 ff). Polarisation, experience of violence and fear influences local relations, as well as the willingness of ordinary people to support military actions against the 'enemy', or to accept negotiations with and concessions to the 'other'.

Civil Society Peace Work

A number of civil society organisations concerned with peace, human rights, and democratic reform were formed in Sri Lanka in the 1970s in response to ethnic riots and government repression. After the 1983 anti-Tamil violence international attention generated an influx of foreign relief funds, much of which was handled by non-governmental organisations. Although civil society actors have been working for peace for decades, a somewhat more forceful peace movement gained momentum, first in connection with the election campaign and then with the subsequent peace process in 1994–95. A wide array of organisations has been working for peace, with activities at national as well as local levels. These are professional conflict resolution organisations such as the National Peace Council and the Foundation for Co-Existence, research institutions such as the International Centre for Ethnic Studies and Centre for Policy Alternatives, cultural groups like Centre for Performing Arts referred to in the introduction, several women's organisations, faith-based organisations, and the large Sarvodaya movement inspired by Gandhian and Buddhist philosophy. There has also been an increased interest among organisations working with development, women's issues, culture, etc., to engage in work for peace and conflict resolution.

The availability of foreign funding has been an important factor enabling the growth of civil society peace work in Sri Lanka. The interest of Western countries in promoting peace—and to channel foreign aid to and through civil society organisations—started in the mid-1990s. With the signing of the ceasefire agreement in 2002, a number of new donors entered and old donors intensified their programmes in a quest to become part of the Sri Lankan peace-building success story. They aspired to lay the ground for sustainable peace by promoting reconciliation and popular support for negotiations. This created space for old peace organisations to expand their work and for new ones to be formed.

Many civil society actors have aimed to raise awareness about the causes of war, and about the grievances of the other side, in order to counter the ethnic polarisation discussed earlier. This has been done, for instance, by promoting cultural exchange, dialogue between religious leaders, visits for youth to other parts of the country, and trips for journalists or civic leaders to the war zone. The long-term goal has been to build the bottom-up support needed to legitimate peace negotiations and political solutions involving power sharing. Advocacy work has been another area of activity; political leaders have been provided with information about the costs of the war, the popular support for peace, ideas on solutions to the conflict, and civic organisations have pressured political leaders to stop human rights abuses and to opt for and keep up dialogue. Mass demonstrations and rallies have been used to show the politicians the view of the 'people'. Many peace organisations also have hoped to prevent popular violence and chauvinism by creating local structures for dialogue and conflict resolution, and by working for just distribution of resources in society.

The impact that this peace work has had on the key parties to the conflict has so far been limited. Peace organisations have not been able to mobilise a vociferous mass-based movement protesting against war, and other factors have had far more influence on the decisions by leaders to pursue the military option or not. However, the peace organisations' many efforts to communicate that a political, negotiated solution is possible, and that reconciliation and dialogue is desirable, has strengthened an alternative discourse that challenges the pro-war agenda and extreme nationalist views, which at times have been picked up by key actors (Orjuela 2004).

Bridging or Maintaining Ethnic Divides?

Providing meeting places and fostering relations between people from different ethnic groups has been a central task for civil society peace groups: 'Like a translator we have to go and speak. Create communication between Sinhalese and Tamils, who don't speak each other's languages.'[5] If people know each other's cultures, peace can be built.[6] A joke told by one interviewee highlights the importance of inter-ethnic relations: 'We must mix people, like in mixed marriages.... The best thing would be to get [President] Chandrika married to [LTTE leader] Prabakaran!'[7]

One important purpose of this 'mixing' is to provide correct information and increase understanding of the other side: 'Sinhalese learn from their teachers that LTTE will shoot them if they go to the north. If ordinary Sinhala people start to [know] what is happening here, then you cannot stop [the peace].'[8] Civil society organisations and leaders in Jaffna have played an important role as contacts and guides for southern civil society groups travelling to the north. They have organised visits to villages, refugee camps, schools, and prisons, shared information and experiences, and organised public meetings.[9] Likewise, Tamil people have visited the south and sometimes changed their images of the Sinhalese. As told by one young activist from Jaffna: 'When we were in Jaffna we were thinking Sinhalese are very bad. Now [that] we came to Colombo we are sharing, we are talking with them.'[10]

In 2001 a number of mothers of army soldiers visited the LTTE-controlled areas and met with women there, something that touched them deeply:

> Now, every time when we hear that there is an attack, we are wondering whether it is their children who were killed. And every time there is an attack on the Army, the mothers on the other side wonder whether our children were killed.[11]

When the Community Development Centre made it possible for Sinhalese women to visit Tamil refugee camps, they wanted to learn some Tamil to be able to communicate, and they brought gifts for the children.[12] Through these visits, the women gained an understanding of the plight of Tamils affected by the war, while the displaced Tamils got to see that not all Sinhalese are enemies. The collections of relief items for people affected by violence in, for instance, border villages, are acts of solidarity that create new understandings of the 'other'. Relief, development work or trauma counselling could also be seen as a symbol of solidarity and cross-ethnic cooperation, if provided by persons from one group to the other, transgressing prejudice about the other as enemy.[13]

The ambition to join together and let go of identity labels has been central in civil society peace work. The Community Development Centre, for instance, brought together Sinhalese, Muslim and Tamil children for peace programmes, where they learnt each others' dances and songs, and sat together and shared their different traditional sweets: 'Gradually they become one, more one than separate sections. Like that we plan every little activity.'[14] Joint labour was a uniting force in camps organised by the Service Civil International among others: 'You cook together, you sleep in the same place. Even these different people can live in the same place, cook and eat and sleep together without... going into a conflict.'[15] A study measuring the trust, empathy, and social distance of Sri Lankan students who had participated in four-day peace camps revealed that camp participants showed significantly greater empathy for persons of the other ethnicity than students from the control group. The camp participants also showed more willingness to donate money to poor children of the other ethnic group (Malhotra and Liyanage 2003).

Civil society peace work thus has provided meeting spaces across the divides between ethnic groups in Sri Lanka. However, the activities have been on a small scale, and diminutive in comparison with the structural segregation and polarisation that has taken place over decades of ethnic politicisation and armed conflict. The ceasefire established in 2002 enabled increased mobility between the north-east and the rest of the country. During the four years it lasted, it created space for more meetings between people from the war zone and the south, eased the work for peace organisations wanting to carry out exchange programmes and study visits, and exposed more southerners to the devastation of the war zone.

Although civil society peace organisations in Sri Lanka have provided cross-ethnic and cross-territorial meeting spaces, they cannot be understood as an 'island of civility', in Mary Kaldor's vocabulary. They are not an isolated piece of 'civil' land in the midst of an unruly sea of conflict. In contrast, civil society actors are very much embedded in society at large, and entail the divisions and conflicts of that society. Although many of the peace NGOs and other civic organisations strive to represent, involve, and reach out to all ethnic groups, this is often not the case. Most large peace organisations have their base in Colombo and many are perceived as Sinhalese-dominated (something that does not necessarily mean that there are no Tamils in the organisations, including in leading positions). Sinhalese peace activists normally do not speak Tamil, and the distances, tardy means of transportation and restrictions on mobility imposed during wartime—Jaffna, for instance, appears very far from Colombo, and has for long times been totally inaccessible—lay the foundations for this divide. The lack of interaction across ethnic boundaries and geographical distances also leads to a lack of understanding by Sinhalese peace workers of Tamil viewpoints. As expressed by one interviewee: 'The Sinhalese peace movement defines peace from a southern perspective.'[16] The Tamil fear of Sinhalese-dominated peace was expressed by one Tamil from a Colombo-based organisation:

> The Tamils are most concerned with equal rights. Suppose we stop fighting today, what will happen? What will be the situation for us? Peace for Tamils is that the Army should get out [from the north-east]. Peace in the south might be LTTE surrendering.[17]

The Sinhalese domination can also be explained by the fact that spaces for political protest have been very limited for Tamils. Tamils who engage politically have been viewed with suspicion by both the government (in whose eyes they are potential terrorists) and the LTTE (who claim the sovereign right to express the will of the 'Tamil people'). This, along with the fact that many Tamils primarily want justice, and mistrust the idea of 'peace at any cost', has restricted their involvement in peace organisations. Peace organisations and protests have thus often been Sinhalese-dominated, while Tamils tend to be involved in more concrete human rights, relief, cultural, and other less explicitly political work. The distances between Colombo (where most larger peace NGOs are based) and the Tamil war-torn areas in the north-east, and the fact that most community-based civil society organisations on the island are mono-ethnic, also contribute to the ethnic divisions of Sri Lankan civil society. But even though many peace organisations in themselves are not ethnically balanced, their activities (in the form of exchanges, meetings, dialogue and study visits) have served to form cross-ethnic meeting spaces. Many of them have been of a temporary nature, but the very fact that people from all ethnic groups have joined in civic peace work provides a more long-term possibility for dialogue. To carry out joint projects, people with different experiences and interpretations of the conflict have had to come together to negotiate peace definitions and strategies.

The ambition to rise above and beyond ethnic divides has definitely been on the peace movement agenda. Two approaches can be distinguished. The first chooses to emphasise difference, and the need to understand and learn about ethnic others, and accept and appreciate inescapable ethnic differences. This is done, for instance, in programmes for cultural exchange, in the learning of each other's language, history and religion, the performing of the other's songs and dances, and sharing of traditional foods. The second approach emphasises a common identity as humans, and downplays ethnic difference. Ethnic differences should, in this view, not be talked about, and instead the focus should be on common needs. For instance, Sarvodaya has chosen this way in its programmes for village awakening (Ariyaratne 2000). Many civic actors have mobilised participants and members around alternative, non-ethnic identities. The identity as poor and oppressed can bring both Tamils and Sinhalese together in the endeavour to improve their lives and unite for peace against what is seen as a pro-war elite. People also have got together for peace in their role as victims of war, mothers, women or artists, thus emphasising these similarities and fostering a unity which de-emphasises, and (at least sometimes) reaches across, ethnicity.

Both these approaches contain inherent dilemmas. The first—emphasising and accepting difference—risks reifying and magnifying ethnic identity, while rendering other cross-cutting identities invisible. The second—downplaying difference—risks running the errands of the dominant group in the conflict by disarming the weaker group of its most efficient weapon of unity—ethnic identity—and thereby maintaining the invisible relations of dominance.

Centre and Periphery in Civil Society Peace Work

'We don't want to take ideas from Colombo and put them into your heads. We want you to take the initiative. We are only facilitators,' said a Colombo-based NGO representative as he addressed a meeting in the southern town of Matara organised to prepare for the Human Rights Day celebrations, which were to be organised under the banner of the umbrella organisation People's Peace Front (PPF). Twenty-five people had turned up and listened when the PPF representatives explained the campaign.

The PPF team left Colombo at 5 A.M. that morning and arrived in Matara in time for the meeting at 10 A.M. When the organiser said that he did not want to 'take ideas from Colombo', Colombo represented much more than a geographical place. It also symbolised upper or middle-class, educated and urban, as different from the people who were to be mobilised for the event.

The postcolonial centralisation of all parts of Sri Lankan society (state, private sector, civil society) around Colombo is clearly reflected in the peace movement. For a peace activity to get a national image or be reported in national or international media, it has to take place in Colombo:

> If you want to get it on television, if you want to get it into the press, if you want to create an impression in Colombo, stop the traffic.... You can stop the traffic in Anuradhapura, it does not make an impact.[18]

The Colombo centrality, however, has been criticised as evidence of NGO professionals' lack of contact with, and activity in, the rest of the country: 'You can see posters for peace in the Colombo area. But only 20 kilometres outside of Colombo there are no such posters. And if you go 100 kilometres away there is definitely nothing'.[19]

The Colombo NGOs were accused of 'trying to build peace in English', and for having closer contact with international diplomats than with grassroots people.

> After 1977, we have opened up our country. This created a lot of opportunities for people [whom it] is easy for the foreign institutions to work with.... They are the mirror image of the West. In terms of ideas, outlook, aspirations, lifestyle. You go to [a five-star] hotel party. [There] foreigners [are] mixing with local people. But these people do not represent the ordinary people in this country at all, far remote from that.[20]

There is, thus, a large gap between the transnational upper strata (who intermingle with Westerners) and the rest of the population. Donor agencies are heavily Colombo-centred and often circumscribed to contacts with an English-speaking elite. Civil society peace work funding has mainly been confined to a limited number of larger Colombo-based organisations, and has only partly 'trickled out' from the capital towards smaller organisations around the island. The limited administrative capacity of donors makes the funding of the professional Colombo NGOs a far more efficient option than attempts at channelling small funds to faraway organisations not yet trained in the intricacies of application, budgeting, and reporting processes. As a consequence, NGOs have often been seen as representing an English-speaking, educated elite. This while civic leaders in remote areas, for instance, in the war-torn north-east, observe great needs for reconstruction and reconciliation, but have heard of no prospects to obtain peace aid.[21] As expressed by one NGO representative in Trincomalee: 'Most organisations are working in Colombo with foreign funding. They do not want to have a foot in the really needy areas.... They want to keep it to themselves.'[22]

A gap between the ideology of (Colombo-based) leaders and the opinions and motivations of participants (from other parts of the country) could often be noted, mainly in the form of a lack of knowledge among participants about the ideological goals they mobilised around. But there are also examples of local enthusiasm in engaging for peace. A leader from the Community Development Centre described how village women engaged in peace work:

> Once they really feel that we are trustworthy [their commitment is] really great. And the way they get themselves involved! Suppose we take a petition, we are pressurising the government to adopt a political solution instead of a military one. Once that is explained in the women's meetings, and once we explain the significance of women being peace makers and working for justice. Once they are convinced, you should see the enthusiasm with which they take these signature lists around the village. Within one week the list will be completed, signed. They go from door to door, house to house, from field to field. Wherever they are working out in the fields, they will get their signatures, and then some of the papers are brown by the time they come back to Colombo. Black and brown![23]

Although initiatives to do peace work have often come from Colombo, many of the NGO leaders have spent much time 'out-stations' and among the grassroots. However, these local connections are often not rewarded in the internal hierarchies of the urban-based NGO sector—class hierarchies that work both within and between organisations. The 'field people' who maintain grassroots links and are good at mobilising sometimes hold a lower status than the 'headquarters people' who are fairly well-known intellectuals, move with diplomats, and are consulted by foreign visitors. The gap between the educated elite and the people of lower classes is thus maintained also through the ways they involve in civil society organisations—the Colombo elite interact with diplomats, while poor people from the periphery are mobilised for mass demonstrations.

Interviews carried out by Markus Mayer with rural youth in southern Sri Lanka in 1998 revealed that 'village life values' were very important.

Young people in these marginal areas identified strongly both with the south and with rural lifestyles, and many articulated a strong animosity towards Colombo, the people there, urban life, and Western influence (Mayer 2000: 161). These youngsters belong to a group of people who are frustrated with their opportunities at life-improvement, and have been easily mobilised in violent movements throughout Sri Lankan history. The fact that they strongly differentiate themselves from the Colombo people who run peace organisations points to a great failure of the peace movement. Moreover, NGOs that work with relief and development often do not live up to the image of being close to the grassroots. As shown by Goodhand et al. (1999: 27), locals in the east were critical of NGOs, whom they saw as unreliable, serving their own agendas, and only favouring wealthier people. The government's ability to reach the poor exceeded that of NGOs; the government was closer to the ground than most NGOs, as it had an ongoing presence through the local officials at the village level (ibid.: 47, 53). Thus, even as NGOs carry out activities at a grassroots level, they are still often seen as transient and distant, failing to build enduring and broad links with local communities.

Concluding Remarks

The postcolonial spatialities that persist in contemporary Sri Lanka also permeate civil society peace efforts. These continued geographies of power build on a spatial imagination of Colombo as the centre—where resources and initiatives come from, and where the powerful, those who can make peace and to whom ordinary people need to demonstrate their will for peace, reside. The Tamil struggle and its attempt to create an alternative centre of power in the north-east has not resulted in a rupture of the geographies of civil society power, something that has much to do with the lack of space for independent civil society initiatives in those areas. The peace movement instead has continued to act out the idea of Colombo as the centre, and the north-east as the faraway periphery. The peace movement, or civil society peace work, in Sri Lanka can be interpreted in terms of a centre and periphery, where Sinhalese, middle-class, Colombo-based actors are centrally positioned, while the war-torn north-east and the poor south is peripheralised and not easily reached by NGO peace work, and where people tend to view the NGO peace work 'fad' with suspicion.

A crucial divide in the peace movement—which mirrors the ethnic polarisation and, to some extent, spatial distances in Sri Lanka at large—is the ethnic divide between Sinhalese and Tamils. This is manifested in the fact that more Sinhalese have been able to engage in national peace NGOs, while Tamils often have had to choose less politically sensitive involvements. The different experiences of conflict and war held by Sinhalese and Tamils, and people from the war zone and outside it, are reflected in different definitions of peace. For many Sinhalese, 'living together in peace' is an unproblematic idea, whereas many Tamils fear a peace with continued subordination. This clash of perspectives is a key to the problem of peace work, and points to the fact that dialogue and inter-ethnic harmony can be seen by the weaker party as an attempt to gloss over their grievances.

The idea of the peace movement as predominantly Sinhalese, male, Colombo-based, Christian and English-speaking is partly a stereotype nurtured, for instance, by counter movements and critics. Nevertheless, the difficulty the peace movement faces bridging the different divides in Sri Lankan society poses questions about the inclusive ambition of the movement and about its legitimacy, as it claims to voice the concerns of the 'people'. In civil society, peace work, identity groups that are traditionally 'dominant' thus speak out on behalf of the subordinate 'other' (Tamils, war victims, the rural masses). This enables the interests of these groups to be heard (for example, as Tamils cannot always freely engage politically, and village people do not easily have a voice in national politics), but has sometimes been criticised as misdirected.

The imbalance between the centre and periphery in peace work has serious implications for the legitimacy and efficiency of civil society peace building. Counter-movements (most importantly the Sinhala nationalist movement) accuse civil society peace organisations for 'brainwashing the people', and being motivated by the lavish incomes generated by foreign aid. The fear of outside intervention (foreign donors as a continuation of a history of intrusion—from South India, from colonial powers and from the Western world), and the perceived threat to traditional Sinhala values and to the Buddhist religion is central to the Sinhala nationalist discourse. Peace NGOs' strong dependency on foreign funds and their good relations with foreign diplomats are looked upon with much suspicion. Efforts to break the polarisation between a centre and a periphery in Sri Lankan society—including in civil society—are hampered by the structures through which foreign development assistance is channelled. The Colombo centrality established during Sri Lankan colonial and post-independence history is reinforced by the Colombo-based nature of foreign donor agencies.

When civil society actors do peace work, they are locked into the structure where Colombo actors provide leadership, power and money, and desperately try to reach out to the grassroots of the marginal areas whose attitudes are to be changed. The Colombo-initiated, foreign-funded attempts at fostering pro-peace attitudes can easily be interpreted as a continuation of the civilising mission of the colonial past. The criticism levelled against NGOs in such a perspective becomes a form of resistance to the continued colonial patterns of political, cultural and material subordination, a protest against the Western propagation of neo-liberal economic development and simplistic peace attempts (where an LTTE–government agreement supported by the people is the main goal).

In the peace promoters' attempts to rise above ethnic identity and cultivate cosmopolitan identity positions, a new polarisation can develop; that between peacemakers and 'war mongers'; cosmopolitan (English-speaking, Colombo-based) NGO workers with good international contacts and foreign support, and locals (non-English speakers, without important international contacts and funding), nurturing parochial and nationalist views; between those who gain from globalisation processes and those who do not fit in. It can be argued that the important conflict to solve in Sri Lanka is not the one between Sinhala and Tamil nationalism, but between extreme nationalists (both Tamil and Sinhalese) on the one side, and a cosmopolitan (non-nationalist) position on the other (*cf.* Kaldor 2006). Sinhalese and Tamil extremists (those who are prepared to fight militarily for their nationalist goals) are in fact interdependent—they are not enemies but counterparts; the actions of one side serve to justify counteraction of the other in an endless spiral of violence and hostility. The challenge for peacemakers is not only to involve the ethnic other in dialogue, but even more so to reach out to the 'hardliners' on both sides.

Those who engage in peace building in Sri Lanka thus face both the challenge of bridging ethnic divides, countering enemy images and providing alternatives to extreme nationalist positions, and of bridging the polarisation between a geographical and class-based centre and periphery in Sri Lankan society.

Notes

1. The chapter is based on research carried out for my Ph.D. thesis '*Civil Society in Civil War: Peace Work and Identity Politics in Sri Lanka* (Orjuela 2004), including 122 interviews conducted in Sri Lanka between 1999 and 2002 with leaders of civil society peace organisations and participants in peace

activities, as well as with key actors outside of civil society peace organisations. Complementary follow-up meetings were held in Sri Lanka during 2005 and 2006.

2. The abbreviation stands for his suggested path to peace from Antagonism, through Resonance, Intervention and Action.
3. Interview, eastern Sri Lanka, 2000.
4. Interview, southern Sri Lanka, 2000.
5. Interview, northern Sri Lanka, 2000.
6. Interview, central Sri Lanka, 2000.
7. Interview, northern Sri Lanka, 2000.
8. Interview, northern Sri Lanka, 2002.
9. Interview, northern Sri Lanka, 2002.
10. Interview, 2000.
11. Interview, central Sri Lanka, 2001.
12. Interview, Colombo, 1999.
13. Interview, eastern Sri Lanka, 2000.
14. Interview, Colombo, 1999.
15. Interview, central Sri Lanka, 2000.
16. Interview, central Sri Lanka, 2000.
17. Interview, 1999.
18. Interview, Colombo, 1999.
19. Interview, Colombo, 1999.
20. Interview, Colombo, 2001.
21. Interview, northern Sri Lanka, 2002.
22. Interview, 2000.
23. Interview, Colombo, 1999.

References

Ariyaratne, A.T. (2000). 'Healing Divided Societies: Sri Lankan Experience'. Presentation at Conference on Religion and Culture in Asia Pacific, RMIT University, Melbourne, Australia, 22–25 October.

Balasingham, A. (2001). *A Will to Freedom: An Inside View of Tamil Resistance*. Mitcham: Fairmax Publishing.

Forut Sri Lanka (2001). 'Capacity Building of Civil Society in the Most Conflict Affected Areas of Sri Lanka'. Unpublished report, Forut. Colombo.

Goodhand, J., N. Lewer and D. Hulme (1999). *NGOs and Peace Building: Sri Lanka Study*. Bradford: Department of Peace Studies, University of Bradford, and Manchester: Institute for Development Policy and Management, University of Manchester.

Hall, S. (1990). 'Cultural Identity and Diaspora', in J. Rutherford (ed.), *Identity: Community, Culture, Difference*, pp. 222–37. London: Lawrence and Wishart.

Hall, S. (1991). 'Old and New Identities, Old and New Ethnicities', in A. King (ed.), *Culture, Globalization and the World-System*, pp. 19–68. London: Macmillan.

Hettige, S.T. (1998). 'Global Integration and the Disadvantaged Youth: From the Centre Stage to the Margins of Society', in S.T. Hettige (ed.), *Globalization, Social Change and Youth*, pp. 71–104. Colombo: German Cultural Institute/ Centre for Anthropological and Sociological Studies.

Jabri, V. (1996). *Discourses on Violence: Conflict Analysis Reconsidered*. Manchester and New York: Manchester University Press.

Kaldor, M. (2006). *New and Old Wars: Organized Violence in a Global Era*. Cambridge and Oxford: Polity Press.

Kandiah, T. (2001). *The Media and the Ethnic Conflict in Sri Lanka* (Marga Monograph Series on Ethnic Reconciliation). Colombo: Marga Institute.

Laclau, E. (1996). 'Universalism, Particularism, and the Question of Identity', in E.N. Wilmsen and P. McAllister (eds), *The Politics of Difference: Ethnic Premises in a World of Power*, pp. 45–58. Chicago: University of Chicago Press.

Lederach, J.P. (1997). *Building Peace: Sustainable Reconciliation in Divided Societies*. Washington, DC: United States Institute of Peace Press.

Malhotra, D.K. and S. Liyanage (2003). 'Assessing the Long-term Impact of "Peace Camps" on Youth Attitudes and Behaviors: The Case of Ethno-political Conflict in Sri Lanka'. Harvard NOM Research Paper 03–24.

Mayer, M. (2000). 'Life Opportunities and Youth Conflict in Sri Lanka. Challenges for Regional Development Planning', in S. Hettige and M. Mayer (eds), *Sri Lanka at Crossroads: Dilemmas and Prospects After 50 Years of Independence*, pp. 156–68. Delhi: Macmillan.

———. (2002). 'Violent Youth Conflicts in Sri Lanka: Comparative Results from Jaffna and Hambantota', in S.T. Hettige and M. Mayer (eds), *Sri Lankan Youth: Challenges and Responses*, pp. 208–46. Colombo: Friedrich Ebert Stiftung.

Melucci, A. (1996). 'The Post-modern Revival of Ethnicity', in J. Hutchinson and A.D. Smith (eds), *Ethnicity*, pp. 367–70. Oxford/New York: Oxford University Press.

Ministry of Finance and Planning (2005). 'Sri Lanka: New Development Strategy: Framework for Economic Growth and Poverty Reduction'. Discussion Paper, Colombo, May.

Nash, C. (2002). 'Cultural Geography: Postcolonial Cultural Geography', *Progress in Human Geography*, 26(2): 219–30.

Orjuela, C. (2004). *Civil Society in Civil War: Peace Work and Identity Politics in Sri Lanka*. Göteborg: Padrigu.

Perera, N. (1999). 'Colonialism and National Space: Representations of Sri Lanka', in S. Gamage and I.B. Watson (eds), *Conflict and Community in Contemporary Sri Lanka: 'Pear of the East' or the 'Island of Tears'?* pp. 23–48. New Delhi: Sage Publications.

Pieterse, J.N. (1997). 'Deconstructing/Reconstructing Ethnicity', *Nations and Nationalism*, 3(3): 365–95.

Polity (2005). 'Tsunami and After: Fault Lines and Shifts in Politics', *Polity*, 2(4): 2.

Sarvananthan, M. (2006). 'Poverty in the Conflict Affected Region of Sri Lanka: An Assessment'. Working Paper 5, Point Pedro Institute of Development.

Richmond, O.P. and H.F. Carey (eds). (2005). *Subcontracting Peace: The Challenges of NGO Peacebuilding*. Aldershot: Ashgate.

Rothman, J. (1997). *Resolving Identity-based Conflict in Nations, Organizations and Communities*. San Francisco: Jossey-Bass Publishers.

Rupesinghe, K. and Naraghi Anderlini (1998). *Civil Wars, Civil Peace: An Introduction to Conflict Resolution*. London: Pluto.

World Bank (2005). *Attaining the Millennium Development Goals in Sri Lanka: How Likely and What Will it Take to Reduce Poverty, Child Mortality and Malnutrition and to Increase School Enrolment and Completion?* Report no. 32134. World Bank, Human Development Unit, South Asia Region. Available online at http://www-wds.worldbank.org/servlet/main?menuPK=64187510&pagePK=64193027&piPK=64187937&theSitePK=523679&entityID=000160016_20050630090640, accessed on 8 October 2008.

8

Rebuilding Lives, Undermining Oppositions: Spaces of War and Peace in the North

Nihal Perera

The way that the Sri Lankan separatist struggle is conceived, discussed, and acted upon by the main parties has constructed an understanding of Sri Lankan society and geography in binary oppositions between Tamils and Sinhalese, the LTTE and government forces, Colombo and Jaffna. The amount of attention given to these binaries in the larger discourse on the 'conflict' privileges the war and the warring parties. Despite these binary geographical imaginations I would like to perceive the conflict in this chapter as a separatist-sovereignist struggle that is one among many processes through which the postcolonial nation-state—including the position of ethnic groups within it—is socially and spatially redefining itself. The last three decades have seen major changes for Sri Lanka, including industrialisation and 'globalisation'. Overall, the country has been transforming since the 1970s from a postcolonial state largely defined by its colonial past to an 'independent' nation-state of its 'own' creation but heavily marked by its colonial and 'traditional' pasts, and influenced by and influencing dynamic global and regional contexts.[1] The descriptions and analyses of this struggle as represented in political statements, military action, newspaper reports, and scholarly work have largely created a totalised view of Sri Lanka defined by two opposite ethnic groups and an 'ethnic conflict' between them.

The trope of the 'ethnic conflict' reifies Sri Lankan society with regard to ethnicity, thus making it common sense to use a ethnicity-based classification of people, and to 'un-mix' the ethnically mixed and hybrid populations within the Sinhala–Tamil duality adopted by the two warring parties (Rajasingham-Senanayake 2002). It also marginalises certain low-income, ethnic, and religious groups, as well as certain gender and class politics that the sign of 'ethnicity' fails to register. The goal of this chapter is to explore other narratives and their correspondent spatialities that lie beyond and in the interstices of this hegemonic ethnic duality.

As the introduction to this volume highlights, space is central to the separatist struggle: territorial claims presume a direct link between a homogeneous Tamil group, and a particular territory identified as the Tamil Eelam. In this chapter, I use Tamil to refer to Sri Lankan Tamils. At the same time, the sovereignists believe in the inviolability of the sovereign territory of a Sri Lanka geographically cognate with the whole island. The struggle thus presumes a geographical determinism. Yet social space—including the nation and Eelam—is neither natural, nor authentic or static, but is socially produced through messy and complex historical processes of contestation, collaboration, accommodation, and negotiation. Inspired by Lefebvre's (1991) seminal work on spaces perceived, conceived, and lived (Perera 1998a), the study explores how social and material spaces are formed, transformed, contested, and adapted. The chapter investigates the unfolding relationships between space and society in the north to pose questions about this ethnic binary, and the larger discourse of conflict built upon the totalisation of this duality. It argues that certain spaces in the north are much more diverse and hybrid than the binary imaginations suggest.

With regard to scholarly work on violence in Sri Lanka, Rogers et al. (1998) highlight three principal strands of thought: historical-revisionist, crowd-centred, and victim-centred scholarships. Despite its richness, this literature lacks well-developed engagements with the role of space in the separatist–sovereignist conflict. These narratives largely tend to treat space as a given or as a container of social action, thus fixing and depoliticising it.Select geographers such as C.M. Madduma Bandara and G.H. Peiris have attempted to apply their physical and ecological frameworks to explain and solve the conflict, but have not questioned the hegemonic duality or examined the conflict from a social production of space standpoint. In keeping with the themes of this book then, this chapter speaks to this gap; it examines the separatist–sovereignist struggle from a spatial standpoint.

It also adopts a vantage point of the 'weak', particularly the inhabitants of the region. With regard to 'weapons of the weak', James Scott (1985) stresses that the relatively powerless typically avoid direct symbolic confrontation with authorities, but engage in 'infrapolitics' using ordinary weapons such as foot-dragging and false compliance that require little or no coordination or planning, and often represent a form of individual self-help. These infrapolitics can be conceived as forms of creative inscription and interstitial articulation. As Homi Bhabha (1994: 1–2) emphasises:

> What is theoretically innovative, and politically crucial, is the need to think beyond narratives of originary and initial subjectivities and to focus on those moments or processes that are produced in the articulation of cultural differences. These 'in-between' spaces provide the terrain for elaborating strategies of selfhood—singular or communal—that initiate new signs of identity, and innovative sites of collaboration, and contestation, in the act of defining the idea of society itself.

Thinking past, or perhaps prior to, the sign of 'resistance' Goh (2002: 202) writes, 'People... always struggle within their own immediate contexts of constraints and opportunities to produce a meaningful life with their own particular values and goals.' As I have demonstrated elsewhere, while the 'weak' inhabit spaces assigned to them by the main political actors, they also produce their own (subversive) spaces (Perera 2002a, 2002b). The spaces of those who live through the separatist struggle are not determined by this struggle alone, but are built through various responses to the context that arise at a tangible scale as part of the process of trying to make the space through which they live meaningfully unto their own lives. Those who live in the war zone both adapt themselves to the social and spatial contexts, and transform space to suit their own needs and practices.

This chapter, thus, focuses on the transformative capacity of the less powerful to effect spatial change (*cf.* Ashcroft et al. 2002), and the impact that everyday practices have had on shaping social space and the built environment (*cf.* Smith and Tardanico 1989). Building on bell hooks' (1990) idea of 'home-places', conceived as 'safe' places that act as positions to negotiate worlds from, Cathrine Brun (2001) argues that re-territorialisation may be understood as the way internally-displaced and local people establish new or expanded networks and cultural practices that define spaces of daily life. Similarly, this chapter investigates how spaces are adopted, adapted, and transformed by examining the changing geographies of war as instigated by the LTTE, and to some extent the government forces, and how people on the ground act upon these geographies. The central question then is, what other spaces and spatial structures have been created beyond, besides and in the interstices of a discursively dominant Sinhala–Tamil duality?

As I examine the spaces in a war zone, it is clear that I am unable to collect sufficient data to map a 'total' geography produced by the LTTE and the people. Neither is this my intention. My objective is to begin a process of mapping out the basic contours of select spaces and spatial structures produced outside and within the interstices of the discursively hegemonic ethnic duality, and thereby make a strong case for the significance of other spaces that lay outside and in the cracks of Sri Lanka's hegemonic binary imaginations. The purpose is not to ameliorate the condition of the 'powerless' who live the struggle by granting them speech or space; quite the contrary. As Gayatri Chakravorty Spivak (2000) points out, such a claim encounters two significant problems: a logo-centric assumption of cultural solidarity among a heterogeneous people, and a notoriously problematic dependence on Western intellectuals to 'speak for' the subaltern condition. Instead, implicit in this chapter is a sense that critical academic discourses that question the above dualities can acknowledge the social agency and the spaces created by those who live in the conflict areas, at times displacing dominant narratives and spatialities, but without losing track of the tensions highlighted by Spivak or descending into a 'voluntarism' of the people. I shall first map out the new spatial duality constructed by the LTTE, both following its separatist agenda and displacing a postcolonial Colombo–Jaffna binary. And then I will highlight some of the burgeoning spaces and hybrid spatial structures of the north performed and inscribed by people.

Remapping Postcolonial Geographies

The ethnic binary is spatially represented as a Colombo–Jaffna opposition. In this paper, I use Jaffna for the city; the Jaffna region and the peninsula will be so mentioned. Ironically, the separatist war itself has displaced the hegemonic geographical imagination of a Tamil homeland, particularly the primacy of Jaffna city and peninsula, the Colombo–Jaffna binary, its hierarchy and directionality. The government has held Jaffna for over a decade now, but is still fighting to bring the north (northern region) under its control. In the meantime, the LTTE has negotiated a territory in the Wanni and created its own spatial structure. This section investigates the alternative spaces, the spatial structure, and the landscape that contest the Colombo–Jaffna duality.

The hegemonic Sinhala–Tamil binary is largely an elite construction of the late 1920s and early 1930s. Yet its spatiality has been vague. The Tamil homelands conceived since the 1920s by leaders such as Ponnambalam Arunachalam and S.J.V. Chelvanayakam were largely social and lacked a well-defined spatiality. Tamil ethno-politics was more focused on the rights of the Tamils. The homeland idea was always present in the discourse, but largely as the electorate from which to draw political power and an area to be protected from Sinhalese encroachments. As the discourses suggest, the cognitive maps of the Tamil leadership loosely envisaged Tamil space as Jaffna-centric. Yet the Tamils did not represent a single community. The Ceylon Tamil League founded in 1922 was largely limited to the Jaffna peninsula; Jeyaratnam Wilson (1994) stresses that even the enormous reputation of Arunachalam was not sufficient to bring the Tamil population from the Northern and Eastern Provinces under one banner. The Tamil United Liberation Front (TULF) not only assumed leadership, but also brought the idea of an independent state to the centre of its campaign in 1976. Still the physical delineation of this social imagination continued to be vague.

As Henri Lefebvre (1991: 54) argues, 'A revolution [a major social transformation] that does not produce new space has not realized its full potential.' The leaders' response to the vague physicality of the Tamil homeland was to ethnicise the colonial maps, making colonial provinces represent ethnic groups. The hegemony achieved by colonial maps in Sri Lanka is indicated in the postcolonial adoption of colonially inscribed provinces, districts and their capitals as culturally and politically neutral objective facts (Perera 1998a, 1998b). As the Tamil political parties relied on the rural voters for power, their imagination was centred upon the electorate. Postcolonial governments have modified and redrawn the electoral map, but within the larger, extant colonial framework of territorial division. Yet electoral power was uneven, and the de facto Tamil territory consisted of a core and a periphery with the political power concentrated in the Jaffna peninsula and reducing with distance from the core, but with spotty concentrations of power in select electorates. Hence, the homeland was demarcated by a frontier very different to the imagination of homogeneous modern states defined by boundaries.

The LTTE, in contrast, paid more attention to the territory of Eelam and produced physical maps. It, too, relied on colonial divisions and faced substantial incongruencies between the social and physical aspects of Eelam. The LTTE created its Eelam primarily out of the northern and Eastern Provinces, and the Puttalam district in the Northwestern Province (see Figure 8.1). It too was ambiguous regarding space. This is evident in how the significant Tiger leader Kittu (Sathasivam Krishnakumar) defined Tamil Eelam in 1990: 'Take a map of the island. Take a paint brush and paint all the areas where Sri Lanka has bombed and launched artillery attacks during these past several years. When you have finished, the painted area that you see—that is Tamil Eelam' (Satyendra 1993).

FIGURE 8.1
Areas Claimed and Controlled by the LTTE

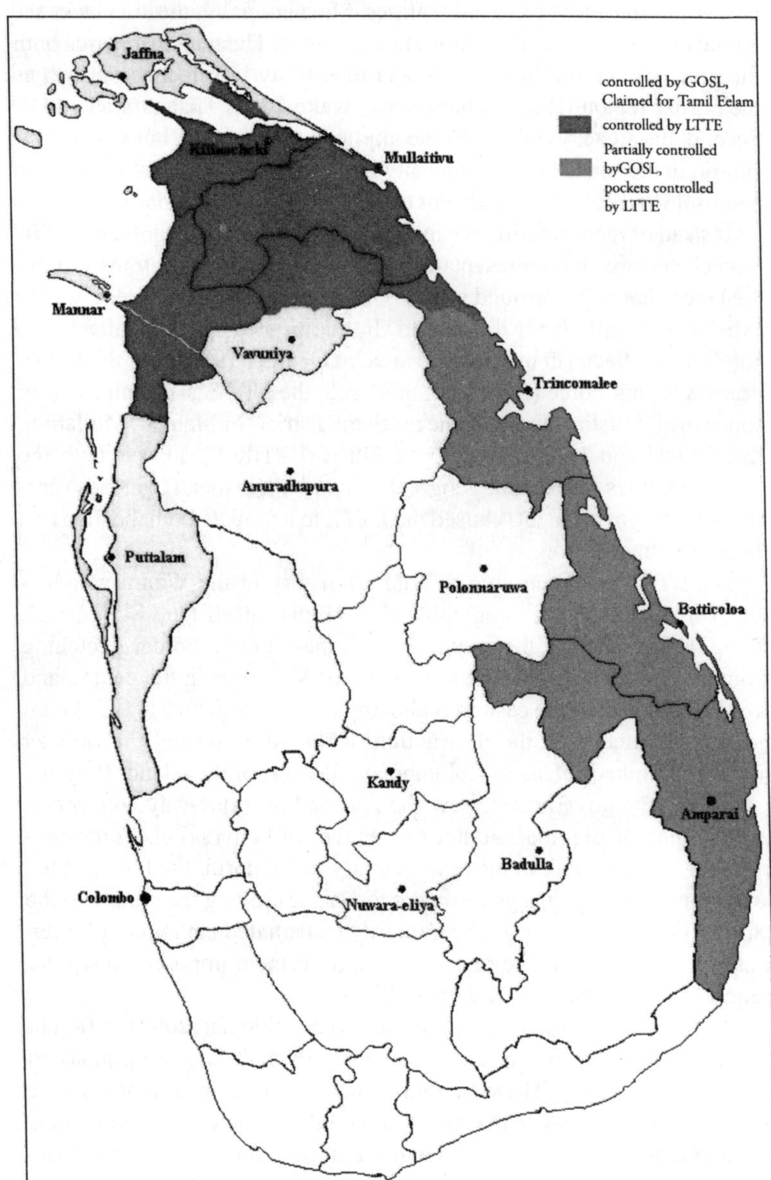

Source: Wikipedia.

Despite having a 'clear' map, there are significant incongruencies between the social and spatial concepts of the Eelam, and also between the representation and the ground realities. Most crucially, the area lacks the ethnic exclusivity that the ethnic state assumes. The map disregards both the diversity within the territory and the mixity in select areas such as the border region (Rajasingham-Senanayake 2002; Thangarajah 1995). Second, the area not only lacks the implied homogeneity, but is also concentric in the sense that the intensity of Tamil-ness is almost total in the peninsula and either non-existent or very thin at the boundaries.

Instead of reconsidering the map, the LTTE opted to negotiate the difference between the representation and the represented by transforming the latter, that is, the ground realities. A notorious LTTE strategy was to expel non-Tamils from the region. In addition to sporadic attacks on non-Tamil villages in the claimed area, in October 1990, after the Indian Peace Keeping Force (IPKF) left in March, the LTTE issued an eviction notice to all Muslims living in the northern districts of Mannar, Mullativu, Kilinochchi and Jaffna: leave or be killed (UTHR 1991). Yet both the ground realities (the extant geographies) and other social agencies (particularly the government) caused the LTTE to negotiate both the map and the larger imagination.

The LTTE has been able to hold a territory in the Wanni which is much smaller than the geography of the Eelam itself (see Figure 8.1). It begins just south of the peninsula with the southern border stretching from Mannar on the west coast, to north of Vavuniya in the centre, and Kokkuthuduwai on the eastern seaboard (Tamilnation 2007). The Wanni became isolated with the destruction of the A9 road and the railway line which linked Jaffna to Colombo and the rest of the island. Both the LTTE and the government view the A9 road as a one-way connection that facilitates Colombo's authority over the northern region. As the government used this link to move its military to the north, the LTTE opted to use landmines against government forces, destroying the roads and the railway lines in the region. The militarily instantiated isolation of Wanni was complemented by the restrictions of movement imposed on regular people by both the LTTE and the military.

The 'closed economy' (especially between 1990 and 2002), different taxes, laws and justice systems introduced by the LTTE gave substance to the de facto geo-body. The separation is highly evident in the maintenance of the old time zone when the rest of the country changed it several times, the adoption of a border tax, and a different no-building zone (200 m as opposed to the national norm of 100 m) in tsunami-hit areas. The tax system, for example, was formalised and justified by engaging in public works projects—like road construction, for example—more vigorously during the truce. This geo-body is not congruent with the maps of the Eelam or the combined Northern and Eastern Provinces within which the government once offered to devolve political power. Instead, it has resulted from the military power of the warring parties.

Along with carving out a territory on the ground and negotiating who will inhabit it, the LTTE has also transformed the regional structure. As part of its fight against the military's dominance over the city, it has deliberately sought to undermine Jaffna's power in the region. In effect, the LTTE has displaced the centrality of both Jaffna and the peninsula with regard to the imaginations of the Tamil homeland.

Jaffna is a European colonial product and home to Westernised, middle-class Tamils, and Tamil parliamentarians. Its coloniality is marked by the continued importance of its location near the lagoon as an external entry point to the peninsula and its grid-like urban layout. Most institutional buildings in the city such as schools and administrative buildings are largely from the British colonial period, built in neo-classical and gothic architectural styles. In positioning Jaffna as a regional centre, colonial authorities also shaped its hinterlands and the spatial structure of the region. This is particularly evident in its radial road connections to all corners of the northern shore of the peninsula, with a fort at the centre to defend the city (see Figure 8.2).

FIGURE 8.2
The Fort and Its Breach

Source: Author.

Jaffna was the centre of the postcolonial Tamil leadership. The most significant monument to it, the Chelvanayakam Column, was built in the city (see Figure 8.3). It was also the city that Sinhala communalists opted to attack and the government desired to recapture. The LTTE also used the fort. After the government takeover in 1995, the LTTE began to develop an alternative. While the government was struggling to reproduce the city's centrality, the LTTE effectively displaced it. The LTTE's failure to recapture the city has thus had little consequence to its struggle.

FIGURE 8.3
Formal (Colonial) Landscapes

Source: Author.

Even before the government takeover of Jaffna, the LTTE did not afford much strategic value to the city. It concentrated on Nallur, the capital of the last (Tamil) kingdom, Nallu Rajadhani—which is similar to Kandy for the Sinhalese—and the outlying areas. Functionally and symbolically, Nallur is today the city of the sacred Kandaswamy Kovil (Hindu temple) located about 4 km to the north-east of Jaffna. In contrast to rebuilding the Chelvanayakam Column by the authorities, the LTTE paid attention to Nallur and other parts of the peninsula such as Valvettithurai and Chavakacheri. Even during the truce, P. Amaratunga, Director of Architecture in Sri Lanka's Central Engineering Consultancy Bureau (CECB), suggested that the LTTE managed to steer to Tellipalai the major cancer hospital that the government wanted to build in Jaffna (see Note 2). The memorial of the martyr Lt Col. Thileepan who died after a 12-day hunger strike protesting the occupation of the IPKF and Kittu are also in Chavakacheri. This way the LTTE have built its own symbolic landscapes outside of Jaffna city, thus displacing the centrality of Jaffna (personal communications with Gopalakrishnan Kalaeswaran, January 15, 2006).

Regionally, the LTTE developed its own urban structure with its dual centre—Kilinochchi and Mullaitivu—in the Wanni. Killinochchi became the unofficial capital of the 'Tiger Territory' in 2000 after it was captured along with a large area occupied by the Sri Lankan army (Dissanayaka 2004). Unlike Jaffna, which was externally produced through colonial encounter, Kilinochchi's significance grew from within the region, as a result of separatist resistance. Further establishing its position, the LTTE used the cessation of hostilities (2002–06) to develop the city and the Wanni region around it (Bulathasinghala 2005). Yet the military and political command centre in Mullaitivu is largely a hideout invisible to many. It represents the LTTE's status as rebel group and not a ruling government. Unlike national capitals that impress its subjects, these are command centres from which the LTTE's authority is exercised and expanded beyond the Wanni through cadres operating in a clandestine landscape. Thus, the LTTE effectively displaced both the centrality of Jaffna city and the significance of the Jaffna peninsula by making Kilinochchi and Mullaitivu its capitals, and the Wanni the heartland of its struggle.

Moreover, the LTTE has also produced new social practices. An exemplary spatialisation of such practices is the grand *mahavira* cemetery in Kopay where fallen fighters are buried (see Figure 8.4). It is maintained to a high standard and profile, indicating that it is one of the most significant symbolic elements in the Tiger landscape. This is one of the structures that the LTTE opted to rebuild after it was destroyed by government forces in 1995. Hindus principally cremate the dead, but the LTTE has begun to attribute special value to the corpses of its fallen cadres. When the government forces entered Jaffna, the LTTE cadres took away and buried the corpse of Thileepan, which was originally donated to the Medical College. They did not want the corpse in enemy hands. Moreover, positions and titles are given to fighters when they pass away. Hence, the cemetery is a means of giving the fallen their 'proper' place, particularly a military

FIGURE 8.4
LTTE Landscapes

Source: Author.

rank and a physical memorial. This spectacle provides an inspiration for living cadres. The cemetery thus plays a highly significant organising and morale-lifting role for the LTTE.

In myriad ways, the LTTE is building its own space and writing its own story in the landscape. Other monuments include those to commemorate watershed events and heroes. These kinds of spatial transformation have displaced the Colombo–Jaffna duality, and former notions of the Tamil homeland, as the LTTE reshape an equally insidious spatialised ethnic polarity in its place wherein Kilinochchi and Mullaitivu displace Jaffna as the centre of the Tamil territory, and the Wanni replaces the Jaffna peninsula as the heartland of the Tamil Eelam. The new landscape that consists of towns, command centres, checkpoints, monuments, and places to perform regular functions and new traditions such as cemeteries contests the landscape of postcolonial Tamil parliamentarians. The military attacks on Kilinochchi and Mullaitivu at the end of 2007 indicate that the government is now engaging the new spatial structure produced by the LTTE. The long-term effects of this spatial politics are unclear, but these emergent spatial structures and practices will have a long-lasting impact. Even if the material traces of conflicts are erased, memory and meaning will influence the future of the landscape.

Rebuilding Lives/Displacing Binaries: Everyday Practice and Emergent Geographies

As the government and the LTTE battle for power and remap the region, people in the north—and the east—have continued to rebuild their lives and subsequently transform space. For those who live in the region, the principal damage is to livelihood. As they adapt their social practices to the context of war and create new practices to fulfil their needs and desires, they develop another layer of social space. This day-to-day geography that materialises on a dwelling scale and shapes both urban and regional scales is not congruent with government or LTTE spatial structures: at times these structures are reinforced and at other times they are contested and/or displaced. This section focuses on these ordinary spaces developed in the north during war, at dwelling, urban, and regional scales. It teases out a 'people's geography' of sorts.

At the immediate level, the conflict made Tamil areas in the north, east, and Colombo materially and perceptually unsafe and unstable for Tamils. After a brief period of relative stability under the LTTE, the IPKF–LTTE war (1987–90) destroyed the region's civilian life and space (Swamy 1994; see Figure 8.5). The instability continued for over 10 years until the ceasefire of 2002, with two brief respites in 1990 and 1995 (Rogers et al. 1998). The current war that began in 2006 is now disrupting the region again. I focus my investigation on the period prior to the breach of the ceasefire in 2006.

FIGURE 8.5
Checkpoints and Voluntary Destruction

Source: Author.

The immediate reaction of those who were concerned about their safety and could afford to leave was to escape the region. By 1992, about 300,000 Tamils had sought asylum in the West, and 200,000 in India (NT 1992; UTHR 1993). Once the strong memories of the 1983 riots subsided, many Tamils also migrated to the Colombo area, first to Wellawatta and later to new areas, especially to Ja-ela and Mabole area, north of Colombo. In 2001, there were over 6,500 Sri Lankan Tamils compared to 15,300 Sinhalese in the Wattla–Mabola Urban Council area. As part of the process, the population of the north-east dropped by almost half within five years from 1.7 million in 1987 to 900,000 in 1992 (NT 1992). The population of the Jaffna peninsula dropped by one-fifth, from 743,000 in 1981 to an estimated 589,000 in 2004 (Department of Census and Statistics, Sri Lanka 1982; District Secretariat 2005a, 2005b in Satyendra 1993).

The remaining population is largely displaced and their livelihood highly disrupted. By July 1990, there were 880,000 people displaced in over 600 camps; Jaffna became a temporary home to 355,000 people in 352 camps (US Committee for Refugees 1991). The war also displaced people of other ethnicities, particularly Sinhalese and Muslims, many of whom were forcibly removed. By 1992, the lost employment in Jaffna district was well over 100,000 jobs (NT 1992; UTHR 1993). In addition to the reduced buying power of the people, the government imposed embargoes, and the LTTE taxation limited the amount of goods entering the region, further increasing the prices. The taxation was reinforced during the ceasefire.

The majority of the people had moved in and out of their homes, hometowns, and refugee camps at various turns of war, peace, and truce, finding safe places and better living conditions. Saving their own lives and building livelihoods are far more central to these moves than taking a side in the war. One of the biggest movements in the region was the exodus from Jaffna that occurred before the government forces entered the city in 1995. The LTTE instigated a panic situation encouraging a large proportion of people to move out with them to the Wanni. Then, in his annual November speech, Prabhakaran exuded: 'We are relieved that our people have safely escaped from the military siege and the political trap behind it' (Swamy 2006: 256). Despite the absorption of this people's reaction within the separatist discourse, most people eventually returned home. The exodus had more to do with people's concern for safety, security, and basic needs than supporting the LTTE. People returning to Jaffna had little to do with any endorsement for government control or sovereignty.

Building Homes

'Returning home' is common desire of those involuntarily displaced. In a particular village in the Wanni, Anna Lena Lösnäs (2005) found that Muslims in it did not trust the LTTE, but still chose to return to live under its control because they wanted to return 'home'. The government also has security zones of about 3,000 ha that have been emptied of people (District Secretariat 2005a). While the coastal belt across Palali, Kankasanturai, and Karainagar, and some thoroughfares, belong to the highest level, towns like Alaveddy and Mavidapuram belong to the next level largely because of nearby military camps. In addition to the designation of the zone, the rumours that there are landmines discourage people from moving back. According to former Alaveddy resident Kalaeswaran,[3] about half the population of Alaveddy has moved back. The 'displaced' Tamils too wish to return home, even though their houses are close to military camps. Sinanona—of a 'displaced' Tamil family at Vinayagapuram, for example—is happy that her family is close to schools, health, and similar facilities, but they can only travel with special passes and frequently face harassment by the military as suspected terrorists. Her wish is to return to her own home (Refugees International 2001).

As the region (context) has changed dramatically, even 'home' has been displaced; for many, the original home is not safe. Home, or familiar space, more generally, is a nostalgia that exists in the memory. The displaced, whether at home or away, have worked hard simply to live and develop a livelihood, identity, and a place within new contexts, as illustrated in Brun's (2005) analysis of Muslim women and LTTE women cadres. The loss of familiar livelihood due to displacement encourages these women to look for new opportunities. One major consequence of this process is the change in patterns of gender control. Many young Tamil women who do not have sufficient social capital to escape violence, by, for example, marrying within the global diaspora, view joining the LTTE as the better local alternative. Many Muslim women who are not otherwise 'qualified' to apply for political asylum abroad have opted to work abroad. Those who can afford to pay employment agencies prefer to go abroad in order to restore assets and rebuild lives than to work locally as agricultural labour. Transforming extant gender roles, many Muslim women are thus playing a greater role in income-generating activities, largely abroad, while Tamil women with low social capital are increasingly involved in military activities locally. Given these new social roles, the northern women are radically transforming their identities and spaces.

At the level of the built environment and shelter, a large number of families live in spaces they see as 'usable', behind the ruined structures as well as quickly built minimum shelters. The human agency in creating social space is evident in how they adapt to the ruined environment, as well as how they adapt the remaining environment to their highly reduced needs (see Figure 8.6). In a situation where the government (national or rebel) pays very little attention to the needs of the people and NGOs are unable to help much, the people have provided their own shelters and more basic spaces by improvising in their (and others') ruined houses, moving into relatives' houses, personalising refugee dwellings, and building temporary shelters.

Many people do not have the luxury of returning home. The majority of those internally displaced were first confined to refugee camps. These camps are shelters of the most basic and temporary nature; they lack water and sanitary facilities. Even after a generation, many still live in temporary shelters. Yet most of them attempt to improve their dwellings, and sometimes build smaller individual shelters of their own. One major location is around the Jaffna railway station: it is allegedly landmined, but people live in self-built housing. By developing particular social interactions that intersect at their present location, they transform the new (and old) locations into their own places (*cf.* Brun 2001); as they familiarise these unfamiliar locations, they also develop their identity in relation to these spaces. The desire to go beyond the minimum shelter provision and regularise life at a domestic scale is evident in the repaired and reconstructed buildings, as well as neatly piled stacks of salvaged material from destroyed houses that testify to the ongoing rebuilding processes (see Figure 8.6).

FIGURE 8.6
Ruined Environments: Living and Reconstruction

Source: Author.

Rebuilding City and Community

In addition to the rebuilding and development of personal lives, the conducting of social and economic interactions such as buying and selling have helped (re)produce neighbourhoods and cities. All towns and small urban centres where people live maintain places of commerce, at least a set of boutiques, along with the social relations they represent. The cities and neighbourhoods so reproduced have their own share of ambivalence: they are not different to what they used to be, but they are not the same either. I shall first focus on Jaffna city.

With a population of 135,000 in 1995, demographically Jaffna is still a second-tier city in Sri Lanka after Colombo (City Population 2006).[4] However, the composition of its population has changed. Jaffna has been home to the educated, economically better-off, and Westernised people in the region. Their lives were intimately connected to the functioning of the formal society and economy. Hence, this is the city that was most affected by the war. Yet, as its upper and middle stratas had the capability, a substantial number of them moved overseas or to Colombo. Similarly, a significant proportion of businessmen of Chavakacheri origin, who had a substantial presence in Jaffna, moved their capital 'back' to their hometown—about 20 km east of Jaffna.

Although the size has not changed much, the composition of the population has changed during the war. It has lost a larger proportion of educated, Westernised, and entrepreneurial people who had the social capital (and opted to leave). The reduction in the original population has been matched by the migrants who moved into the city in search of a better place. Most notably, the business-oriented '*tivu* people' (the islanders) from the surrounding islands where the economic life is badly affected have moved in to fill part of the investors' gap. Making use of the relative stability during the 2002–06 truce and the opening of roads, the city regained a strong population and economic base. Jaffna continues to be the primary city in the peninsula.

Moreover, it is a nationally and internationally significant city. Although the roles have changed, various national and international interventions have maintained and revived the downtown area. As the city is of strategic significance to the government, it spends on limited public infrastructure necessary to keep the city and the government-controlled areas safe and functioning, and to win the support of the local people. In addition, it also maintains government functions, connections with Colombo and public transportation, including the use of the air force base in Palali as the airport for civilian flights services by Lionair and Serendib Express. Small improvements in services such as these have substantially upgraded the quality of life in Jaffna. Being the government centre in the region, it also attracts foreign missions and NGOs. Jaffna thus has a large public sphere and public space. The intervention of institutions, organisations, and people is key to the reconstruction of day-to-day life. Public amenities such as the city administration, schools, university, library, and market are maintained by the government. The remaining local leaders, the business community, and upper classes with stakes in their businesses, schools, or private residences have used their limited leverage to find resources from various sources, including NGOs. Despite the damaged buildings and environments in surrounding areas, there is not much destruction in the city centre. Most buildings are reasonably well maintained.

The entrepreneurs have also striven to maintain the economy. They have attempted to serve the region during a long period of isolation. As the north was isolated due to the war and the embargo, investors attempted to produce basic provisions such as soap and aerated water within the region. While many of these factories are in ruins, some still operate. The ceasefire increased the amount of visitors to Jaffna city and the peninsula, and investors were quick to identify new opportunities. As foreigners, members of the diaspora, and other Sri Lankans began to visit the area during the truce, a tourist industry began to capitalise on the economic opportunity. Although few in number, guest houses have sprung up, mainly for foreigners, and are largely located in the area of foreign missions. Old cars—particularly Austins—that represent Jaffna's isolation have become fashionable. Like the landscape of disaster in which they are driven, these old cars exist, now, for the consumption of tourists. The landscape of war and the images of economic stagnation are being commodified.

Nevertheless, new buildings are a rarity, and Jaffna continues to be substantially defined by the architecture of its colonial past. Main institutional buildings, including the City Hall and the university, were built during the colonial period. Outside the city centre, the conflict has also preserved 'traditional' buildings with courtyards, entrance structures, *thinnai*s (verandas), and Dutch-influenced houses with gables and verandas. With regard to dwellings, traditional courtyard houses with traditional entryways and Dutch-influenced houses with open verandas are still in use (Mayoornathan 2002) (see Figure 8.7). The stagnant economy has done much to conserve these climatically suitable and culturally identifiable built forms. All of this makes Jaffna a unique city in Sri Lanka with regard to its built environment and society.

FIGURE 8.7
Courtyard Houses

Source: Author.

With regard to personal identity, although wealth is unevenly distributed, the display of wealth in the landscape is not conspicuous; the landscape, in fact, is conservative. Except for a few large houses built during the colonial period, almost none of the others visually stand out. The houses are more or less functional places to 'live in', and Jaffna citizens have not 'modernised' these as in Colombo, nor have they added embellishments (Arasaratnam 1994: 28). According to Jaffna resident and architect Shanthini Balasubramanium (in a personal communication with the author, 2005), the lack of modernisation is not a direct effect of the war. Even before the war, the people of Jaffna did not invest much money in building grand houses. Savings usually took the form of land, a house to live in, houses for children, and gold. The war has made security an extra reason for conservative building practices. In addition to the fear of looting, many people fear that display of wealth might attract the undue attention of the LTTE and government forces.

While being conservative, Jaffna's landscape is also dynamic. In addition to rebuilding, to a very limited degree new construction and the renovation of public buildings also take place. Although this may not be highly apparent, the process of modernisation continues in the midst of conflict, but incrementally, at a slow pace. The movement of goods, people, and ideas during the truce began to transform the city. The most apparent new buildings are evident outside of Jaffna; the market complex and private commercial buildings, particularly the Millennium Restaurant in Chavakacheri stand out (see Figure 8.8). With blue glass curtain walls, this building does not demonstrate much conservativeness. Two main restaurants in Kilinochchi also demonstrate the use of imported materials and building styles from Colombo.

These 'modern' buildings, when taken in isolation, look very much like those in Colombo or similar cities around the world, and they perform

FIGURE 8.8
Emerging Environments

Source: Author.

similar economic roles. Hence, the 'people's struggle', as read from the business landscape, is by no means simply a rejection of Colombo, but instead a form of emulation and competition with Colombo and other 'large' cities in the region. However, the inflow of ideas, particularly from the Tamil diasporic community, struggles against the censorship and constraints of war. Transcultural ideas can be seen in the investments made by the diasporic community in the Tamil neighbourhoods of Colombo: a recent trend being to build luxury condominiums targeting Tamil customers. These also bear names like Sellamaal Court, making them modern and Tamil simultaneously. This way, the overall landscape is made up of components that represent destruction, reproduction, and growth. The largely destroyed environment is mixed with buildings that continue to be maintained, and is punctuated with temporary housing and more permanent modern buildings that imply possible future trends.

Shaping the Region

In developing livelihoods, inhabitants in the north have also been making new urban centres and a regional structure in the cracks, and the margins of the same systems created by the government and the LTTE. While Jaffna and Killinochchi have become significant nodes in the system, a series of towns such as Chavakacheri, Mullaitivu, Pathukudiyirippu, and Point Pedro have developed the second tier of a larger settlement structure of the north.

Chavakacheri is a town that has produced entrepreneurs who had invested in Jaffna. Many entrepreneurs who did not emigrate moved their capital to Chavakacheri and also made new investments in the town. It was heavily damaged by the war; for example, its hospital is totally destroyed. Yet, with the investment of more capital, it has become the other significant town in the peninsula. In this sense, it replaces other secondary towns such as Kankasanturai. Unlike in the more subdued Jaffna, the new investments are represented in Chavakacheri's 'modernising' built environment, as stressed previously.

Some of the towns that managed to avoid large-scale destruction, particularly to their infrastructure, also belong to this tier. For example, Pathukudiyirippu, about 20 km from Mullaitivu, still has its historic landscape, and the hospital is intact. It is relatively more vibrant in comparison to Mullaitivu. It also benefits from the instability surrounding Mullaitivu. Less damage to infrastructure makes it a desirable place for people who strive to reconstruct their lives and livelihoods. The population increases in towns such as Valvettithurai and Mullaitivu highlight that they are perceived as safe, and more desirable.

Kilinochchi is a substantial city. Before the LTTE established its centre, Kilinochchi was not much of a town; most of its 65,000 people had fled to the jungles. According to Kilinochchi Government Agent R. Rasanayagam, over 90 per cent of its population are displaced people. With outside agencies such as the Peace Secretariat and other major LTTE institutions located in it, it is the visible locus of the LTTE's political and administrative machinery. After the truce of 2002, the government provided funds for factories in the city. New buildings are being built in the town; some of these house various LTTE functions, some are built by NGOs, and others by private citizens. The air-conditioned restaurants with tinted glass walls stand as testimony to its modernisation.

In addition to being an administrative and industrial centre, Kilinochchi is also a commercial hub and an active town located on the Colombo–Jaffna road. The city lost its former function as the regional vegetable collection centre to cities such as Vavuniya and Dambulla. The town has electricity during the day, but most live in the dark by night. Yet the people's (civil society's) efforts, on top of those of the LTTE, have turned it into an inhabited and lively city. Shops and restaurants line the main road, and they also sell various food items brought from outside the region. People and institutions are adapting to the conditions of the town, and adapting its environment for their daily practices. The Kilinochchi Central College building, which was bombed leaving a shell with no walls, no windows and no doors, is now operational. According to its Principal, Veerakarthy Rajakulasingham, there were about 1,500 landmines in the playing field when he returned. Now it is a place where about 1,500 students study maths and languages (*Daily News* 2003). The opening of the A9 road, the less-restricted movement of people, and the greater access to goods have all worked in its favour. Its population had risen sharply to 149,000, more than doubling its pre-war dimensions, and matching Jaffna in size.

The biggest town that people have created outside of government and LTTE centres is Vavuniya. Vavuniya and Mullaitivu had the highest annual growth rates of 2.2 per cent per annum for the period of 1981–2001 (Department of Census and Statistics, Sri Lanka 2001). Vavuniya's population grew from 18,500 in 1981 to 53,000 in 2001, and the population of the Vavuniya district almost doubled from 95,500 to 164,000 during that period (City Population 2006). During its 1996 offensive in the Wanni region, the LTTE asked people to leave the town, but its population swelled due to the migration of northerners who wanted to flee the war but did not want to enter Sinhalese areas, and due to others—especially Sinhalese and Muslims—who wanted to do business in this expanding gateway city. Most crucially, its Tamil population increased dramatically.

Vavuniya is thus the town of choice for most people who remained in the region. It is a place with a substantial social and physical infrastructure that can support the rebuilding of lives; it is also the furthest city from the war that is not 'inside' Sinhalese territory. It is safe for Tamils, but quite far from the core LTTE area. It is government-controlled, but not fully. Except for a few interruptions, bus services from the south have operated throughout the conflict period; it has also been linked to the north most of the time. It has, thus, been the nexus between the north and the south.

Ironically, within the context of a struggle to construct 'authentic' ethnic groups, what the people have created in Vavuniya is a mixed city. This is built upon the same city that had a pattern of coexistence that consisted of ethnic and caste-based spatial segregation, counterbalanced and interpolated by social mingling and linguistic hybridity (Rajasingham-Senanayake 2002). Vavuniya is not in the centre of any ethnic territory, but is both a liminal space in between the north and the south, and a hybrid place where the Tamil and Sinhalese lands overlap. It puts into question the validity of an absolute and ethnicised Sinhala–Tamil duality.

During the strife the ethnically mixed town has developed into a gateway and frontier town between north and the south. As it is on the main Colombo–Jaffna highway and because it might be the least 'dangerous' of the towns discussed in this chapter, the opening of the highway has turned the city into a pivotal connection between the north and the south, and a highly desirable place for business. The government has also provided some of the basic infrastructure facilities such as roads, wells, and electricity. Demonstrating its competitiveness, it has taken over some of the collection and distribution of goods from Kilinochchi. The high number of internally displaced persons and the ongoing pass system for movement between government- and LTTE-controlled areas continue to cause hardships for local people. Although less affected by the war compared to northern towns, the constant patrol of army vehicles and heavy security are stark reminders of its location on the frontlines of the war. According to Vavuniya District Secretary, K. Ganesh, the people have begun to feel that there is free movement between government- and LTTE-controlled areas during the truce (Herath 2002). Nonetheless, in response to the war, people have reinforced but redefined its hybridity, ambivalence, and its role as a nexus between the north and the south.

In short, in response to the conditions imposed by the conflict, and to their own needs, people are rebuilding their lives, and in so doing, are creating a whole series of new social spaces and spatial structures. Along with creating living spaces, they have restructured the urban system along the A9 road. Its principal nodes are Jaffna, Killinochchi, and Vavuniya, and the second-tier cities include Chavakacheri, Valvettithurai, Point Pedro, Padikudirippu, and Mullaitivu. Vavuniya, which is located at the most ambiguous location and intersection of Tamil- and Sinhalese-dominated areas, is the defining articulation of people's agency and their intervention into the larger spatial organisation: it defies the notion of 'ethnic conflict' based on absolute and essential Sinhala–Tamil opposition.

Conclusions

The stories and spaces of war and peace are multi-layered, multifaceted, interwoven, and changing. It is impossible to understand these within any simple binary oppositions creating polemical, binarised, and ethnicised understandings that efface the activities of the majority of social actors in the region, that is, regular people. The spaces they produce are much more contested, messy, complex, and ultimately hybrid. For example, there are multiple Tamil–Sinhala binaries: the parliament-based postcolonial duality and the government–LTTE conflict produce and represent different realities and spatialities.

As part of the struggle, many postcolonial spatial discourses have also been inverted. Jaffna has been in government hands for over a decade, but the government is still struggling to bring the north under its control because Jaffna has not proved as strategically powerful as the conventional Colombo–Jaffna duality suggests. Jaffna is no longer the undisputed centre of the north or of the Tamil people.

The LTTE has been accomplishing its own objectives on its own terms. Yet the territory it controls in the Wanni is very different to its map of the Eelam. Despite the neat spatial perceptions and mappings of formal articulations of both the government and the LTTE, the messy spaces of the conflict are defined by the non-contiguous territories held by the government and the LTTE, and the contested spaces within and outside of these landscapes that are lived, performed, and (re)produced anew by people on the ground. In accommodating, building upon, and adapting to the context, less powerful social actors—regular people—have created new spatial and temporal structures within, in the cracks, beyond, and besides those of the separatist–sovereignist struggle. At one level, they have adopted, reinforced, and expanded the spatialities created by the warring parties, for example, in Jaffna, Killinochchi, Mullaitivu, and Mannar. At the same time, these have been undermined and redefined by adapting these to their daily practices. As I have shown in this chapter, the Jaffna peninsula and the city have been subjected to demographic change, and Chavakacheri is developing into a significant, enterprising, and modernising town. The people have also moved into and developed small towns such as Padikudirippu and Point Pedro. Most significant is the people's choice to move away from the war zones to Vavuniya, the southernmost city in the northern region, a liminal space between the north and the south. With Vavuniya becoming a major city in Sri Lanka, a new structure of cities has emerged; it is made up of Jaffna, Killinochchi, Vavuniya, and the second-tier towns such as Chavakacheri, Padikudirippu, and Point Pedro. These new spatialities present new political constraints and possibilities.

The spatial organisation of the north is, therefore, different than what the well-organised hegemonic discourses suggest; it is a palimpsest of spaces negotiated—by the government, by Tamil parliamentarians, by the LTTE, and most importantly by the people—through war as well as through daily social and cultural practices. These cannot easily be captured within mappings that fix and reify a system of (post)colonial provinces and districts, because these spaces simultaneously evidence multiple narratives. It is significant for any analysis to take this multiplicity of space into consideration, and for any development effort in the north to bring these multiple spatial narratives into representation—to show their awkward, tense, but extremely hopeful, coexistence.[5]

Notes

1. For the context of this chapter at large, see Perera (1998a, 1998b).
2. The CECB have led a number of construction projects in Sri Lanka's north and east. In this section I draw on personal conversations with Praneeth Amaratunga, head of the architecture section of the CECB, on 28 December 2007.
3. Gopalakrishnan Kalaeswaran, personal communication, 22 June 2006.
4. Before the war, Jaffna's population was 118,000, and the peninsula had about 750,000 (City Population 2006).
5. I wish to thank Wes Janz, Arijit Sen, Ryan Smith, and the anonymous reviewers for their valuable comments on the manuscript. I also thank Shanthini Balasubramanium, Professor Balasubramanium, Gopalakishnan Kalaeswaran, Praneeth Amaratunga and many local residents who helped me develop a small idea of the larger spatial transformation that is taking shape in the north.

References

Arasaratnam, S. (1994). 'Sri Lanka's Tamils: Under Colonial Rule', in C. Manograran and B. Pfaffenberger (eds), *The Sri Lankan Tamils: Ethnicity and Identity*, pp. 28–53. Boulder, CO: Westview Press.

Ashcroft, Bill, Gareth Griffiths and Helen Tiffin (2002). *The Empire Writes Back: Theory and Practice in Post-colonial Literatures (New Accents)*. London, New York: Routledge.

bell hooks (1990). *Yearning, Race, Gender, and Cultural Politics*. Boston, MA: South End Press.

Bhabha, H.K. (1994). *The Location of Culture*. London and New York: Routledge.

Brun, C. (2001). 'Reterritorializing the Relationship between People and Place in Refugee Studies', *Geografiska Annaler*, 83(B): 15–25.

———. (2005). 'Women in the Local/Global Fields of War and Displacement in Sri Lanka', *Gender, Technology and Development*, 9(1): 57–80.

Bulathasinghala, F. (2005). 'Report: Dateline Jaffna', *Himal: South Asian*, February. Available online at http://www.himalmag.com/2003/february/report_1.htm, accessed 10 December 2005.

City Population (2006). Available online at http://www.citypopulation.de/SriLanka.html, accessed February 2006.

Daily News (2003). 'Kilinochchi Residents Yearn for Peace', 15 November. Available online at http://www.dailynews.lk/2003/11/15/sec03.html, accessed 5 February 2006.

Department of Census and Statistics, Sri Lanka (1982). *Census of Population and Housing: 1981*. Colombo: Government Press.

———. (2001). *Census of Population and Housing 2001*. Available online at http://www.statistics.gov.lk/census2001/index.html, accessed 3 August 2006.

Dissanayaka, T.D.S.A. (2004). *War or Peace in Sri Lanka*. Mumbai: Popular Prakashan.

District Secretariat (2005a). *Statistical Information: Jaffna District*. Jaffna: District Secretariat.

———. (2005b). *Statistical Information: Kilinochchi District*. Kilinochchi: District Secretariat.

Goh, B.L. (2002). *Modern Dreams: An Inquiry into Power, Cultural Production, and the Cityscape in Contemporary Urban Penang, Malaysia*. Ithaca, NY: Southeast Asia Program, Cornell University.

Herath, A. (2002). 'Vavuniya'. Available online at http://www.priu.gov.lk/Vavuniya/Home.htm, accessed 3 August 2006.

Lefebvre, H. (1991). *The Production of Space*. Oxford: Basil Blackwell.

Lösnäs, A.L. (2005). 'Resettlement and Rehabilitation of IDPs in Post-conflict Sri Lanka: A Case Study of a Village in Vanni'. Master's thesis, Lund University, Lund, Sweden.

Mayoornathan, R. (2002). 'Understanding the Architectural Traditions of Jaffna', *Sri Lanka Architect* (special issue on 'War and Architecture'), 104(1): 21–28.

Perera, N. (1998a). *Society and Space: Colonialism, Nationalism, and the Postcolonial Identity in Sri Lanka*. Boulder, CO: Westview.

———. (1998b). 'Territorial Spaces and National Identities: Representations of Sri Lanka', *South Asia*, xx, Special issue on Conflict and Community in Contemporary Sri Lanka: 23–50.

———. (2002a). 'Feminizing the City: Gender and Space in Colonial Colombo', in Sonita Sarker and Esha Niyogi De (eds), *Trans-Status Subjects: Genders in the Globalization of South and Southeast Asia*, pp. 67–87. Durham, NC: Duke University Press.

Perera, N. (2002b) 'Indigenising the Colonial City: Late 19th-Century Colombo and Its Landscape', *Urban Studies: Contested Landscapes, Asian Cities*, 39(9): 1703–21.

Rajasingham-Senanayake, D. (2002). 'Identity on the Borderline: Modernity, New Ethnicities, and the Unmaking of Multiculturalism in Sri Lanka', in N. de Silva, ed., *The Hybrid Island: Culture Crossings and the Invention of Identity in Sri Lanka*, pp. 41–70. Colombo: Social Scientists' Association.

Refugees International (2001). 'IDPs in Sri Lanka: Visual Mission March 2001', *Refugees International*. Availbale online at http://www.refintl.org/files/1900, accessed 10 July 2007.

Rogers, J.D., J. Spencer and J. Uyangoda (1998). 'Sri Lanka: Political Violence and Ethnic Conflict', *American Psychologist*, 53(7): 771–77.

Satyendra, N. (1993). 'Tamil Eelam Struggle for Freedom: Boundaries of Tamil Eelam'. Available online at http://www.tamilnation.org/tamileelam/boundaries/index.htm, accessed 15 December 2007.

Scott, J.C. (1985). *Weapons of the Weak: Everyday Forms of Peasant Resistance*. New Haven, CT: Yale University Press.

Smith, M.P. and R. Tardanico (1989). 'Urban Theory Reconsidered: Production, Reproduction and Collective Action', in M.P. Smith and J.R. Feagin (eds), *The Capitalist City*, pp. 87–110. Cambridge: Basil Blackwell.

Spivak, G.C. (2000). 'The New Subaltern: A Silent Interview', in Vinayak Chaturvedi (ed.), *Mapping Subaltern Studies and the Postcolonial*, pp. 324–40. London: Verso.

Sunday Times, 13 December 1992.

Swamy, M.R.N. (1994). *Tigers of Lanka: From Boys to Guerillas*. Delhi: Konark.

———. (2006). *Inside an Elusive Mind: Prabhakaran*. Colombo: Vijitha Yapa.

Tamilnation. (2007). Available online at http://www.tamilnation.org/tamileelam/defacto/index.htm, accessed 21 January 2007.

Thangarajah, Y. (1995). 'Narratives of Victimhood as Ehnic Identity among the Veddas of the East Coast', in P. Jeganathan and Q. Ismail (eds), *Unmaking the Nation: The Politics of Identity and History in Modern Sri Lanka*, pp. 191–218. Colombo: The Social Science Association.

U.S. Committee for Refugees (1991). 'Sri Lanka: Island of Refugees'. Issue Paper, US Committee for Refugees, Washington, DC.

University Teachers for the Human Rights (UTHR) (1991). 'The Politics of Destruction & the Human Tragedy', Report No. 6. Available online at http://www.uthr.org/Reports/Report6/Report6.htm, accessed 3 August 2006.

———. (1993). 'Rays of Hope Amidst Deepening Gloom', Report No. 10. Available online at http://www.uthr.org/Reports/Report10/Report10.htm, accessed 15 January 2006.

Wilson, A.J. (1994). 'The Colombo Man, the Jaffna Man, and the Batticaloa Man: Regional Identities and the Rise of the Federal Party', in C. Manograran and B. Pfaffenberger (eds), *The Sri Lankan Tamils: Ethnicity and Identity*, pp. 126–42. Colombo: Social Science Association.

9

Fractured Sovereignty: The LTTE's State-Building in an Interconnected World

Øivind Fuglerud

> *It is necessary to distinguish clearly between sabotage, a revolutionary and highly effective method of warfare, and terrorism, a measure that is generally ineffective and indiscriminate in its results, since it often makes victims of innocent people and destroys a large number of lives that would be valuable to the revolution.* (Guevara 1985: 140)

As indicated by the title of this chapter, my wish is to reflect upon the Liberation Tigers of Tamil Eelam's (LTTE's) effort to build a separate Tamil state. Since the early 1980s, Sri Lanka's political agenda has increasingly been dominated by the ongoing conflict between the government of Sri Lanka and the LTTE. The declared goal of the latter is a separate state, Tamil Eelam, comprising the Tamil-speaking parts of Sri Lanka's north-east. At present, the LTTE militarily and politically control large tracts of land in the Wanni. Until recently, they also controlled parts of the Eastern Province. As a result of the ceasefire agreement signed in February 2002, freezing the military situation existing at that time, their control over the Wanni has been strengthened and stabilised. From the LTTE's current administrative centre in Kilinochchi, state-like structures of government are being built. What I will do here is to locate this state building within the framework of a discussion on the nature of states in general, and the situation of postcolonial nation-states at the present time in particular.

Building the LTTE State

In a recent paper first made internationally available on the pro-LTTE website TamilNet,[1] later published through academic channels (Stokke 2006), Kristian Stokke, professor at the University of Oslo, reviews the development of Tamil Eelam. Having been given the official tour provided by the LTTE Peace Secretariat to researchers, Stokke notes in particular the workings of the legal sector: 'It can be observed that the police and judiciary maintain a high degree of rule of law in LTTE-controlled areas' (ibid.: 10). The judiciary operates a system of District Courts in the Wanni and in LTTE-controlled areas of the Eastern Province and Mannar, handling both civil and criminal cases. Police officers are reported to be recruited from the general public, many of them victims of oppression under the Sri Lankan armed forces. The author observes that: 'The manner in which these institutions operate, seem to give them a substantial degree of legitimacy among the Tamil civilian population' (ibid.). Next to the legal sector, 'social welfare is the other state function that has been given a central place in the building of the LTTE state' (ibid.). But Stokke also observes that after the ceasefire in 2002 there has been a new focus on economic development with the establishment of a central Planning and Development Secretariat and a central role given to LTTE-affiliated NGOs like Tamil Rehabilitation Organisation and The Economic Consultancy House (TECH). Stokke discusses these developments within a framework of theory on peace building, which focuses on peace being closely related to 'what is conventionally seen as the three core functions of any modern state: security, welfare and representation' (ibid.: 5). While he admits that in the emerging LTTE state there is 'clearly an overarching emphasis on the question of security' (ibid.), he argues that this has gradually been supplemented with an additional focus on welfare and development. In this, he sees a potential for more democratic forms of representation and governance.

Stokke's presentation raises at least two issues. One is the factual correctness of the information provided. In a sharp rejoinder to Stokke, Tamil academic Muttukrishna Sarvananthan (2006)[2] has rejected Stokke's understanding of what is under construction in areas under LTTE rule. He points out that the situation of the common man in the Wanni is worse now than before the LTTE took control. While the excesses committed by the state security forces could be appealed to courts of law or the

Human Rights Commission, under 'the jungle laws of the LTTE in the Wanni, Tamils living there cannot mutter a word against the irrationality, arbitrariness, and excesses of the security apparatus of the LTTE' (ibid.: 11). With respect to welfare, Sarvananthan argues that the main purposes of LTTE institutions are 'coercing state services to provide employment to family members of their cadres and steal goods from these government welfare services' (ibid.). He also criticises Stokke's reliance on information provided by the LTTE themselves.

The other issue, which I will pursue a bit further, has to do with the nature of the LTTE and their state in particular, and with the nature of states in general. There is little doubt that the picture drawn by Stokke remains very close to the one projected by the LTTE in its struggle for international legitimacy: that of a pre-existing national formation with a collective aspiration for independence, which, if left in peace and security, will progress steadfastly towards freedom and prosperity for all. On the official webpage of the LTTE,[3] the organisation's struggle for independence is framed within a legal discourse familiar to Western readers. We are told that the fight of the Tamil people for freedom is a quest for 'reversion to sovereignty', since:

> the alleged territorial jurisdiction and sovereignty for the whole Island claimed by the Sri Lankan Government are constructed on a false premise. Sri Lanka has no legitimate or legal claim to encompass the North and East, the homeland of the Tamils' Tamil Eelam.

In legal terms the basis for the present-day claim for an independent Tamil state is argued in two ways. One argument is that Sri Lanka not only violates, in a contingent way, principles of human rights, but that its state system, in all its political, economic, social, cultural, and educational aspects, is based upon the racial discrimination of the Tamil people. With reference to the UN Declaration on the principles of Equal Rights and Self-Determination (G.A. Resolution 1970), it argues that the Sri Lankan government has no legitimate right to exercise authority over the Tamil population of the north-east because of this. The second argument, made with reference to the UN International Covenant on Civil and Political Rights (G.A. Resolution 1966) declaring the rights of self-determination of all people, is that Sri Lanka Tamils, as one people, are entitled to their own state.

This justification for separation under LTTE leadership is not unproblematic. In political terms one particular difficulty with the lines of argument presented by the LTTE, in particular the second one, is that the 'peoplc' cannot really 'self-determine' before someone decides who the people to make such determinations are. As there are members of Tamil background in the central government and armed Tamil groups cooperating with the Sri Lankan army fighting the LTTE on the ground, it is not obvious that the ones to make this decision are the LTTE alone. Framed with reference to Stokke's presentation the question is: why should we assume that, because there are institutional structures being built in the LTTE-controlled areas, a development and expansion of the 'core functions' of welfare and representation will follow, which in the end will allow the Tamil people as a totality to decide their own fate in a democratic manner?

The Nature of States

One possible answer to this question is, of course, that this is what happens when states take shape. As noted by Blom Hansen and Stepputat (2005: 3), the assumption within the academic discipline of international relations has for decades been that states are *normal*, that is, with de facto legitimate control of their populations and territory, and that they are *identical*, that is, with similar interests, strategies, and expected patterns of action. However, this concept of the state conceals more than it reveals. As an alternative, the two authors suggest that sovereignty of the state is an aspiration that seeks to create itself in the face of internally fragmented, unevenly distributed, and unpredictable configurations of political authority, that exercise more or less legitimate violence in a territory (ibid.). This is in line with Philip Abrams' (1988) well-known constructivist understanding of the state. Abrams argues that the state as understood by political science, that is in the sense of a concrete political agency or structure, distinct from the social agencies and structures of the civil society in which it operates, simply does not exist. What do exist, however, are two things. On the one hand, real power exists. That is, armies are real, and so are police officers, prisons, and deportation orders. On the other hand, the state does exist as an *idea*, as an ideological project. The state comes into being as a structuration *within* political and public practice; it starts its life as an implicit construct of action and then acquires a life of its own as a public reification. What we need to study is not the state as one abstract–formal entity, but the coming together of *two* entities: ideas of the state, produced and transformed under specific historical conditions, and public and political practices carried out in the name of the state.

Under the present conditions of globalisation, we see a two-fold development relevant to the role of the state, constructing it as simultaneously indispensable and inadequate (Blom Hansen and Stepputat 2001): on the one hand, there is an increased focus on the need for states to confer rights and entitlements on citizens, organisations, and movements; to fight corruption and nepotism, and to promote human rights not only domestically but world-wide. On the other, we can observe within nation-states an increased emphasis on ethnic identity and a gradation of citizenship (Fuglerud 2005; Ong 1999)—in the postcolonial periphery often developing into a pattern of civilian strife in which state institutions apply brutal force against segments of their own population (Kapferer 2001). I believe that the terms of this apparent paradox are in fact not contradictory, but are, rather, complementary responses to the opening of borders to international capital flows and the reconfiguring of global political relations. That is, the projection of the state as the ultimate guarantee of citizenship and human rights is a way of dealing with the actual fragmentation and increasing socio-economic divides accompanying the forces of economic globalisation. This universalising and empowering rhetoric is part of what the state has to offer organised interests acting in its name.

With respect to the postcolonial world, the constructivist understanding is a more fruitful starting point for exploration than the one found in international relations. The concept of the state in independent postcolonial nation-states comprises a wide range of differently constituted aspirations for power and sovereignty, continuing earlier forms of exercising dominance, ranging from the rhetoric of race in Latin America via brutal *commandment* in Africa (Mbembe 2001), to the varied forms of legal regulation and bureaucratisation developed in South Asia. Within the neo-liberal global order taking shape after the Cold War, postcolonial regimes perform balancing acts between outside pressure (most commonly applied by institutions like the World Bank and the IMF) to open up and dismantle whatever welfare mechanisms there are, and the need to show agency and make themselves visible to their own constituencies. While the constitution and execution of state power cannot be seen as separate from the society in which it unfolds, we must take into account the point made by Bourdieu (1999) that in order to protect its legitimacy each institutional field that sees itself as a part of the state must develop rites, classifications, and hierarchics in order to keep a distance between itself and 'society'. As Blom Hansen and Stepputat (2001: 6) write:

> The state not only strives to be a state for its citizen-subjects, it also strives to be a state for itself and is expected by populations, politicians, and

bureaucrats to employ 'proper' languages of stateness in its practices and symbolic gestures.

The use of force is an effective language to this end.

LTTE and the Homeland of Tamil-speaking People

While unlike Sarvananthan (2006), I will not seek to prove the empirical incorrectness of Stokke's presentation of LTTE's state building summarised earlier, there is a need to point out a few things that remain unsaid both in his paper and in the presentation provided by the LTTE on their website. I will comment briefly on four such issues.

The Question of Political Unity among Tamils

The central question concerns what it means to be 'one people'. While Sri Lanka–Tamil nationalism has been a factor in Sri Lankan society since the mid-1970s, serving as a *raison d'être* for Tamil political parties and militant groups, until recently it has not been an idea or ideological framework unifying the separate sectors of the Tamil population. Rather, nationalism has served as a factor of internal contention and conflict. In fact, one may argue that to the extent that a common Sri Lanka–Tamil national identity exists today, it has quite literally been constructed during the lifespan of the LTTE—that is, from the mid-1970s—and is to a large extent a result of the war situation itself. For example, Pfaffenberger (1994) has noted that when he interviewed untouchable labourers in Jaffna in the 1970s, they referred to local members of the landowning Vellala caste as 'Tamils'. Neither they nor the Vellalas, it turned out, considered the labourers themselves to be Tamil.

An historic landmark in the history of Sri Lanka–Tamil nationalism is the Vaddukodai resolution adopted by the party Tamil United Front at its national convention in 1976, a convention where the party also decided to change its name into Tamil United Liberation Front (TULF). In the resolution it is stated that:

> This convention resolves that the restoration and reconstitution of the Free, Sovereign, Secular, Socialist State of Tamil Eelam based on the right to self-determination inherent in every nation has become inevitable in order to safeguard the very existence of the Tamil nation in this country.[4]

The Vaddukodai resolution, and the new name of the party adopting it, reflect the increasing desperation felt by many Tamils as a result of high-handed Sinhala majoritarianism after Sri Lanka's independence in 1948. Among the reasons for adopting the resolution listed in the text itself are, Sinhalese colonisation of Tamil areas, the institution of Sinhala as the official language, giving Buddhism the foremost place among religions of the country, and the denial of equality to Tamils in employment, education, and economic life. This political chauvinism was accompanied by the recurrent flaring up of ethnic violence of which members of the Tamil-speaking community were the main victims, and which governments and their institutions did little to prevent.

The resolution, however, also represents the culmination of a long process of Tamil politicians resisting the intrusion of the central government into Tamil affairs, particularly caste affairs. To understand the particular trajectory of Sri Lanka–Tamil nationalism, it is important to realise that what are the best interests of the Tamil community in Sri Lanka has always been a disputed question, interlinked with caste issues. For the British colonial regime this was a concern from the 1920s onwards. The commission preparing the Donoughmore Constitution with specific reference to the Tamil areas noted in their report that universal suffrage would be the only way to prevent 'placing an oligarchy in power without any guarantee that the interests of the remainder of the people would be consulted by those in authority' (Russel 1982: 16). The most conservative of the Vellala elite, on the other hand, argued that the giving of the vote to non-Vellala castes and women was not only a mistake leading to 'mob rule', but 'an anathema to the Hindu way of life' (ibid.). S.W.R.D. Bandaranaike, then Minister of Local Government, in 1939 observed that 'the caste problem is much more acute in Jaffna than in any other district' (ibid.). In Jaffna, the first 30 years after independence were plagued by 'temple-entry conflicts', conflicts over the possibility of low-caste people entering Hindu temples, and conflicts over successive central governments' efforts of putting a stop to Tamil discriminatory practices. One noteworthy instance was in 1968 when an organisation of Jaffna Minority Tamils, a euphemism for low-caste Tamils, aligned with the Sinhala nationalist Sri Lanka Freedom Party opposition in stopping the tabling of the Bill on District Development Councils, which would have devolved a modest amount of authority to the districts. The Minority Tamils argued that the Bill would provide high-caste Tamils 'with a weapon to reduce our people to slavery' (Pfaffenberger 1994: 159). Pfaffenberger (1994) points out that the Federal Party, the main constituent of the later Tamil United Front, instead of taking a principled stand on the temple and caste questions, tried to divert public attention away from issues dividing the Tamil community by focusing on common ethnic grievances. While this, in a sense, was successful, it was also the beginning of the end not only for the TULF, but for Tamil democratic politics as such. As Pfaffenberger (1994: 163) says: 'If the FP [Federal Party] and TULF met with short-term success in constructing a politics of confrontation, the parties' confrontational policy also helped to set off a process of political upheaval that political moderates could not control.' After the demise of the TULF in the elite division of Sri Lankan politics, the Vaddukodai resolution was lifted as a banner by the emerging Tamil militant groups—without further concern for the depth of support among the people, one may add. Thus, in 1983, the LTTE submitted a memorandum to the Seventh Summit Meeting of the Non-Aligned nations in Delhi, where it says that:

> The struggle for national freedom, having failed in its democratic popular agitations, having exhausted its moral power to mobilise the masses for peaceful campaigns, gave rise to the emergence of armed resistance movement in Tamil Eelam in the early seventies.... The armed struggle therefore is the historical product of intolerable national oppression; it is an extension, continuation and advancement of the political struggle of our oppressed people. (quoted in Balasingham 2004: 36)

This understanding, that it has inherited a popular mandate that is not possible to implement through democratic means, is a recurrent theme in LTTE's self-presentations. These presentations normally avoid mentioning that one of several reasons why democratic popular agitations have failed is because the LTTE themselves have systematically exterminated Tamil politicians with a democratic leaning, including—but in no way limited to—one leader and two Members of Parliament from the TULF, and three mayors of Jaffna. The armed struggle itself has throughout been characterised by brutal 'fratricide' among a large number of groups. The LTTE, however, has come out on top, forcing the remaining others to flee the country, or seek protection with the government and the Sri Lankan army.

The Nature of LTTE's Political Project

A description of the LTTE's state building in terms of the Western concepts of security, welfare and representation provides a somewhat inadequate understanding of the organisation's political project, if not a simple distortion. Despite the legal rhetoric found on their website, concepts derived from Western political science are not the ones through which the organisation seeks legitimacy and mobilises support from its constituency. While there is no room here for a lengthy discussion of this complex issue, their project is not a modernist one aiming for individual civic and political rights, but a revivalist one seeking to re-establish pre-colonial social conditions. It, therefore, needs to be framed in terms of South Asian social organisation and local traditions. Indeed, one notable characteristic of the LTTE is their systematic effort of 'embedding' their own activity in cultural constructions that are new and innovative, but which nevertheless are historically rooted and resonate with people's—especially poor and uneducated people's,—familiar life-worlds. For example, while the LTTE oppose discriminating caste practices and have enacted laws within their territory to end such practices, in substantiating its own claim to prominence, it draws on the organisation's rooting in Jaffna's Karyar community, a caste community that historically provided soldiers to the Tamil king. As observed by Hellmann–Rajanayagam (2005; Schalk 1997; Sivaram 1992), the success of the LTTE is founded in components of collective memory, among them the Tamil military tradition. This mobilisation of beliefs 'only succeeds because tradition has been redefined within a framework that accepts the Karyars as guardians of the culture' (Hellmann-Rajanayagam 2005: 152).

In terms of operational ideology, the LTTE's political project revolves around three relationships involving the LTTE warriors and potential martyrs: their relationship to territory, their relationship to their leader, and their relationship to non-combatants or the Tamil people in general. The central element in the first is the conceptualisation of territory as Motherland (*Tamiltay*) or, rather, the land as mother, and the death of the soldiers as 'seed' for the liberation/regeneration of this mother/land. The relationship is portrayed as a mutual one, where the life of the soldier (through birth) is a debt to be repaid through individual sacrifice securing the continued fertility of the mother. As it says in a message from Prabhakaran, the leader of the LTTE, spread on video in the early 1990s: 'The death of a liberation fighter is not a normal event of death. This death is an event of history, a lofty ideal, a miraculous event which bestows life.' In the songs and lyrics now part of the LTTE's own martial tradition, we find documented how this and the other two relationships are perceived by more common members and sympathisers. For example, in a poem called 'They Go On to Live as History', from the collection *Curiyap Putalvar* ('Children of the Sun'), the lyrics assert:

They go, the great heroes, they go—
Having
won the war with the enemy they go to
their death…

Having paid the great debt to the soil of
the good Tamil Mother
Crowned with the golden band they
go—their
mothers to wail and our country's people
In sobbing rows they go…

Names mentioned they go on to live as
history
In the hearts of the Tamils tomorrow.

(Ko. Tirunamam, reproduced in Hellmann-Rajayanagam 2005: 129)

This debt to the land, however, is often conflated with loyalty to the *talaivar*, the leader. LTTE martyrs do not die for the right to vote. It is to the LTTE's leader, Prabhakaran, that soldiers pledge loyalty. It is for him they die. The poem 'We Children of the Sun', written by a female soldier who later died in battle, offers an example of the conflation between land and leader. Hellmann–Rajanayagam (2005: 127) suggests that the theme of sacrifice, here handled through the metaphor of the sun and its rays, refers to the LTTE flag, which portrays a tiger's head on a sunburst, and to the god Murukan, 'the radiant one', the Tamil god of love and war. However, it is well-known that Prabakaran, LTTE's leader, among followers is revered as *Soorya Devan*, the 'Sun God'. I would argue that a more plausible interpretation is that the poem is about Prabhakaran himself:

We Children of the Sun
Oh Sun
Your rays are we,
Therefore only us to singe
Nobody is capable.
You
Father of heat
We
Children of heat therefore only
All adversaries
Can we torch.
You
Even if you hide, again and again

You continue to rise
Therefore only we also,

Even if we fall, we become the seed
And sprout a new shoot
As heroes having painted Grand pictures
For paintings in red
In your name
We continue to shine
Sun
Your rays
You never singe
Similarly,
The sun to burn
No Sun
Will ever rise.

(Hero Major Amuta, Malty Battallion, reproduced in Hellmann-Rajanayagam: 128)

Regarding the last of the relationships mentioned, that between the martyrs and the Tamil public, the poem also partakes in the Tamil military tradition that provides the basis for LTTE's claim to be the 'sole representative' of the Tamil nation. As I have argued elsewhere, it is through willingness to die, and through actually dying in battle, that LTTE cadres become connected to the unfolding of history and subsequently become part of Tamil destiny (Fuglerud 1999: 170). Non-combatants have in principle no other role than to support the struggle of the fighters, which establishes an asymmetrical relationship between the LTTE and its political constituency. This puts the concept of 'representation' into a rather different perspective from that found in Western political science.

Ethnic and Regional Identities

The existence of competing social identities to the one propagated by the LTTE has always been a difficult issue in their struggle. Rajasingham–Senanayake (1999: 101) argues that the construction of Sinhalese and Tamil national identities is the outcome of what she calls a 'bi-polar ethnic imagination', an ethnic identity politics that 'constructs Sinhalas and Tamils as mutually exclusive and collectively exhaustive of the island's diverse and hybrid communities.' While I share her general understanding of what is going on, it must be noted that the ethnic imagination in Sri Lanka at the present time in fact is not bipolar. What is notable is the extent to which the LTTE has *not* been able to build a broad-based and inclusive conception of the Tamil nation. Of major importance in this respect is what in public debates is normally referred to as 'the Muslim question'. The LTTE gained its dominant position only during the latter part of the 1980s, a period when the relationship between this movement and the Muslim population became strained. In 1990, the LTTE drove the Muslim population of the Jaffna peninsula—approximately 16,000 families—out of the Northern Province. During the same period, the LTTE conducted several large-scale massacres on Muslims in the Eastern Province, and Muslim farmers were expelled from villages in Paduvankarai, their lands taken over by Tamils. Now, 18 years later, although the LTTE in theory acknowledges 'that the Tamil speaking Muslim people constitute themselves as a unique ethnic group with distinct religio-cultural identity, forming an integral part of the Tamil national formation', and that 'Tamil Eelam, constituting Northern and Eastern Provinces, is also the homeland of the Muslim people' (LTTE 2005), Jaffna Muslims are still languishing in temporary settlements in Puttalam, and farmers in the east are still afraid to take back their land.

While the exact reasons for the sudden Muslim pogrom in 1990 have never been made clear, the political consequences are clearly visible. Until the late 1980s, the Muslim population, particularly in the Eastern Province, saw itself as part of the Tamil-speaking minority. Muslim youth joined both the LTTE and other 'Tamil' militant organisations. From 1990 onward, a separate Muslim national consciousness developed. As noted recently by Ismail et al. (2005: 195): 'The reason for a pronounced nationalist Muslim discourse emerging only recently, is that the Muslims were evicted from the Tamil nationalist movement, not that they were "asleep".' But recently or not, it *is* emerging. While the most important driving force in this development so far, the Sri Lankan Muslim Congress (SLMC), has focused on a separate Muslim identity rather than the concept of a Muslim nation as such, the demand for some form of self-determination is growing increasingly stronger among members of the Muslim minority. In what is called the 'Oluvil Declaration' of 2003 the Student Council of the (Muslim) South Eastern University states that: 'We, the North-eastern Muslims, a separate political category, have political equality and the right of self-rule' (ibid.).

As a result of developments taking place after the ceasefire of 2002, new alignments are emerging, further undermining the hegemony of the Jaffna-based nationalism of the LTTE. In March 2004 the former high-ranking eastern commander of the LTTE, Karuna, broke away from the main organisation. Theories about the causes for this split have been many among people claiming inside information, ranging from economic irregularities on the part of Karuna, to resistance from him and his men against the 'rule of law' implemented from the Wanni. The causes highlighted by Karuna himself have been the discrimination of the East (as a region) and the eastern wing of the LTTE by the northern wing in terms of positions within the organisation and the allocation of soldiers (Athas 2004). Within the Tamil population the social division between the north and the east is an old one, the areas having different caste structures and separate cultural traditions. In the east 'Jaffna people' are regarded as generally arrogant and high-handed—'Jaffna people have brains, Batticaloa-people have a heart' being one local saying to that effect. After having lost a decisive battle in April 2004, Karuna discharged most of his soldiers while a smaller number of hardcore followers remained in the east as one more armed element. Their attacks on the LTTE, and their presence in general, has since been one of the most complicating factors with respect to upholding the ceasefire, in that the LTTE has accused the Sri Lankan Army of providing protection to his men.

The discrimination of the east by the north resonates with the feelings of many eastern Muslims. Muslims in the east have something of the same relationship to the Muslim community on the west coast; a feeling of being looked upon as backward and 'primitive'. In spite of Karuna's track record of ruthlessness towards the Muslim community while he was a commander in the LTTE, the possibility of Karuna-sympathisers and Muslim radicals coming together on a basis of regional identification should not be ruled out. The Muslims I interviewed in Kathankudy in January 2006, openly stated that if their grievances were not taken note of, 'there is always Karuna'. Since then this possibility has materialised with the establishment of the Defenders of Eastern People's Rights,[5] an alliance between different Sinhala, Tamil, and Muslim groups from the east. While there is no reason to believe that this or similar groups at the moment pose a military challenge to the LTTE, they do complicate the bipolarity on which the ongoing peace process is based.

The Diaspora and the 'Transnational State'

The Sri Lankan conflict has brought approximately one-third of the pre-war population of the Northern Province, the one predominantly Tamil province in Sri Lanka, out of the country in search of physical security and alternative livelihoods. The most important explanation for the relative success of Tamils in securing emigration and protection as refugees in Western countries was the previous existence of family members outside Sri Lanka. In the post-independence period, Tamils started migrating to find work, when Sinhala politicians in the 1950s consciously sought ways of reducing Tamil entry into the public sector in Sri Lanka (Daniel and Thangaraja 1995). When the war started and Western countries tightened their immigration and asylum controls, these early emigrants became instrumental in assisting relatives in need of a safe haven (Fuglerud 1997, 1999).

In earlier works I have argued that internal tensions among Tamil exiles may be understood as a struggle over two different models of culture (Fuglerud 1999, 2001). The 'revolutionary model', propagated by the LTTE, links Tamil exile identity to the vision of the Tamil Eelam—the traditional Tamil homeland and future liberated Tamil state—as based upon the principle of all members being equal under the enlightened leadership of their own organisation. The 'traditional model' in exile upheld and articulated by the early migrant workers and non-political refugees, centres on hierarchical relationships of age, gender, and social origin ('caste'). These models or identity projects are also linked with two versions of transnationalism (Fuglerud 2001). While the LTTE keeps alive a diaspora identity and an allegiance based on ideas of national liberation and the possibility of return, recent ethnographic research with non-activist immigrants in Oslo showed that ordinary Tamils' actual contact with Sri Lanka in terms of travel, business, and political engagement is less than what could perhaps be expected—in fact, it is quite limited (Fuglerud and Engebrigtsen 2006). Admittedly, these two dispositions may to some extent be interconnected, in the sense that the LTTE in Western countries seeks to monopolise home country engagement. However, I would argue that there is also an element of the traditionally strong village identity in Tamil Sri Lanka being transposed into exile. In fact, the Tamil Home Village Associations existing in certain Western countries is one indication of this (Cheran, n.d.). While earning money to bring relatives out of the war zone was an overriding concern among Tamils in Norway in the early phase of emigration/immigration (Fuglerud 1999), when this immediate need was taken care of many seem to have put their energy into cultural activities and into providing increasingly better economic and educational conditions for the next generation of Tamil children where they live at present.

There is little doubt that not everyone wholeheartedly accepts the LTTE's conception of the diaspora being part of, and sharing responsibility for, the political destiny of the Eelam. Jeganathan (1998) captures some of this when he reflects on the design of one of the more important websites serving the Tamil national cause; the LTTE's own website *Eelam.com*. He points out that the site carries a graphic representation of the Eelam. The mapped-out contour of what the LTTE looks upon as the Tamil homeland in fact dominates its design, but without any reference to the battles fought or the lives actually lived on this piece of territory. Jeganathan (ibid.) argues that this graphic representation reflects the understanding of the Eelam itself as an icon within the Tamil diaspora:

> Not as a lived-in-place of old, the kind of nation one can return to and die in. But rather as an emptied-out map, that can be believed in. This works for all those nationals of Tamileelam who click onto eelam.com from New York, Oslo, Sidney, or Amsterdam, who have no wish to return to Eelam, no wish to live there, but who must believe in it if they are to keep living where they are.... For them, Eelam is real, it is lived—not as a place but as an image. (ibid.: 527)

This is tantamount to saying that transnational geographical imaginations may be important to people's projects of integration. While the LTTE no doubt would gladly use such imaginations for their own purposes, which is also implied by Jeganathan, there is a potential contradiction between the 'emptied-out map' and the LTTE's need for hard cash support for their military project in Sri Lanka. According to *Jane's Intelligence Review* of August 2007, the LTTE's annual revenue from its external operations has reached an astonishing USD 200 to 300 million. The money comes from different sources. While the organisation has invested in different forms of legitimate economic activity, voluntary and coerced contributions from individuals and Tamil businesses have formed the main source of income.

Lately there are signs that the willingness to contribute is wearing thin among an increasingly large part of the exile population. In early 2006 Human Rights Watch published the report called 'Funding the Final War' that described the ruthless methods used by the LTTE in collecting money for their cause in the exile communities. The publication of the report is a landmark not because the stories were new to observers familiar with the Tamil scene, but because for the first time a number of people made a choice to provide information, although most of them anonymous, for a report critical of the LTTE. While, undoubtedly, the LTTE still has many ardent supporters also in the diaspora, an increasingly larger section of this population seems to think, and now also say, that the political coercion of the LTTE in exile has lasted long enough.

The most important contradiction between the LTTE's *realpolitik* and the imaginary homeland, however, lies in the simple fact of generational change in the diaspora population. The children of the young men and women who fled Sri Lanka during the 1980s are now approaching 20 to 25 years of age. In another 10 years they will be breadwinners and parents to yet another generation of children to whom Sri Lanka will not even be a distant memory and the concept of the Eelam will have little meaning. It is very unlikely that the LTTE will be able to hold its grip on the exile population when the generation having actually experienced the war starts ageing. In fact, one may already observe this changing attitude unfold on websites and chatrooms, like the one in Denmark called *Denunge.dk* ('*theyoung.dk*'), where second-generation Tamils voice their opinions, including their incomprehension as to their parents' acceptance of pressure and extortion. The experiences of these youngsters clearly provide for a different conception of space from the one propagated by the LTTE.

The National Order of Things?

Uyangoda (1998: 178) has criticised analysts of the Sri Lankan ethnic question for treating the Sri Lankan case in isolation from the rest of South Asia. He makes the important point that the ethnic problem in Sri Lanka is a symptom of the dying of the nation-state in South Asia in general, and in order to be understood correctly requires a broader political imagination than Sri Lankan exceptionalism. I would like to use this insight to frame the question in another way: In what way does the LTTE's state formation compare with the state from which the organisation seeks independence? To what extent does it represent something new?

At first sight the Sri Lankan and the emerging Tamil state constructions appear to be very different. While the historical basis for, and legitimacy of, the Sri Lankan nation-state—like all other nation-states—lies in control over territory, the LTTE seemingly operates a truly transnational state, collecting taxes and dispensing justice among its constituency with no regard for national borders. While the LTTE is at present banned in a large number of countries, including India, the EU member states, the USA and Canada, the Sri Lankan state has all the international recognition and diplomatic privileges a state can ask for. Throughout the war period, and in spite of its horrible track record with respect to human rights, it has received generous support from the international donor community.

Still, my own answer to the questions posed is that the similarities between the two state formations are more significant that the differences. This is not because there is reason to believe that Tamil Eelam will grow into a well-functioning welfare state, but because they both in unusually transparent ways make visible the moorings of state formations in geopolitical structures of power stretching beyond their own borders. As we saw earlier in the reasoning presented on its website, the ambition of the LTTE is not to overcome the limitations of the nation-state as a form of political organisation, or to work out an alternative to the existing majoritarian state, but only to replace one with another. While the sources from which they draw support and economic sustenance are different, the Tamil diaspora and the international donor community respectively, representatives of both states adhere to what Malkki (1994: 41) has described as 'internationalism… as a transnational cultural form for imagining and ordering differences among people'. Rather than depicting a willingness to overlook national interests in favour of the welfare of humanity as a whole, internationalism, the understanding of globality as interrelations among discrete nations, should be seen as constitutive of the national order of things, the order where 'for any piece of land, and for any human being, there should be a definite answer to the question "which nation is responsible?"' (Rée quoted in ibid.: 42). The fact that Sri Lanka's relatively privileged international position goes together with a deep scepticism among a large portion of Sinhalese voters and politicians towards the international donors assisting it and towards Western countries in general, should, therefore, come as no surprise. On the Tamil side, this is paralleled by the efforts of the LTTE to keep alive the overriding loyalty to the Eelam among its diasporic constituency, and to limit the integration into host societies of members of this constituency (Fuglerud 1999).

Further, both the Sri Lankan and the Eelam state formations show the importance of sectional interests to state building projects and the inherent brutality of their day-to-day reproduction. In many nation-states, ethnic hostility is related to competition and fractionising not between ethnic groups, but between elite groups of similar cultural or linguistic backgrounds. In the Sri Lankan case it has been argued that there is a direct relationship between the opening up of the economy from 1977 onward and the increase in ethnic violence (Gunasinghe 1984), this liberalisation bringing to power a new class of Sinhala-only background. A similar development, but favouring a different elite segment, has taken shape from 2004 onwards when the Sinhala electorate turned their back on Ranil Wickremasinghe's United National Front (UNF) government and its effort to privatise government institutions holding up the remains of the Sri Lankan welfare society. In spite, or indeed because, of Wickremasinghe's signing of the ceasefire agreement, combined with his allies in the international community increasing the total amount of aid by close to an astonishing 350 per cent after his coming to power in 2002 (Bastian 2006), voters at the next election brought the current militaristic regime of Mahinda Rajapakse into power on a promise to safeguard the unity of the country. In doing so, the electorate provided political space to even more anti-Tamil players like the Janatha Vimukthi Peramuna (JVP) and the Jathika Hela Urumaya (JHU). After being elected president in 2005 (an electoral success assisted by the LTTE-enforced boycott of the election by Tamil voters), Rajapakse has installed 138 of his relatives in key official positions, the family dynasty controlling more than 80 per cent of public finances (*Morning Leader* 2007). On the Tamil side, the LTTE in functional terms represents a relatively recent coming together of the Karyar caste, from which most of their senior leaders have been recruited, and sections of the landowning and traditionally dominant Vellalar caste, who support their political programme economically now mostly from exile. Using the low-caste and destitute as recruiting material for their army, these elite groups act in the name of the future state. If the Eelam should ever become independent, they would constitute its political core.

Rather than seeing the two state formations as different, one legitimate and the other not, we need to look for the ways in which the reorganisation of world order in the age of Empire (Hardt and Negri 2000) affects both old and new claims to sovereignty. If so, we may find that the marginalisation of refugees in Western countries, making them susceptible to the influence of movements like the LTTE, and the international pressure to dismantle welfare mechanisms in countries like Sri Lanka are connected in complex ways. Joxe (2002), for example, has suggested that at present the strategy of control in the outer regions of imperial interest is one of low-intensity warfare rather than peace. This is cost-effective, and deflects local resentment onto puppet regimes. As noted by Kapferer (2004: 11): 'Peace is no more the ultimate objective of order. Order and chaos is functionally intertwined.'

In the Sri Lanka–Eelam case, both formations respond to the promises and pressures of globalisation with a combined dynamics of centralisation and fragmentation. What the case illustrates is that 'ethnic conflicts' and the violence they entail should be seen not as results of 'primordial loyalties' or of individual subjectivities, but as part of the projection and reproduction of the 'myth of the state' (Cassirer 1946) under shifting circumstances. As pointed out by Castoriadis (in Mbembe 2005), what a society, a community or particular individuals are prepared to live and die for is, in most cases, neither material nor 'real'. More often than not the politics of life and death is shaped around 'imaginary social symbolisations' made concrete and implemented by institutions in which the use of force is constituted and organised as struggles about power, through power and for power. Violence is, therefore, a productive force, a way of 'embedding into the structures of everyday life the ideas of which violence is itself a discursive practice' (Kapferer 2001: 71). If anything, this general dynamic is even more visible on the Tamil side due to the directness of LTTE's political symbolism. Here, the parallel processes of incorporation and exclusion present in any state formation are grounded in political submission pure and simple—and they are deadly. The emerging LTTE state is a state born in and through violence; not only ethnic but also intra-ethnic violence. While Sinhala elite competition is couched in Buddhist slogans of protecting the unity of the motherland, the sectional interests represented by the LTTE are articulated in rhetoric of national liberation. Fundamental to the activity of the LTTE is a *sacrilisation* of politics where the vision of an independent Tamil Eelam is made the holy aim of the movement. Around this vision the LTTE in a very conscious way has established:

> an elaborate symbolism of death and resurrection, a sacrificial commitment to the nation; there is a demand for 'faith', a mysticism of blood and sacrifice, a cult of heroes and martyrs, and an intimate communion of brotherhood such as we find in mystery cults. (Schalk 1997: 152)

This is the language through which the organisation seeks to appear as a state both to its subjects and to itself (*cf.* Blom Hansen and Stepputat 2001). What runs through the history of the LTTE is an emphasis on ethno-political purity; the understanding that the LTTE are the sole representatives of the Tamil people, and that the only pure Tamil is the one accepting their supremacy. Their systematic targeting and killing of politicians and human rights workers of Tamil background critical of their position is, therefore, no accident. The sad fact of the Sri Lankan situation is that at present the two sides at war need each other and the violence they have in common in order to sustain their own, largely imaginary, states. They exist in a mutual relationship of life-support.

Notes

1. In the following my references are to the Internet version, accessed at http://www.tamilnet.com/art.html?catid=79&artid=17291.
2. My references here are to the original publication of Sarvananthan paper. This paper was later published in *Third World Quarterly*, 28(6): 1185–95.
3. See http://www.eelam.com.
4. See http://www.eelam.com/introduction/vaddukoddai.html.
5. See http://www.tamilnet.com/art.html?catid=13&artid=17532.

References

Abrams, P. (1988). 'Notes on the Difficulty of Studying the State', *Journal of Historical Sociology*, 1(1): 58–89.

Athas, Iqbal (2004). 'East on Powder-keg', *Sunday Times*, 14 March.

Balasingham, A. (2004). *War and Peace. Armed Struggle and Peace Efforts of Liberation Tigers*. Fairmax Publishing: Mitcham.

Bastian, S. (2006). 'How Development Undermined Peace', in Kumar Rupesinghe (ed.), *Negotiating Peace in Sri Lanka. Efforts, Failures and Lessons, Vol. II*, pp. 245–77. Colombo: Foundation for Co-Existence.

Blom Hansen, T. and F. Stepputat (2001). 'Introduction', in T. Blom Hansen and F. Stepputat (eds), *States of Imagination. Ethnographic Explorations of the Postcolonial State*, pp. 1–38. Durham, NC, and London: Duke University Press.

———. (2005). 'Introduction', in T. Blom Hansen and F. Stepputat (eds), *Sovereign Bodies. Citizens, Migrants, and States in the Postcolonial World*, pp. 1–36. Princeton, NJ, and Oxford: Princeton University Press.

Bourdieu, P. (1999). 'Rethinking the State: Genesis and Structure of the Bureaucratic Field', in G. Steinmetz (ed.), *State/Culture: State-formation after the Cultural Turn*, pp. 53–75. Ithaca, NY: Cornell University Press.

Cassirer, E. (1946). *The Myth of the State*. New York: Doubleday Anchor.

Cheran, R. (no date). 'Transnationalism, Diasporicity and Social Capital: Tamil Community Networks in Canada'. Draft paper. Department of Sociology and Anthropology, University of Windsor.

Daniel, V.E. and Y. Thangarajah (1995). 'Forms, Formations, and Transformations of the Tamil Refugee', in V.E. Daniel and J.C. Knudsen (eds), *Mistrusting Refugees*, pp. 225–256. Berkeley, Los Angeles and London: University of California Press.

Fuglerud, O. (1997). 'Ambivalent Incorporation: Norwegian Policy towards Tamil Asylum-Seekers from Sri Lanka', *Journal of Refugee Studies*, 10(4): 443–62.

———. (1999). *Life on the Outside: The Tamil Diaspora and Long Distance Nationalism*. Cambridge: Pluto Press.

Fuglerud, O. (2001). 'Time and Space in the Sri Lanka-Tamil Diaspora', *Nations and Nationalism*, 7(2): 195–215.

———. (2005). 'Inside Out: The Reorganization of National Identity in Norway', in T. Blom Hansen and F. Stepputat (eds), *Sovereign Bodies: Citizens, Migrants, and States in the Postcolonial World*, pp. 291–311. Princeton, NJ, and Oxford: Princeton University Press.

Fuglerud, O. and E. Engebrigtsen. (2006). 'Culture, Networks and Social Capital', *Ethnic and Racial Studies*, 29(6): 1118–34.

Government Agent (GA). (1966). 'International Covenant on Economic, Social and Cultural Rights'. 16 December, G.A. Res. 2200 (XXI), 21 U.N. GAOR Supp. (No. 16), U.N. Doc. A/6316.

———. (1970). 'Declaration on Principles of International Law Concerning Friendly Relations and Co-operation among States in Accordance with the Charter of the United Nations'. G.A. Res. 2625, U.N. GAOR, 25th Sess., Supp. No. 28, at 121, UN Doc. A/8028.

Guevara, E.C. (1985). *Guerilla Warfare*. Manchester: Manchester University Press.

Gunasinghe, P.A.T. (1984). *The Tamils of Sri Lanka: Their History and Role*. Colombo: Nugegoda Press.

Hardt, M. and A. Negri (2000). *Empire*. London and Cambridge, MA: Harvard University Press.

Hellmann-Rajanayagam, Dagmar (2005). 'And Heroes Die: Poetry of the Tamil Liberation Movement in Northern Sri Lanka', *South Asia: Journal of South Asian Studies*, 23(1): 112–53.

Human Rights Watch (2006). 'Funding the Final War'. Human Rights Watch, 18(1[C]), March.

Ismail, M., R. Abdullah and M. Mohamed Fazil (2005). 'The Other Side of the Muslim Nation', in Georg Frerks and Bart Klems (eds), *Dealing with Diversity: Sri Lankan Discourses on Peace and Conflict*, pp. 191–200. Netherlands Institute of international Relations: The Hague.

Jane's Intelligence Review (2007). 'Feeding the Tiger—How Sri Lankan Insurgents Fund their War'. Available online at http://jir.janes.com/public/jir/terrorism.shtml, accessed on 1 August 2007.

Jeganathan, P. (1998). 'Eelam.com: Place, Nation, and Imagination in Cyberspace', *Public Culture*, 10(3): 515–28.

Joxe, A. (2002). *Empire of Disorder*. Los Angeles and New York: Semiotext(e).

Kapferer, B. (2001). 'Globalization: The State and Civil Violence in Sri Lanka', *Bulletin of the Royal Institute for Inter-faith Studies*, 3(2): 59–111.

———. (2004). 'Introduction: Old Permutations, New Formations? War, State, and Global Transgression', in B. Kapferer (ed.), *State, Sovereignty, War: Civil Violence in Emerging Global Realities*, pp. 1–15. New York and Oxford: Berghahn Books.

Liberation Tigers of Tamil Eelam (LTTE) (2005). 'Socialist Tamil Eelam: Political Programme of the LTTE', reprinted in Georg Frerks and Bart Klems (eds),

Dealing with Diversity: Sri Lankan Discourses on Peace and Conflict, pp. 291–306. The Hague: Netherlands Institute of international Relations.

Malkki, L. (1994). 'Citizens of Humanity: Internationalism and the Imagined Community of Nations', *Diaspora*, 3(1): 41–68.

Mbembe, A. (2001). *On the Postcolony*. Berkeley: University of California Press.

———. (2005). 'Sovereignty as a Form of Expenditure', in T. Blom Hansen and F. Stepputat (eds), *Sovereign Bodies: Citizens, Migrants, and States in the Postcolonial World*, pp. 148–166. Princeton and Oxford: Princeton University Press.

Morning Leader (2007). 'Enter the Blood Brothers', 26 September.

Ong, A. (1999). *Flexible Citizenship: The Cultural Logic of Transnationality*. Durham, NC: Duke University Press.

Pfaffenberger, B. (1994). 'The Political Construction of Defensive Nationalism: The 1968 Temple Entry Crisis in Sri Lanka', in C. Manogaran and B. Pfaffenberger (eds), *The Sri Lankan Tamils: Ethnicity and Identity*. San Francisco and Oxford: Westview Press.

Rajasingham-Senanayake, D. (1999). 'Democracy and the Problem of Representation: The Making of Bi-polar Ethnic Identity in Post/Colonial Sri Lanka', in J. Pfaff-Czarnecka, D. Rajasingham-Senanayake, S. Sagnik Nandy and E.T. Gomez (eds), *Ethnic Futures: The State and Identity Politics in Asia*, pp. 99–134. New Delhi: Sage Publications.

Russel, Jane (1982). *Communal Politics under the Donoughmore Constitution 1931–1947*. Tisara Press: Dehiwala.

Sarvananthan, M. (2006). 'In Pursuit of a Mythical State of Tamil Eelam. Rejoinder to Kristian Stokke: A Long Distance Propagandist'. PPID Working Paper Series, Point Pedro Institute of Development, Point Pedro, May.

Schalk, P. (1997). 'The Revival of Martyr Cults among Ilavar', *Temenos*, 33: 151–90.

Sivaram, D.P. (1992). 'Tamil Militarism', *Lanka Guardian*, 1 May–1 November (series).

Stokke, K. (2006). 'Building the Tamil Eelam State: Emerging State Institutions and Forms of Governance in LTTE-controlled Areas in Sri Lanka', http://www.tamilnet.com/art.html?catid=79&artid=17291, accessed 27 February 2006.

Uyangoda, J. (1998). 'Biographies of a Decaying Nation-State', in Mithran Tiruchelvam and C.S. Dattathreya (eds), *Culture and Politics of Identity in Sri Lanka*, pp. 168–186. Colombo: International Centre for Ethnic Studies.

10
Concluding Thoughts

Cathrine Brun and Tariq Jazeel

> *The green fatigues had vanished. The trademark cyanide capsule was tucked away. After 20 years of waging war against the Sri Lankan government and ruthlessly eliminating his enemies, the Tamil leader Velupillai Prabhakaran emerged from the jungle yesterday in a clean grey shirt: a clear sign that his career of violence and revolutionary mayhem is now over. Probably.* (Harding 2002)

And so began a brief four-year window of peace from February 2002 to April 2006, packed full of half successful negotiations, mandates, and agreements. The A9 road into Jaffna was reopened, having been closed for several years during the war, to facilitate Prabharkaran's symbolic emergence in 2002, an emergence caught by the glare of the world's media. The road remained open and many ordinary people from the north and south were physically able to travel the entire length of the island for the first time since war broke out. Soon after, they were also able to travel from the east to west, and vice versa. Island-ness, in the wake of the 2002 peace accord, became more than just a chimera, more than an imaginative geography. It became a material spatiality around which people were no longer losing their lives with the alarming frequency of the previous 19 years of war.

This glimmer of hope was fuelled by a geographical awakening of sorts, an opening up of the heterogeneous political possibilities that an enlivened spatial imagination offered within Sri Lanka. For it was the ability of both the UNP government at the time and the LTTE to converse about their respective spatial imaginations in ways less uncompromising than ever before that led us closer to the materialisation of a less introverted mode of post-independence island-ness than ever existed at any period before; an island-ness in which it was not impossible for the government to also conceive of relative northern and eastern political autonomy and historical/cultural connections to South India, and an island-ness that it seemed the LTTE thought not antithetic to these goals. It is, of course, a gross oversimplification to suggest that stable and sustainable peace in Sri Lanka might be achieved via bipartite agreements that pander to a polarised ethnic imagination (see the chapters by Orjuela and Perera in this volume). In fact, the resumption of hostilities in 2005 suggests that, if anything, the enlivened spatial imagination conceived in 2002 was not imaginative enough. Nevertheless, what this slight opening up of the spatial imagination did achieve was significant, and points to the tangible rewards that *spatialising politics*, or thinking and working politics through creative and nuanced spatial registers, might bring. Probably.

It is in this spirit that this book has been written. Despite the breadth and diversity of the chapters that gives rise to its richness, each has in different ways made two common intellectual manoeuvres. First, to show that postcolonial Sri Lankan politics has—discursively and materially—produced a plethora of uncompromising, often exclusive, spatialities in and through which everyday life, everyday social and political realities do not just occur, but have been and continue to be actually produced and signified. Second, as we have sketched earlier, and in the introduction to this volume, each chapter has either explicitly or implicitly pointed to the political potential that engaging space *as* political offers. Cultural politics are always spatial; politics happens through meaningful spatial formations, not *in* inert container-like spaces. The postcolonial geographical challenge that this volume poses is to think and mobilise the alternatives to Sri Lanka's often uncompromising spaces of identity, difference, and nationhood.

Politics, Space, and Boundary in Everyday Life: Situating Sri Lanka

> *Boundaries are never established gratuitously. Society does not form divisions purely for the pleasure of breaking the social universe into compartments. The institutionalized boundaries dividing the parts of society express the recognition of power in one part at the expense of the other. Any transgression of the boundaries is a danger to the social order because it is an attack on the acknowledged allocation of power.* (Mernissi 1975: 137)

Our imaginations of Sri Lanka today are strongly shaped by the language of segregated territories, of different worlds materialised through the distinction between 'cleared' (under government control) and 'uncleared'

(LTTE-controlled) areas. These territorialised spatial imaginations situate particular understandings of Sri Lanka, and these understandings of the island-state in turn encompass polarised—often savage—understandings of the 'other'. Increasingly, these prevailing geographical imaginations of Sri Lanka are shaped by disaster, conflict, and human suffering, but engaging with Sri Lanka involves much more than engaging just with the contemporary territorialised dimensions of conflict, and understanding the conflict itself necessitates engaging dimensions and spatialities less frequently evoked than those territorialised and polarised understandings of difference immediately identified with the conflict. The imaginative spatial interrogations in this book remind us of the consequences of language and the various stabilised meanings we attach to the sign 'Sri Lanka'. The chapters have contributed to an understanding of the heterogeneous spatial incarnation of politics; of how the present condition has been spatially produced in a number of different ways.

If, as we have argued throughout, space is much more than just a container, then politics must be understood both in and through the physical and social spaces and relationalities that people live in their lives. In contemporary Sri Lanka, relational spatialities and ethnicised boundaries are lived through everyday lives. Identity politics becomes lived experience of conflict and displacement, segregated neighbourhoods and villages, different school systems or attendance to different religious institutions, for example—all of which (re)create the uncompromising spaces of the conflicting parties.

As some of the authors in this volume have suggested, however, physical meetings and movement also have the potential to destabilise sedimented boundaries. Such meetings and productive spatial formations hold out new possibilities for new understandings of difference. The peace process enabled for a short period of time people from different social and geographical locations to meet. The (albeit differential) island-wide openings and physical mobility that the opening of the A9 road facilitated allowed people who were curious of what places of the other looked like to become spectators and strangers within their own state. People living in Sri Lanka, but never having had the chance to visit the war-affected areas of the country, witnessed landscapes of war and destruction that gave new understandings of how war was experienced for those physically present in the war zones.

Another set of movements involved Sri Lankan Tamils living abroad who finally had an opportunity to go 'back home' to Jaffna and other places in order to visit relatives and friends and see to—or sell off—their properties.

For many, these physical meetings and movements made clear the fundamental changes that had taken place in the relationships between those who left and those who stayed behind. 'Our foreigners', as the diaspora Tamils were called by the Jaffna people, dressed and behaved differently, and their children could often not communicate with their relatives. People from the Tamil diaspora could with their own eyes see the effects of the LTTE's spatial politics of control. Now in 'post'-conflict Sri Lanka, since the hostilities broke out again from November 2005, social and physical boundaries, it seems, are being reconstituted differently.

But 'outer-national' movements are not new. Various chapters of the book have strongly pointed to the postcolonial histories of transnational geographical imaginations and practices that have shaped various ways of situating contemporary Sri Lanka and its competing nationalisms in the present. Positioning Sri Lanka and Eelam in the national order of things (Fuglerud), the location of Sri Lanka in the empire (Duncan, Wickramasinghe), the slippery distinctions between, and the roles of, 'insiders'/'outsiders' in constructing and challenging the idea and institutions of Sri Lanka and alternative nations (Duncan, Fuglerud, Jazeel, Wickramasinghe)—all emphasise the importance of refusing to contain the spatiality of the nation-state within its borders (Jazeel). Bell's identification of her role not just as a foreign researcher, but also as a member of a community into which she has been incorporated as a professional colleague, friend and sometimes even relative, serves as a lucid and productive reminder of how even knowledge spaces are not so easily divided between 'inside' and 'outside'. Situating postcolonial Sri Lanka is a lot more slippery than we might imagine at first, and this is the productive challenge that this book has committed to working through.

From a critical geographical perspective, one of the challenges within Sri Lankan studies that this volume throws down is to reconceptualise the nature of 'politics' in society in ways that recognise the politics that inheres in these and many more mundane spaces and spatialities of everyday life. Each of the chapters has been less concerned with the abstractions and generalities of political debate in South Asia in what often become quite hermetically sealed yet notionally 'public' political spheres, to which the public are granted access through constitutionally convoluted channels. Rather, we have been concerned variously with the ways that politics is lived through the private, personal, historical, and familiar dimensions of the worlds that surround us in Sri Lankan life: material cultures (Wickramasinghe), coffee economies and histories (Duncan), literature and reading (Jazeel), or disciplinary geographical knowledge itself (Korf).

As the book has shown, these are worlds striated with the markings of the island-state's colonial and post-independent histories; histories that have folded, crumpled, and moulded space into the familiar and powerful forms whose agency all those connected with the island-state must now negotiate somehow. Here, we situate Sri Lanka as an articulation of practices at various scales from the body to the transnational. As such, this book explicitly connects to reworkings of the 'political' in feminist (de Alwis 1995; Giles and Hyndman 2004; Jayawardena 1986), postcolonial (Fanon 1968; Said 1978; Tiruchelvam and Dattathreya 1998), and recent South Asian studies literature (Blom Hansen 2002; Mines and Lamb 2002) that insist on the inseparability of politics from the private sphere and everyday life. We hope that the manoeuvres this book makes can contribute a more widespread understanding of these types of political workings within Sri Lankan society, for understanding is the first stage of being able to effect change. And the term 'spatial politics' represents as much a challenge to come as it describes a condition. As we stated in the introduction to this volume, our geographies are hopeful in this respect.

Epilogue: Speaking to Sri Lanka

We realise that our academic discussions often appear to peer at the intern-ally displaced, the war-dead, the government, the LTTE, or the question of peace through theoretical goggles of scholarly abstraction. This is inevitable, particularly for two editing authors who enjoy the comforts of academic tenure in the diasporic spaces of Sri Lankan studies. So ques-tions remain on how our academic discussions about Sri Lanka might have relevance to the people who are living their lives with conflict, people who are manoeuvring in the uncompromised spaces of which we speak, spaces where creativity is a main source of survival?

These are not easy questions, but one of the challenges that this book has consistently tried to face up to is the challenge to 'speak to' Sri Lanka, or to be more precise, 'to' the question of politics in post-colonial Sri Lanka. By this we mean that we, along with the contributors to this volume, believe that academics must work hard to make their iterations do more than merely speak of, or for, Sri Lanka as a kind of case study in an exercise of abstract knowledge production. Whilst some of us must recognise our positions 'outside', this volume and all its chapters are, in the main, partisan, they stake out forms of opposition and politics in attempts to engage debate and stimulate discussion on Sri Lanka's spatial politics. Part of the methodological complexity here revolves around embracing a sense of the inalienable connections between theory and politics; a sense that any discourse about Sri Lanka produces it anew in some sense (Ismail 2005). This is to understand Sri Lanka as more than just the pre-existing geopolitical object that, of course, it is. For it is also a textual object, knowledge of which is (re)produced slightly differently each time we render it through representation. It is a textual object whose colonial constructed-ness and uncompromising Sinhala history, to take just one example, is mobilised, perhaps subtly solidified, each time we utter the very phrase 'Sri Lanka'.

As well as the object of 'enlightened' anthropological investigation, we choose the island-state as the subject of our representations in the hope that we can—as we have suggested—stimulate discussion of the role and potential of space in Sri Lankan politics' past, present, and future. Thus, despite our location 'outside' the contested spaces of the island, we position ourselves within the terrain of political debate. This politics of location and intellectual intervention is itself a politics that involves intensely spatial dilemmas; dilemmas about who gets to speak, where and why, and how 'conversations' within and without the nation-state might transpire? We hope this book opens up to that challenge. Yet, whilst we agree that the role of Sri Lankan studies researchers should necessarily be placed under scrutiny, we bemoan the fact that as we finish writing this book, spaces for thinking differently are shrinking in Sri Lanka. Sri Lankan universities are politicised and polarised, and 'speaking'—even in the spirit of stimulating debate—is increasingly dangerous. With due humility, we hope here to produce 'an imminent politics of openings' (Gidwani 2006: 17) in respect of the issues we raise. In this way we hope our research connects to, speaks to, political imaginations in postcolonial Sri Lanka.

References

Blom Hansen, T. (2002). *Wages of Violence: Naming and Identity in Postcolonial Bombay*. Princeton, NJ: Princeton University Press.

de Alwis, M. (1995). 'Gender, Politics and the "Respectable Lady"', in P. Jegenathan and Q. Ismail (eds), *Unmaking the Nation: The Politics of Identity and History in Modern Sri Lanka*, pp. 137–57. Colombo: Social Scientists' Association.

Fanon, F. (1968). *Black Skin, White Masks* (translated by C.L. Markham). London: MacGibbon and Kee.

Gidwani, Vinay. (2006). 'What's left? Subaltern cosmopolitanism as politics', *Antipode*, 38 (1), pp. 8–21.

Giles, W. and J. Hyndman (eds). (2004). *Sites of Violence: Gender and Conflict Zones*. Berkeley, Los Angeles and London: University of California Press.
Harding, L. (2002). 'Tamil Leader Signals the End of Civil War', *Guardian*, 11 April: p. 19.
Ismail, Q. (2005). *Abiding by Sri Lanka. On Peace, Place, and Postcoloniality*. University of Minnesota Press, Minneapolis.
Jayawardena, K. (1986). *Feminism and Nationalism in the Third World*. London and New Jersey: Zed Books.
Mernissi, F. (1975). *Beyond the Veil: Male–Female Dynamics in Muslim Society*. London: Al Saqi Books.
Mines, D. and S. Lamb (eds). (2002). *Everyday Life in South Asia*. Bloomington, IN: Indiana University Press.
Said, E. (1978). *Orientalism*. London: Penguin.
Tiruchelvam, M. and C.S. Dattathreya (eds). (1998). *Culture and Politics of Identity in Sri Lanka*. Colombo: International Centre for Ethnic Studies.

Afterword

Pradeep Jeganathan

> *'American movies, English books—remember how they all end?' Gamani had asked that night. 'The American or Englishman gets on a plane and leaves. That's it. The camera leaves with him. He looks out of the window at Mombassa or Vietnam or Jakarta, someplace he can look through the clouds. The tired hero... the war, to all purposes, is over.'* (Ondaatje 2000: 285–86)

I

I begin my afterword to this important collection of essays that thematises the 'spatial' with an evocation of a memorable passage from the celebrated Sri Lankan–Canadian novelist Michael Ondaatje, one which seems increasingly well known in the quarters his work circulates in (*cf.* Jazeel, this volume).

This was also a pivotal passage for me in a recent argument I have made on the limits of post-enlightenment anthropological disciplinarity and the category of 'violence', but the resonances of the passage increase given a concern with the 'spatial' (Jeganathan 2005a). Location, the place where one is, physically and discursively, must be constitutive of any spatial argument, I suggest, and as such an elaboration on the importance of location in general—and then my own location—seems crucial at the beginning.

Before I do so, I will also point out that I have organised my analytical remarks in this afterword as a delineation of, and then a brief engagement with, the different locations that can be detected within the logic of the chapters. These notes come after a few introductory paragraphs, and in them the chapters are discussed not in sequence of the volume, but through another sequencing that makes location itself the guiding thread.

II

I write from a post-national location, from within the uncomfortable place of a nation that never was, and never will be.[1] I write as a national who does not celebrate the possibility of the nation or its eventual becoming, who is unpersuaded by the vision of a heroic utopia that is nationalism's torch, and who has only uncertain and unstable knowledge of the descent of national life into a grotesque world that has become ordinary. To write from this location, then, is to write of a place of loss that is so singular, that the fullness of this loss cannot be known completely—as perhaps in Freud's description of melancholia. It is telling, I find, that in a sophisticated discussion of space and place that moves through both Lefebvre and Massey, Malathi de Alwis (2004) touches on the importance of 'home' as a category that is always already defined by loss and a melancholy wake. I have, in other work, tried to think through what is clearly an impossible construction: 'the work of melancholia'—and have called that lost home 'the island formally called Ceylon'. This is not simply to mark the passing of a colonial proper name, but to mark our own incomprehension as to what was lost when Ceylon became Sri Lanka (Jeganathan 2004b).

Insisting that location matters, as home, is not a claim to more or less 'authenticity'. All locations, if they are worked through and delineated honestly, might well be equally sincere and authentic. Location matters, firstly, because it relates to the stakes of an argument. The contrast that Ondaatje, who is not located in Sri Lanka, draws between Anil Tissera, the forensic anthropologist, a concerned expatriate like himself, and Sarath Diyasena, the archeologist who practises in the island that he will never leave, is stark. They collaborate on an argument that identifies a skeleton and implicates the state in his murder; Sarath is killed over it and Anil leaves. Stakes matter, even though they may not always be about life and death.

Location matters, secondly, and perhaps even more importantly, in relation to the intellectual traditions of inquiry and scholarship that appear before it. For example, if one is located in the metropolitan university system, the questions one asks are often conditioned by the currently authoritative theoretical text that appears before one as the answer to a lack in a previously widely read text; as Agamben might be held up as a mirror to Foucault's omissions. In another location, as in Sri Lanka, my colleagues and I, battling the categories of International Non-Governmental Organizations (INGOs)—such as 'participation,' 'empowerment' and 'psycho-social'—that govern the frame of grants and grant proposals, place value on arguments that problematise these very categories. And at other times, when faced with mounting daily terror, I may worry about 'checkpoints' or 'identity cards' (Jeganathan 2004a), or the legality of evictions and deportations. I do not think one effort is less intellectual than the other; yet they are products of different locations, each quite parochial in its own way.

Nevertheless, it should also be obvious that in the world as it were, outside any claims we as scholars may wish to make for ourselves, epistemological locations are not all equally authoritative. Euro-American or northern locations, descendents of colonial ones, are indeed far more authoritative than southern ones, say, in Sri Lanka. The world has never been equal, and perhaps never will be. Thinking through location, then, requires consideration of this imbalance of authority.

III

Benedikt Korf's chapter in this volume speaks quite directly to this matter. Following Jennifer Robinson (2003), his is a concern to postcolonialise geography—and one tactic he adopts after her, is to engage with scholars of the subject who are in fact located in the regions studied, recognising, as I do, the built-in imbalances of global scholarly production. That is laudable, and Korf's engagement with G. H. Peiris' and C. M. Maduma Bandara's work on the spatial categories of rule in the island of Ceylon serves both to demonstrate the centrality of the category space to debates in and about nationalism in Ceylon over a long period, and also to raise questions about fact and evidence, political claims and scholarly claims.

I do agree with Korf that Peiris's work, for example, is to be understood as a contribution to Sinhala nationalist thought, and both his engagement with and his critique of it are important. But it should also be noted that this work, and work like it, represents but one side of positions articulated from locations within or engaged with nationalist thought on the island. Peiris has been associated with the International Centre for Ethnic Studies, Kandy, for many years, and both of his articles with which Korf engages are published by one of the major journals of the centre. It is important to note, however, that I am located, as a scholarly practitioner, at the parallel campus of the research centre in Colombo where my colleague Sunil Bastian's work (1995), which Korf also cites in passing, might well be understood as the other side of that represented by Peiris. Bastian, who is embedded in a series of dense debates located in the island, offers a counterpoint to Peiris and Maduma Bandara's arguments from what is a scholarly location in the same (extended) institution that has been, from time to time, identified with liberal Tamil nationalism. Nevertheless, Bastian is neither Tamil nor a Tamil nationalist, and we see that the plot thickens. In other words, one might suggest that the specificities of Korf's locative argument stops too soon; a more granulated understanding of location would perhaps have yielded richer results.

When one considers the novelty of an approach such as Korf's, it seems clear that it has taken us long to fully understand the enormous role that location has played in the very constitution of modern authoritative knowledge about Sri Lanka. In the early years of scholarship enabled by the work of Michel Foucault and Bernard Cohn, a good deal was made of the 'colonially constructed' nature of knowledge. But this only touches the tip of the iceberg if the texture of the epistemological apparatus that produces that knowledge is not examined in detail on the one hand, and on the other hand if the appropriation of those knowledges by postcolonial nationalisms is not taken into account.

IV

The translations of the series of Pali texts that have come to be called chronicles, and are now understood as clustered around the proper name *Mahavamsa*, are a case in point. As Jonathan Walters (2000) has demonstrated in his erudite and unchallenged reading of their Orientalist (Inden 1990; Said 1978) appropriation by George Turnour and others of the Royal Asiatic Society of Bengal in the first half of the 19th century, what emerged as the printed and bound *Mahavamsa* by the second half of that century, is really epistemologically quite different from what he, Walters, or another differently located person might read out of it. But what is more, as I have argued at length elsewhere, this textual reading is linked to the entire landscape of Ceylon and imbues places with new meanings that are simultaneous with a series of material practices. These practices, which were hydraulic, archaeological, and aesthetic, transform the spatial formation of the island in an irreducible way throughout the 19th century (Jeganathan 1995). One of the consequences of these formations of practice is the racialisation of the landscape of Ceylon. So much so that by 1887, John Ferguson, the colonial editor of a newspaper published in Colombo, could write in a special commemorative annual of the 'determined and constant… southward flow of the successors of the old South India invaders'. He means to place on one landscape 'the influx of Tamils' in the second half of the 19th century, to which he is a supposed witness, and 'old...invaders' as from the *Mahavamsa*, in the ancient but now well-known past (cited in Jeganathan 1995: 122). Herein lies the problem of 'Ceylon'. It is constituted as a divided unity by certain kinds of colonial knowledge at its very inception. Sinhala and Tamil nationalisms have competed to appropriate these knowledges, but have not, and perhaps can never, transcend them.

V

Given this perspective, I find Tariq Jazeel's choice to work with Ondaatje's *Anil's Ghost* an exemplar of both the dilemmas of scholarly location within as well as without the island, and as a text that is sensitive to socio-historical construction of space in its most minute form, to be apt. He understands that new spatialities were made in the wake of archaeological practice in the 19th century, as I have in previous work, and then goes on to grapple with the continuation of this in the 20th century by a careful reading of the Palipana/Paranavitana double in Ondaatje's novel. His point, that life and lives are constitutive of—and constituted by in turn—politicised, racialised spaces, is an important one. What I find harder to fully grasp is his own location. On the one hand, I agree that while Ondaatje lives most of his life physically out of Sri Lanka, *Anil's Ghost* is not simply a Canadian novel. It can perhaps be considered a contribution to the tradition of Sri Lankan English literature, which in an old and venerable one, but I would not (Jeganathan 2005b; *cf.* Jazeel, this volume). Nevertheless, I could consider it a contribution to cosmopolitan Sinhala nationalist thought, which as I have argued elsewhere is inaugurated by Ananda Coomaraswamy's *Medieval Sinhalese Art* (Jeganathan 2005a). It should go without saying surely that Ondaatje's acclaimed *The English Patient* (1992) or *In the Skin of the Lion* (1987) are not contributions to either of these traditions. Then again, given the logic of the location of *Anil's Ghost*, I would want to distinguish it from say Romesh Gunesekera's *Reef* (1994) which is, I would argue, the product of a different kind of location: that of the exile who does not wish to return. I have detoured here through the multiple locations of Ondaatje's work, wondering if in this chapter Jazeel wants his location to be close to the Ondaatje/Tissera double in *Anil's Ghost*. If so, I think it a most productive one. Nevertheless, I would also like to suggest that a scholarly or literary work can gain traction from an articulation between different locations, taken both materially and discursively. I expand on this later.

Øivind Fuglerud's chapter, 'Fractured Sovereignty', presents a subtle contribution to our understanding of the question of sovereignty in that aspect of Sri Lanka's conflict. It is both an attempt to rethink the 'state' and its distribution, and also to argue in very located ways with the claims of a certain strand of Tamil nationalism. I see Fuglerud's location as a triangulation between three points of reference: a Scandinavian scholar such as Stokke whose work may have some sympathy with the official ideology of the LTTE, a critic of the LTTE located within the island of Ceylon such as Saravanandan (quoted by Fuglerud), and Fuglerud's own voice that at times is embedded with, and sensitive to, a second or third generation of European Tamils who might inhabit the cyberspace of 'denunge.dk', demonstrating, I would argue, how a location outside the island can lead to epistemological purchase. This triangular location ultimately strengthens his argument that the claims of the territoriality of 'the emerging LTTE state' are tenuous at the level of interpellated citizenship, but even more importantly, something of a chimera given that the very idea of the state such claims pursue may be impossible.

Nihal Perera's chapter can also be read, I would argue, as triangularly located. One point of reference for him, as for a volume as a whole, is the category 'space' that he pursues with the conviction that a new category might well lead to new conceptual purchase on the old chestnuts of Sri Lankan studies. This I will suggest—if I can do so in a non-pejorative way—is a metropolitan preoccupation. However, I am not persuaded of Perera's claim that Sri Lankanist literature 'lacks well developed engagements with the role of space in Sri Lanka's ethnic conflict'. It seems the work of Peiris, Madduma Bandara and Bastian would be worth pausing over at this point; and there are others that come to mind as well. But that does not matter, apart from the claim of 'firstness'. Space is surely an important category.

Another more puzzling locational point for Perera seems to be within a well-known, but hardly well-worked-through, populist Sinhala nationalist narrative that does not take cognisance of the socio-historical emergence of Tamil nationalism within Ceylon, but suggests that it was a quick invention of a communalist Tamil elite of the 1920s consolidated by an unexplained and socio-historically unmoored TULF electoral victory in 1977 (Perera, this volume). On another view, which I confess I share, the 'Sinhala–Tamil binary' does not emerge full blown out of elite machinations in the 1920s, but is one that emerges from the very colonial reading and remaking of the landscapes of Ceylon after the 1830s, and is consolidated as modern, that is, horizontal, 'Sinhala-ness' and 'Tamil-ness' under the signs of persons such as Dharmapala and Bandaranaike on the one side, and Navalar and Chelvanayakam on the other. This view then is produced from a different location from Perera's account.

Perera's location is important for his third and most important one, which seeks to displace the putative centrality of 'Jaffna' in this congealed Tamil-ness. This re-description does take up most of his chapter, and it is rich with details that seem to want to navigate close to the perspective of northern Tamils, claiming at times an affinity with the views of Tamil resident informants in the north. Yet this remains confusing to me, since it is well known that Tamil nationalism seeks to claim and build its centre in Trincomalee, not Jaffna or Kilinochchi. While Jaffna is certainly central to a particular parochial Tamil imagination, the possibilities of linguistic nationalism and electoral politics, certainly by the 1950s, propelled the Federal Party and then the TULF to look east to Trincomalee as the capital of a (federal) state that would encompass the 'Tamil-speaking people', which at the time certainly included the Muslims as well. And hence the enormous, continuing importance of the question of merging or de-merging the two provinces, North and East, to Sinhala, Tamil, and Muslim nationalisms. I find that Perera's constant and consistent avoidance of some of the basic nuances of the Tamil nationalist narrative risks repositioning him within the eddies of, populist Sinhala nationalism.

Nira Wickramasinghe's chapter is an effective contrast to Perera's while located within the scholarly traditions of the historiography of the island. As Brun and Jazeel have already noted in their introduction, Wickramasinghe's detail helps render afresh, and with new insights, the well known permeability of Ceylon's boundaries (*cf.* Roberts 1974). But furthermore, as she prises apart tea from gin and tonic, and machine-sewn, block-patterned sari blouses from top hats and tailcoats, she also, in her quiet way, retells and then decentres Sinhala nationalism's own biography that might insist on a different division of foreign and indigenous. Yet, what one misses is a doubling of location that might also have considered the issues raised from a location outside the one that a critical historian of empire might have adopted. Perhaps then, Wickramasinghe may have been able to address the founding of the Empire Marketing Board in 1926, and its role it in the economy of imperial commodities (Constantine 1986; Hitchens 2004: 61).

James Duncan's paper occupies this very location—that of the metropolitan critic of imperialism. His is a location outside Ceylon, but it is an important one for it allows him to grasp the place of coffee both as crop and drink, and plantations, both in relation to labouring bodies and ecosystems. It is this location that allows for the insight that the effects and consequences of imperialism have to be understood as a relationship between the colony and the metropolis, and that the massive changes wrought by imperial incursions, such as coffee plantations in Ceylon, may have unintended and devastating consequences. The coffee blight, for example. But then, as contrasted with Wickramasinghe, Duncan does not engage with the historiography of Ceylon, and so we can not fully compute the space his insights may have on that tradition.

Camilla Orjuela's chapter attempts to trace, through spatial metaphors and categories, fault lines in the field of 'peace work' in the country. While the categories centre and periphery are common to those working out of diverse locations, and arguments about what we might call after Raymond Williams *The Country and the City* (1973) are also common in many intellectual traditions, I detect in Orjuela's analysis a point of view frequent in scholars, and even others, who are visitors to this country. In this view the binaries 'Westernised/indigenous', 'rich/poor', 'Colombo/village' can be seen as oppositions of great substance and then naturalised as such. In another view, these oppositions may be seen as the products of the relatively recent past, and encompassed in a more robust category of the 'modern' as in a 'Sri Lankan modern'. Furthermore, it is not often understood that as measured by the most widely used economic indicator, economic inequality in Sri Lanka is less than that of the United States and the United Kingdom. Since this is counter-intuitive, perceived inequality seems to loom large, and easily begins to be treated as a 'natural' social fact, which then can be folded into a Colombo/village binary. It is not that this simply is a view of outsiders; often it is a view shared by some, located elsewhere, who are concerned with inequality, and populist nationalists located in Sri Lanka. From my own location, the perceived relationship between categories like centre/periphery, country/city, Westernised/indigenous must themselves be subject to inquiry and understood as rendered contingent to shifting political alliances and enmities. It is that political field that we need to grasp if we want to dissect what has come to be called 'peace work'.

I turn to Sharon Bell's chapter at the end of this afterword as it considers in some detail the question of the social identity of the investigator, often taken to be key, in contemporary understandings of location. My own effort has been an attempt to displace simplistic arguments about identity and its politics that seem common to contemporary, metropolitan scholarship. As such, I find Bell's chapter helpful in some ways, for while she is clear that her own identity, and perceptions of it, structure her interactions with informants, she also points to nodes in her biography that are not as strongly structured by her 'whiteness'. Importantly, she places some emphasis on her intellectual training and scholarly interests as constituent elements of her approach to things—an argument that I have elaborated on at length elsewhere through a detour into the history of early modern experimental science, returning to the limits of disciplinary anthropological knowledge, including my own (Jeganathan 2005c).

VI

But it is when Bell touches on the intersection of location and stakes that I find myself marvelling at the echo of Ondaatje's Anil:

> Unlike many of my colleagues [in the island] I am free to divorce myself from intractable social and political problems and even physically leave, or not engage, if I feel at risk. This is…an extra-ordinarily privileged position—any pretext to equality is shallow. (Bell, this volume)

Note

1. I owe this formulation to M.S.S. Pandian. I owe the idea of the post-national, to the discussions of the postnational collective, particularly at the Institute of Economic Growth (IEG) Delhi, in August 2005.

References

Bastian, S. (1995). *Control over Land: the Devolution Debate*. Colombo: International Center for Ethnic Studies.

Constantine, S. (1986). *Buy & Build: The Advertising Posters of the Empire Marketing Board*. London: HMSO.

de Alwis, M. (2004). 'Purity of Displacement', in J. Hyndman and W. Giles (eds), *Sites of Violence: Gender and Conflict Zones*, pp. 213–31. Berkeley and Los Angles: University of California Press.

Gunesekera, R. (1994). *Reef*. London: Granta.

Hitchens, C. (2004). *Blood, Class and Empire: The Enduring Anglo-American Relationship*. New York: Nation Books.

Inden, R. (1990). *Imagining India*. Oxford: Basil Blackwell.

Jeganathan, P. (1995). 'Authorizing History, Ordering Land: The Conquest of Anuradhapura', in P. Jeganathan and Q. Ismail (eds), *Unmaking the Nation: The Politics of Identity and History in Modern Sri Lanka*, pp. 106–36. Colombo: Social Scientist's Association.

Jeganathan, P. (2004a). 'Checkpoint: Anthropology and Cartographies of Violence', in Veena Das and Deborah Poole (eds), *Anthropology in the Margin of the State*, pp. 67–80. Santa Fe, NM: School of American Research Press.

———. (2004b). 'The Work of Melancholia: Aspects of Nationalist Thought in the Island Formerly called Ceylon'. Keynote Address, University of Munich, Munich, Institute of Postcolonial Studies, Bi-Annual Conference, July.

———. (2005a). '*Discovery*: Anthropology, Nationalist Thought, Thamotharampillai Shanaathanan, and an Uncertain Descent into the Ordinary', in N. Whitehead (ed.), *Violence,* pp. 185–202. Santa Fe, NM.: School of American Research Press.

———. (2005b). 'The De Kretser Case: A Note on Sri Lankan Writing in English', *Inter-Asia Cultural Studies*, 6(3): 446–51.

———. (2005c). 'Pain, Politics & the Epistemological Ethics of Anthropological Disciplinarity', in P. Pells and L. Maskell (eds), *Beyond Ethics: Anthropological Moralities on the Boundaries of the Public the Professional* (Papers Presented at the 130th Wennergren International Symposium), pp. 147–68. Oxford and New York: Berg.

Ondaatje, M. (2000). *Anil's Ghost*. London: Bloomsbury.

Roberts, Michael. (1974). 'Problems of social stratification and the demarcation of national and local elites in British Ceylon', *Journal of Asian Studies,* 23: 549–77

Robinson, J. (2003). 'Postcolonialising Geography: Tactics and Pitfalls', *Singapore Journal of Tropical Geography*, 24(3): 273–89.

Said, E. (1978). *Orientalism*. New York: Vintage.

Walters, J. (2000). 'The Pali Vamsa's of Sri Lanka', in R. Inden, D. Ali and J. Walters (eds), *Querying the Medieval: Texts and the History of Practices in South Asia*, pp. 99–164. Oxford: Oxford University Press.

Williams, R. (1973). *The Country and the City*. New York: Oxford University Press.

About the Editors and Contributors

Editors

Cathrine Brun is Associate Professor in Geography at the Norwegian University of Science and Technology, Norway. With a geographical focus on Sri Lanka, her teaching, research, and writing are in the fields of forced migration, humanitarianism, and development geographies.

Tariq Jazeel is Lecturer in Human Geography at the University of Sheffield, UK. His research and teaching interests are in social and cultural geography, South Asian Studies, and postcolonial and critical theory.

Contributors

Sharon Bell is anthropologist and film-maker, and Senior Programme Developer at the L.H. Martin Institute in the Graduate School of Education, University of Melbourne, Australia.

James Duncan is Reader in Cultural Geography and Fellow of Emmanuel College at the University of Cambridge, UK.

Øivind Fuglerud is Professor of Anthropology at the University of Oslo, Norway.

Pradeep Jeganathan is a Senior Research Fellow at the International Centre for Ethnic Studies (ICES), Colombo, Sri Lanka, and has held professorial appointments and fellowships at Chicago, Minnesota, The New School, and Delhi University.

Benedikt Korf is Assistant Professor in the Department of Geography, University of Zürich, Switzerland.

Camilla Orjuela is a Research Fellow at the School of Global Studies, University of Gothenburg, Sweden.

Nihal Perera is Associate Professor in the Department of Urban Planning, Ball State University, Indiana, US.

Nira Wickramasinghe is Professor of History at the Department of History and International Relations, University of Colombo, Sri Lanka.

Index